Sunset

BEST HOME PLANS

Country Home Plans

Covered porches front and rear offer a gracious connection with the outdoors.
See plan E-1811 on page 86.

Sunset Books Inc. ■ **Menlo Park, California**

SUNSET BOOKS INC.
Director, Sales & Marketing:
Richard A. Smeby
Editorial Director:
Bob Doyle
Production Director:
Lory Day
Group Marketing Manager:
Becky Ellis
Art Director:
Vasken Guiragossian
Assistant Editor:
Jody Mitori
Contributing Editor:
Don Vandervort

A Dream Come True

Whether you're seriously considering building a new home or just dreaming about it, this *Best Home Plans: Country Home Plans* book offers a wealth of inspiration and information to help you get started. Containing the latest, most popular home designs, this volume features more than 200 proven home plans created by architects and professional designers for families just like yours. In addition, you'll learn how to plan and manage a home-building project—and how to ensure its success.

Peruse the following pages and study the floor plans; you're sure to find a home that's just right for you. When you're ready to order blueprints, you can simply call or mail in your order, and you'll receive the plans within days.

Enjoy the adventure!

Photographers: Mark Englund/
HomeStyles: 4, 5; Philip Harvey:
10 top; Stephen Marley:
11 top left and right; Russ Widstrand:
10 bottom; Tom Wyatt: 11 bottom.

Cover: Pictured is plan J-90013 on page
121. Cover design by Vasken
Guiragossian. Photography by Mark
Englund/HomeStyles.

First printing September 1997
Copyright © 1997, Sunset Books Inc.,
Menlo Park, CA 94025.
First edition. All rights reserved, including
the right of reproduction in whole or in part
in any form. ISBN 0-376-01186-6. Library of
Congress Catalog Card Number: 96-61981.
Printed in the United States.

For more information on Sunset's *Best Home Plans: Country Home Plans* or any other Sunset book, call (800) 526-5111.

Contents

Ideal for both entertaining and family life, this imposing home positions public spaces around a two-story foyer downstairs and situates the master suite and three additional bedrooms upstairs. See plan AHP-9020 on page 93.

Country Living

In recent years, the popularity of country-style architecture has soared, and with good reason. Country-style homes offer a touch of nostalgia and a sense of being rooted in simpler times. The architecture is friendly, straightforward, and full of character.

If you're considering building a country-style home, you'll find a wealth of inspiration and information in this book. It offers you an opportunity to browse through a broad selection of country home ideas. It will even get you started on the process of building your dream home.

The two keys to success in building are capable project management and good design. The next few pages will walk you through some of the most important aspects of project management: You'll find an overview of the building process, directions for selecting the right plan and getting the most from it, and methods for successfully working with a builder and other professionals.

The balance of the book presents professionally designed stock plans for country houses in a wide range of configurations and expressions. Once you find a plan that will work for you—perhaps with a few modifications made later to personalize it for your family—you can order construction blueprints for a fraction of the cost of a custom design, a savings of many thousands of dollars (see pages 12-15 for information on how to order).

Behind this home's classic façade with its columned porch is a spacious contemporary plan that includes an island kitchen, separate dining and living rooms, a two-story family room, and four-plus bedrooms. See plan FB-5016-MARY on page 219.

Informal living begins on the country-style front porch of this cozy, two-story home. The main floor features a large family room and a bay-windowed formal dining room. On the second floor, two bedrooms and a shared bath nestle behind the dormers. See plan C-8645 on page 167.

Double doors open to an elegantly symmetrical plan in this compact charmer. The roomy master suite is situated on one side of the foyer; the living room, dining room, and other public spaces are on the other. Upstairs are two bedrooms and a bath. See plan VL-2360 on page 217.

Charming gazebo adds a note of yesteryear to a thoroughly modern, up-to-the-minute home. A grand foyer welcomes guests to generous entertaining spaces on the main floor. Upstairs, a balcony that overlooks the family room below leads to the master suite and three more bedrooms. See plan GL-3027 on page 206.

The Art of Building

As you embark on your home-building project, think of it as a trip—clearly not a vacation but rather an interesting, adventurous, at times difficult expedition. Meticulous planning will make your journey not only far more enjoyable but also much more successful. By careful planning, you can avoid—or at least minimize—some of the pitfalls along the way.

Start with realistic expectations of the road ahead. To do this, you'll want to gain an understanding of the basic house-building process, settle on a design that will work for you and your family, and make sure your project is actually doable. By taking those initial steps, you can gain a clear idea of how much time, money, and energy you'll need to invest to make your dream come true.

The Building Process

Your role in planning and managing a house-building project can be divided into two parts: prebuilding preparation and construction management.

■ **Prebuilding preparation.** This is where you should focus most of your attention. In the hands of a qualified contractor whose expertise you can rely on, the actual building process should go fairly smoothly. But during most of the prebuilding stage, you're generally on your own. Your job will be to launch the project and develop a talented team that can help you bring your new home to fruition.

When you work with stock plans, the prebuilding process usually goes as follows:

First, you research the general area where you want to live, selecting one or more possible home sites (unless you already own a suitable lot). Then you choose a basic house design, with the idea that it may require some modification. Finally, you analyze the site, the design, and your budget to determine if the project is actually attainable.

If you decide that it is, you purchase the land and order blueprints. If you want to modify them, you consult an architect, designer, or contractor. Once the plans are finalized, you request bids from contractors and arrange any necessary construction financing.

After selecting a builder and signing a contract, you (or your contractor) then file the plans with the building department. When the plans are approved, often several weeks—or even months—later, you're ready to begin construction.

■ **Construction management.** Unless you intend to act as your own contractor, your role during the building process is mostly one of quality control and time management. Even so, it's important to know the sequence of events and something about construction methods so you can discuss progress with your builder and prepare for any important decisions you may need to make along the way.

Decision-making is critical. Once construction begins, the builder must usually plunge ahead, keeping his carpenters and subcontractors progressing steadily. If you haven't made a key decision—which model bathtub or sink to install, for example—it can bring construction to a frustrating and expensive halt.

Usually, you'll make such decisions before the onset of building, but, inevitably, some issue or another will arise during construction. Being knowledgeable about the building process will help you anticipate and circumvent potential logjams.

Selecting a House Plan

Searching for the right plan can be a fun, interactive family experience—one of the most exciting parts of a house-building project. Gather the family around as you peruse the home plans in this book. Study the size, location, and configuration of each room; traffic patterns both inside the house and to the outdoors; exterior style; and how you'll use the available space. Discuss the pros and cons of the various plans.

Browse through pictures of homes in magazines to stimulate ideas. Clip the photos you like so you can think about your favorite options. When you visit the homes of friends, note special features that appeal to you. Also, look carefully at the homes in your neighborhood, noting their style and how they fit the site.

Mark those plans that most closely suit your ideals. Then, to narrow down your choices, critique each plan, using the following information as a guide.

■ **Overall size and budget.** How large a house do you want? Will the house you're considering fit your family's requirements? Look at the overall square footage and room sizes. If you have a hard time visualizing room sizes, measure some of the rooms in your present home and compare.

It's often better for the house to be a little too big than a little too small, but remember that every extra square foot will cost more money to build and maintain.

■ **Number and type of rooms.** Beyond thinking about the number of bedrooms and baths you want, consider your family's life-style and how you use space. Do you want both a family room and a living room? Do you need a formal dining space? Will you require some extra rooms, or "swing spaces," that can serve multiple purposes, such as a home office–guest room combination?

■ **Room placement and traffic patterns.** What are your preferences for locations of formal living areas, master bedroom, and children's rooms? Do you prefer a kitchen that's open to family areas or one that's private and out of the way? How much do you use exterior spaces and how should they relate to the interior?

Once you make those determinations, look carefully at the floor plan of the house you're considering to see if it meets your needs and if the traffic flow will be convenient for your family.

■ **Architectural style.** Have you always wanted to live in a Victorian farmhouse? Now is your chance to create a house that matches your idea of "home" (taking into account, of course, styles in your neighborhood). But don't let your preference for one particular architectural style dictate your home's floor plan. If the floor plan doesn't work for your family, keep looking.

■ **Site considerations.** Most people choose a site before selecting a plan—or at least they've zeroed in on the basic type of land where they'll situate their house. It sounds elementary, but choose a house that will fit the site.

When figuring the "footprint" of a house, you must know about any restrictions that will affect your home's height or proximity to the property lines. Call the local building department (look under city or county listings in the phone book) and get a very clear description of any restrictions, such as setbacks, height limits, and lot coverage, that will affect what you can build on the site (see "Working with City Hall," at right).

When you visit potential sites, note trees, rock outcroppings, slopes, views, winds, sun, neighboring homes, and other factors. All will impact on how your house works on a particular site.

Once you've narrowed down the choice of sites, consult an architect or building designer (see page 8) to help you evaluate how some potential houses will work on the sites you have in mind.

Is Your Project Doable?

Before you purchase land, make sure your project is doable. Although it's too early at this stage to pinpoint costs, making a few phone calls will help you determine whether your project is realistic. You'll be able to learn if you can afford to build the house, how long it will take, and what obstacles may stand in your way.

To get a ballpark estimate of cost, multiply a house's total square footage (of livable space) by the local average cost per square foot for new construction. (To obtain local averages, call a contractor, an architect, a realtor, or the local chapter of the National Association of Home Builders.) Some contractors may even be willing to give you a preliminary bid. Once you know approximate costs, speak to your lender to explore financing.

It's a good idea to discuss your project with several contractors (see page 8). They may be aware of problems in your area that could limit your options—bedrock that makes digging basements difficult, for example. These conversations are actually the first step in developing a list of contractors from which you'll choose the one who will build your home.

Working with City Hall

For any building project, even a minor one, it's essential to be familiar with building codes and other restrictions that can affect your project.

■ **Building codes,** generally implemented by the city or county building department, set the standards for safe, lasting construction. Codes specify minimum construction techniques and materials for foundations, framing, electrical wiring, plumbing, insulation, and all other aspects of a building. Although codes are adopted and enforced locally, most regional codes conform to the standards set by the national Uniform Building Code, Standard Building Code, or Basic Building Code. In some cases, local codes set more restrictive standards than national ones.

■ **Building permits** are required for home-building projects nearly everywhere. If you work with a contractor, the builder's firm should handle all necessary permits.

More than one permit may be needed; for example, one will cover the foundation, another the electrical wiring, and still another the heating equipment installation. Each will probably involve a fee and require inspections by building officials before work can proceed. (Inspections benefit *you*, as they ensure that the job is being done satisfactorily.) Permit fees are generally a percentage (1 to 1.5 percent) of the project's estimated value, often calculated on square footage.

It's important to file for the necessary permits. Failure to do so can result in fines or legal action against you. You can even be forced to undo the work performed. At the very least, your negligence may come back to haunt you later when you're ready to sell your house.

■ **Zoning ordinances,** particular to your community, restrict setbacks (how near to property lines you may build), your house's allowable height, lot coverage factors (how much of your property you can cover with structures), and other factors that impact design and building. If your plans don't conform to zoning ordinances, you can try to obtain a variance, an exception to the rules. But this legal work can be expensive and time-consuming. Even if you prove that your project won't negatively affect your neighbors, the building department can still refuse to grant the variance.

■ **Deeds and covenants** attach to the lot. Deeds set out property lines and easements; covenants may establish architectural standards in a neighborhood. Since both can seriously impact your project, make sure you have complete information on any deeds or covenants before you turn over a spadeful of soil.

Recruiting Your Home Team

A home-building project will inject you and your family into the building business, an area that may be unfamiliar territory. Among the people you'll be working with are architects, designers, landscapers, contractors, and subcontractors.

Design Help

A qualified architect or designer can help you modify and personalize your home plan, taking into account your family's needs and budget and the house's style. In fact, you may want to consider consulting such a person while you're selecting a plan to help you articulate your needs.

Design professionals are capable of handling any or all aspects of the design process. For example, they can review your house plans, suggest options, and then provide rough sketches of the options on tracing paper. Many architects will even secure needed permits and negotiate with contractors or subcontractors, as well as oversee the quality of the work.

Of course, you don't necessarily need an architect or designer to implement minor changes in a plan; although most contractors aren't trained in design, some can help you with modifications.

An open-ended, hourly-fee arrangement that you work out with your architect or designer allows for flexibility, but it often turns out to be more costly than working on a flat-fee basis. On a flat fee, you agree to pay a specific amount of money for a certain amount of work.

To find architects and designers, contact such trade associations as the American Institute of Architects (AIA), American Institute of Building Designers (AIBD), American Society of Landscape Architects (ASLA), and American Society of Interior Designers (ASID). Although many professionals choose not to belong to trade associations, those who do have met the standards of their respective associations. For phone numbers of local branches, check the Yellow Pages.

■ **Architects** are licensed by the state and have degrees. They're trained in all facets of building design and construction. Although some can handle interior design and structural engineering, others hire specialists for those tasks.

■ **Building designers** are generally unlicensed but may be accredited by the American Institute of Building Designers. Their backgrounds are varied: some may be unlicensed architects in apprenticeship; others are interior designers or contractors with design skills.

■ **Draftspersons** offer an economical route to making simple changes on your drawings. Like building designers, these people may be unlicensed architect apprentices, engineers, or members of related trades. Most are accomplished at drawing up plans.

■ **Interior designers,** as their job title suggests, design interiors. They work with you to choose room finishes, furnishings, appliances, and decorative elements. Part of their expertise is in arranging furnishings to create a workable space plan. Some interior designers are employed by architectural firms; others work independently. Financial arrangements vary, depending on the designer's preference.

Related professionals are kitchen and bathroom designers, who concentrate on fixtures, cabinetry, appliances, materials, and space planning for the kitchen and bath.

■ **Landscape architects, designers, and contractors** design outdoor areas. Landscape architects are state-licensed to practice landscape design. A landscape designer usually has a landscape architect's education and training but does not have a state license. Licensed landscape contractors specialize in garden construction, though some also have design skills and experience.

■ **Soils specialists and structural engineers** may be needed for projects where unstable soils or uncommon wind loads or seismic forces must be taken into account. Any structural changes to a house require the expertise of a structural engineer to verify that the house won't fall down.

Services of these specialists can be expensive, but they're imperative in certain conditions to ensure a safe, sturdy structure. Your building department will probably let you know if their services are required.

General Contractors

To build your house, hire a licensed general contractor. Most states require a contractor to be licensed and insured for worker's compensation in order to contract a building project and hire other subcontractors. State licensing ensures that contractors have met minimum training standards and have a specified level of experience. Licensing does not guarantee, however, that they're good at what they do.

When contractors hire subcontractors, they're responsible for overseeing the quality of work and materials of the subcontractors and for paying them.

■ **Finding a contractor.** How do you find a good contractor? Start by getting referrals from people you know who have built or remodeled their home. Nothing beats a personal recommendation. The best contractors are usually busily moving from one satisfied client to another prospect, advertised only by word of mouth.

You can also ask local real estate brokers and lenders or even your building inspector for names of qualified builders. Experienced lumber dealers are another good source of names.

In the Yellow Pages, look under "Contractors–Building, General"; or call the local chapter of the National Association of Home Builders.

■ **Choosing a contractor.** Once you have a list of names of prospective builders, call several of them. On the telephone, ask first whether they handle your type of job and can work within your schedule. If they can, arrange a meeting with each one and ask them to be prepared with references of former clients and photos of previous jobs. Better still, meet them at one of their current work sites so you can get a glimpse of the quality of their work and how organized and thorough they are.

Take your plan to the meeting and discuss it enough to request a rough estimate (some builders will comply, while others will be reluctant to offer a ballpark estimate, preferring to give you a hard bid based on complete drawings). Don't hesitate to probe for advice or suggestions that might make building your house less expensive.

Be especially aware of each contractor's personality and how well you communicate. Good chemistry between you and your builder is a key ingredient for success.

Narrow down the candidates to three or four. Ask each for a firm bid, based on the exact same set of plans and specifications. For the bids to be accurate, your plans need to be complete and the specifications as precise as possible, call-

ing out particular appliances, fixtures, floorings, roofing material, and so forth. (Some of these are specified in a stock-plan set; others are not.)

Call the contractors' references and ask about the quality of their work, their relationship with their clients, their promptness, and their readiness to follow up on problems. Visit former clients to check the contractor's work firsthand.

Be sure your final candidates are licensed, bonded, and insured for worker's compensation, public liability, and property damage. Also, try to determine how financially solvent they are (you can call their bank and credit references). Avoid contractors who are operating hand-to-mouth.

Don't automatically hire the contractor with the lowest bid if you don't think you'll get along well or if you have any doubts about the quality of the person's work. Instead, look for both the most reasonable bid and the contractor with the best credentials, references, terms, and compatibility with your family.

A word about bonds: You can request a performance bond that guarantees that your job will be finished by your contractor. If the job isn't completed, the bonding company will cover the cost of hiring another contractor to finish it. Bonds cost from 2 to 6 percent of the value of the project.

Your Building Contract

A building contract (see below) binds and protects both you and your contractor. It isn't just a legal document. It's also a list of the expectations of both parties. The best way to minimize the possibility of misunderstandings and costly changes later on is to write down every possible detail. Whether the contract is a standard form or one composed by you, have an attorney look it over before both you and the contractor sign it.

The contract should clearly specify all the work that needs to be done, including particular materials and work descriptions, the time schedule, and method of payment. It should be keyed to the working drawings.

A Sample Building Contract

Project and participants. Give a general description of the project, its address, and the names and addresses of both you and the builder.

Construction materials. Identify all construction materials by brand name, quality markings (species, grades, etc.), and model numbers where applicable. Avoid the clause "or equal," which allows the builder to substitute other materials for your choices. For materials you can't specify now, set down a budget figure.

Time schedule. Include both start and completion dates and specify that work will be "continuous." Although a contractor cannot be responsible for delays caused by strikes and material shortages, your builder should assume responsibility for completing the project within a reasonable period of time.

Work to be performed. State all work you expect the contractor to perform, from initial grading to finished painting.

Method and schedule of payment. Specify how and when payments are to be made. Typical agreements specify installment payments as particular phases of work are completed. Final payment is withheld until the job receives its final inspection and is cleared of all liens.

Waiver of liens. Protect yourself with a waiver of liens signed by the general contractor, the subcontractors, and all major suppliers. That way, subcontractors who are not paid for materials or services cannot place a lien on your property.

Personalizing Stock Plans

The beauty of buying stock plans for your new home is that they offer tested, well-conceived design at an affordable price. And stock plans dramatically reduce the time it takes to design a house, since the plans are ready when you are.

Because they were not created specifically for your family, stock plans may not reflect your personal taste. But it's not difficult to make revisions in stock plans that will turn your home into an expression of your family's personality. You'll surely want to add personal touches and choose your own finishes.

Ideally, the modifications you implement will be fairly minor. The more extensive the changes, the more expensive the plans. Major changes take valuable design time, and those that affect a house's structure may require a structural engineer's approval.

If you anticipate wholesale changes, such as moving a number of bearing walls or changing the roofline significantly, you may be better off selecting another plan. On the other hand, reconfiguring or changing the sizes of some rooms can probably be handled fairly easily.

Some structural changes may even be necessary to comply with local codes. Your area may have specific requirements for snow loads, energy codes, seismic or wind resistance, and so forth. Those types of modifications are likely to require the services of an architect or structural engineer.

Plan Modifications

Before you pencil in any changes, live with your plans for a while. Study them carefully—at your building site, if possible. Try to picture the finished house: how rooms will interrelate, where the sun will enter and at what angle, what the view will be from each window. Think about traffic patterns, access to rooms, room sizes, window and door locations, natural light, and kitchen and bathroom layouts.

Typical changes might involve adding windows or skylights to

bring in natural light or capture a view. Or you may want to widen a hallway or doorway for roomier access, extend a room, eliminate doors, or change window and door sizes. Perhaps you'd like to shorten a room, stealing the gained space for a large closet. Look closely at the kitchen; it's not difficult to reconfigure the layout if it makes the space more convenient for you.

Above all, take your time—this is your home and it should reflect your taste and needs. Make your changes now, during the planning stage. Once construction begins, it will take crowbars, hammers, saws, new materials, and, most significantly, time to alter the plans. Because changes are not part of your building contract, you can count on them being expensive extras once construction begins.

Specifying Finishes

One way to personalize a house without changing its structure is to substitute your favorite finishes for those specified on the plan.

Would you prefer a stuccoed exterior rather than the wood siding shown on the plan? In most cases, this is a relatively easy change. Do you like the look of a wood shingle roof rather than the composition shingles shown on the plan? This, too, is easy. Perhaps you would like to change the windows from sliders to casements, or upgrade to high-efficiency glazing. No problem. Many of those kinds of changes can be worked out with your contractor.

Inside, you may want hardwood where vinyl flooring is shown. In fact, you can—and should—choose types, colors, and styles of floorings, wall coverings, tile, plumbing fixtures, door hardware, cabinetry, appliances, lighting fixtures, and other interior details, for it's these materials that will personalize your home. For help in making selections, consult an architect or interior designer (see page 8).

Each material you select should be spelled out clearly and precisely in your building contract.

Finishing touches can transform a house built from stock plans into an expression of your family's taste and style. Clockwise, from far left: Colorful tilework and custom cabinetry enliven a bathroom (Design: Osburn Design); highly organized closet system maximizes storage space (Architect: David Jeremiah Hurley); low-level deck expands living space to outdoor areas (Landscape architects: The Runa Group, Inc.); built-ins convert the corner of a guest room into a home office (Design: Lynn Williams of The French Connection); French country cabinetry lends style and old-world charm to a kitchen (Design: Garry Bishop/Showcase Kitchens).

What the Plans Include

Complete construction blueprints are available for every house shown in this book. Clear and concise, these detailed blueprints are designed by licensed architects or members of the American Institute of Building Designers (AIBD). Each plan is designed to meet standards set down by nationally recognized building codes (the Uniform Building Code, Standard Building Code, or Basic Building Code) at the time and for the area where they were drawn.

Remember, however, that every state, county, and municipality has its own codes, zoning requirements, ordinances, and building regulations. Modifications may be necessary to comply with such local requirements as snow loads, energy codes, seismic zones, and flood areas.

Although blueprint sets vary depending on the size and complexity of the house and on the individual designer's style, each set may include the elements described below and shown at right.

■ **Exterior elevations** show the front, rear, and sides of the house, including exterior materials, details, and measurements.

■ **Foundation plans** include drawings for a full, partial, or daylight basement, crawlspace, pole, pier, or slab foundation. All necessary notations and dimensions are included. (Foundation options will vary for each plan. If the plan you choose doesn't have the type of foundation you desire, a generic conversion diagram is available.)

■ **Detailed floor plans** show the placement of interior walls and the dimensions of rooms, doors, windows, stairways, and similar elements for each level of the house.

■ **Cross sections** show details of the house as though it were cut in slices from the roof to the foundation. The cross sections give the home's construction, insulation, flooring, and roofing details.

■ **Interior elevations** show the specific details of cabinets (kitchen, bathroom, and utility room), fireplaces, built-in units, and other special interior features.

■ **Roof details** give the layout of rafters, dormers, gables, and other roof elements, including clerestory windows and skylights. These details may be shown on the elevation sheet or on a separate diagram.

■ **Schematic electrical layouts** show the suggested locations for switches, fixtures, and outlets. These details may be shown on the floor plan or on a separate diagram.

■ **General specifications** provide instructions and information regarding excavation and grading, masonry and concrete work, carpentry and woodwork, thermal and moisture protection, drywall, tile, flooring, glazing, and caulking and sealants.

Other Helpful Building Aids

In addition to the construction information on every set of plans, you can buy the following guides.

■ **Reproducible blueprints** are helpful if you'll be making changes to the stock plan you've chosen. These blueprints are line drawings produced on erasable, reproducible paper for the purpose of modification. When alterations are complete, working copies can be made.

■ **Itemized materials list** details the quantity, type, and size of materials needed to build your home. (This list is extremely helpful in obtaining an accurate construction bid. It's not intended for use to order materials.)

■ **Mirror-reverse plans** are useful if you want to build your home in the reverse of the plan that's shown. Because the lettering and dimensions read backwards, be sure to buy at least one regular-reading set of blueprints.

■ **Description of materials** gives the type and quality of materials suggested for the home. This form may be required for obtaining FHA or VA financing.

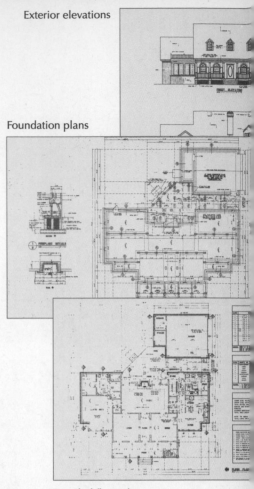

Exterior elevations

Foundation plans

Detailed floor plans

■ **How-to diagrams** for plumbing, wiring, solar heating, framing and foundation conversions show how to plumb, wire, install a solar heating system, convert plans with 2 by 4 exterior walls to 2 by 6 construction (or vice versa), and adapt a plan for a basement, crawlspace, or slab foundation. These diagrams are not specific to any one plan.

NOTE: Due to regional variations, local availability of materials, local codes, methods of installation, and individual preferences, detailed heating, plumbing, and electrical specifications are not included on plans. The duct work, venting, and other details will vary, depending on the heating and cooling system you use and the type of energy that operates it. These details and specifications are easily obtained from your builder or local supplier.

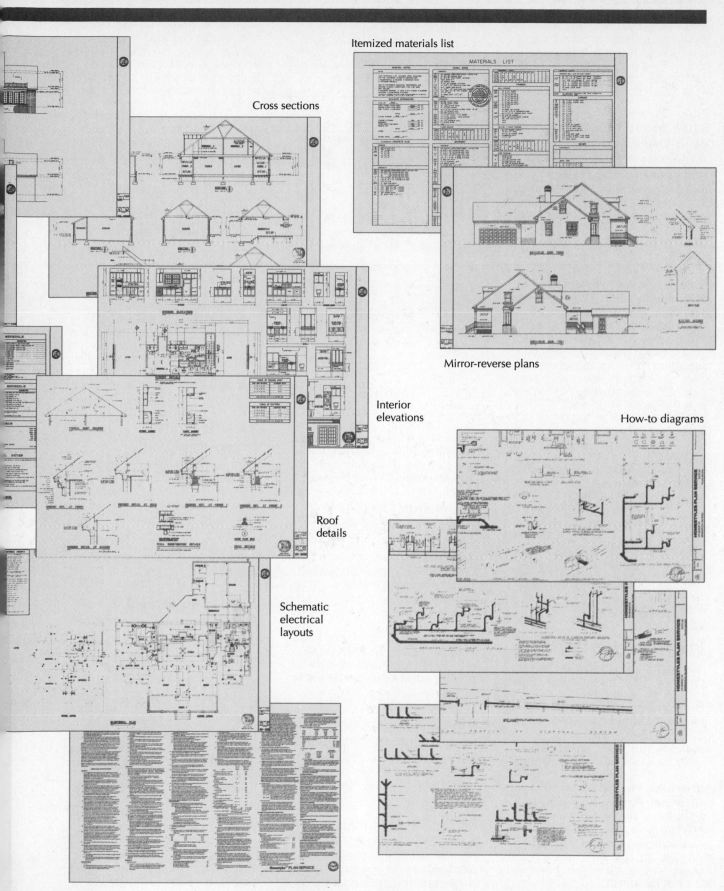

Cross sections

Itemized materials list

Mirror-reverse plans

Interior elevations

Roof details

Schematic electrical layouts

How-to diagrams

General specifications

Before You Order

Once you've chosen the one or two house plans that work best for you, you're ready to order blueprints. Before filling in the form on the facing page, note the information that follows.

How Many Blueprints Will You Need?

A single set of blueprints will allow you to study a home design in detail. You'll need more for obtaining bids and permits, as well as some to use as reference at the building site. If you'll be modifying your home plan, order a reproducible set (see page 12).

Figure you'll need at least one set each for yourself, your builder, the building department, and your lender. In addition, some subcontractors—foundation, plumber, electrician, and HVAC—may also need at least partial sets. If they do, ask them to return the sets when they're finished. The chart below can help you calculate how many sets you're likely to need.

Blueprint Checklist

____ Owner's set(s)

____ Builder usually requires at least three sets: one for legal documentation, one for inspections, and a minimum of one set for subcontractors.

____ Building department requires at least one set. Check with your local department before ordering.

____ Lending institution usually needs one set for a conventional mortgage, three sets for FHA or VA loans.

____ TOTAL SETS NEEDED

Blueprint Prices

The cost of having an architect design a new custom home typically runs from 5 to 15 percent of the building cost, or from $5,000 to $15,000 for a $100,000 home. A single set of blueprints for the plans in this book ranges from $245 to $685, depending on the house's size. Working with these drawings, you can save enough on design fees to add a deck, a swimming pool or a luxurious kitchen.

Pricing is based on "total finished living space." Garages, porches, decks and unfinished basements are not included.

Building Costs

Building costs vary widely, depending on a number of factors, includ-

Price Code (Size)	1 Set	4 Sets	7 Sets	Reproducible Set
AAA (under 500 sq. ft.)	$245	$295	$330	$430
AA (500-999 sq. ft.)	$285	$335	$370	$470
A (1,000-1,499 sq. ft.)	$365	$415	$450	$550
B (1,500-1,999 sq. ft.)	$405	$455	$490	$590
C (2,000-2,499 sq. ft.)	$445	$495	$530	$630
D (2,500-2,999 sq. ft.)	$485	$535	$570	$670
E (3,000-3,499 sq. ft.)	$525	$575	$610	$710
F (3,500-3,999 sq. ft.)	$565	$615	$650	$750
G (4,000-4,499 sq. ft.)	$605	$655	$690	$790
H (4,500-4,999 sq. ft.)	$645	$695	$730	$830
I (5,000 & above)	$685	$735	$770	$870

ing local material and labor costs and the finishing materials you select. For help estimating costs, see "Is Your Project Doable?" on page 7.

Foundation Options & Exterior Construction

Depending on your site and climate, your home will be built with a slab, pier, pole, crawlspace or basement foundation. Exterior walls will be framed with either 2 by 4s or 2 by 6s, determined by structural and insulation standards in your area. Most contractors can easily adapt a home to meet the foundation and/or wall requirements for your area. Or ask for a conversion how-to diagram (see page 12).

Service & Blueprint Delivery

Service representatives are available to answer questions and assist you in placing your order. Every effort is made to process and ship orders within 48 hours.

Returns & Exchanges

Each set of blueprints is specially printed and shipped to you in response to your specific order; consequently, requests for refunds cannot be honored. However, if the prints you order cannot be used, you may exchange them for another plan from any Sunset home plan book. For an exchange, you must return all sets of plans within 30 days. A nonrefundable service charge will be assessed for all exchanges; for more information, call the toll-free number on the facing page. Note: Reproducible sets cannot be exchanged.

Compliance with Local Codes & Regulations

Because of climatic, geographic and political variations, building codes and regulations vary from one area to another. These plans are authorized for your use expressly conditioned on your obligation and agreement to comply strictly with all local building codes, ordinances, regulations and requirements, including permits and inspections at time of construction.

Architectural & Engineering Seals

With increased concern about energy costs and safety, many cities and states now require that an architect or engineer review and "seal" a blueprint prior to construction. To find out whether this is a requirement in your area, contact your local building department.

License Agreement, Copy Restrictions & Copyright

When you purchase your blueprints, you are granted the right to use those documents to construct a single unit. All the plans in this publication are protected under the Federal Copyright Act, Title XVII of the United States Code and Chapter 37 of the Code of Federal Regulations. Each designer retains title and ownership of the original documents. The blueprints licensed to you cannot be used by or resold to any other person, copied or reproduced by any means. The copying restrictions do not apply to reproducible blueprints. When you buy a reproducible set, you may modify and reproduce it for your own use.

Blueprint Order Form

Complete this order form in just three easy steps. Then mail in your order or, for faster service, call toll-free.

1. Blueprints & Accessories

BLUEPRINT CHART

Price Code	1 Set	4 Sets	7 Sets	Reproducible Set*
AAA	$245	$295	$330	$430
AA	$285	$335	$370	$470
A	$365	$415	$450	$550
B	$405	$455	$490	$590
C	$445	$495	$530	$630
D	$485	$535	$570	$670
E	$525	$575	$610	$710
F	$565	$615	$650	$750
G	$605	$655	$690	$790
H	$645	$695	$730	$830
I	$685	$735	$770	$870

A reproducible set is produced on erasable paper for the purpose of modification. It is only available for plans with prefixes A, AG, AGH, AH, AHP, APS, AX, B, BOD, BRF, C, CC, CDG, CPS, DCL, DD, DW, E, EOF, FB, G, GA, GL, GSA, H, HDS, HFL, HOM, IDG, J, JWA, K, KD, KLF, L, LRD, LS, M, NBV, NW, OH, PH, PI, RD, S, SDG, SG, SUL, SUN, THD, TS, U, UD, UDA, UDG, V, WH. Prices subject to change

Mirror-Reverse Sets: $50 surcharge. From the total number of sets you ordered above, choose the number you want to be reversed. *Note: All writing on mirror-reverse plans is backwards. Order at least one regular-reading set.*

Itemized Materials List: One set $50; each additional set $15. Details the quantity, type, and size of materials needed to build your home.

Description of Materials: Sold in a set of two for $50 (for use in obtaining FHA or VA financing).

Typical How-To Diagrams: One set $20; two sets $30; three sets $40; four sets $45. General guides on plumbing, wiring, and solar heating, plus information on how to convert from one foundation or exterior framing to another. *Note: These diagrams are not specific to any one plan.*

2. Sales Tax & Shipping

Determine your subtotal and add appropriate local state sales tax, plus shipping and handling (see chart below).

SHIPPING & HANDLING

	1–3 Sets	4–6 Sets	7 or More Sets	Reproducible Set
U.S. Regular (5–6 business days)	$17.50	$20.00	$22.50	$17.50
U.S. Express (2–3 business days)	$29.50	$32.50	$35.00	$29.50
Canada Regular (2–3 weeks)	$20.00	$22.50	$25.00	$20.00
Canada Express (5–6 business days)	$35.00	$40.00	$45.00	$35.00
Overseas/Airmail (7–10 businessdays)	$57.50	$67.50	$77.50	$57.50

3. Customer Information

Choose the method of payment you prefer. Include check, money order, or credit card information, complete name and address portion, and mail, fax, or call using the information at the right.

SS20

COMPLETE THIS FORM

Plan Number _____ **Price Code** _____

Foundation _____
(Review your plan carefully for foundation options—basement, pole, pier, crawlspace, or slab. Many plans offer several options; others offer only one.)

Number of Sets: $_____
- ☐ One Set   (See chart at left)
- ☐ Four Sets
- ☐ Seven Sets
- ☐ One Reproducible Set

Additional Sets _____ $_____
($40 each)

Mirror-Reverse Sets _____ $_____
($50 surcharge)

Itemized Materials List $_____
Only available for plans with prefixes AH, AHP, APS*, AX*, B*, BOD, C, CAR, CC, CDG*, CPS, DD*, DW, E, G, GSA, H, HFL, HOM, I*, IDG, J, K, L, LMB*, LRD, NW*, P, PH, R, S, SG, SUN, THD, U, UDA, UDG, VL, WH, YS.
*Not available on all plans. Please call before ordering.

Description of Materials $_____
Only for plans with prefixes AHP, C, DW, H, J, K, P, PH, SUL, VL, YS.

Typical How-To Diagrams $_____
- ☐ Plumbing ☐ Wiring ☐ Solar Heating ☐ Foundation & Framing Conversion

SUBTOTAL $_____

SALES TAX Minnesota residents add 6.5% $_____

SHIPPING & HANDLING $_____

GRAND TOTAL $_____

☐ Check/money order enclosed (in U.S. funds) payable to HomeStyles
☐ VISA   ☐ MasterCard   ☐ AmEx   ☐ Discover

Credit Card # _____ **Exp. Date** _____

Signature _____

Name _____

Address _____

City _____ **State** ____ **Country** _____

Zip _____ **Daytime Phone** (____) _____
☐ Please check if you are a contractor.

Mail form to: Sunset/HomeStyles
P.O. Box 75488
St. Paul, MN 55175-0488

Or fax to: (612) 602-5002

FOR FASTER SERVICE CALL 1-800-820-1283

SS20

15

Adorable and Affordable

- This charming one-story home has much to offer, despite its modest size and economical bent.
- The lovely full-width porch has old-fashioned detailing, such as the round columns, decorative railings and ornamental molding.
- An open floor plan maximizes the home's square footage. The front door opens to the living room, where a railing creates a hallway effect while using very little space.
- Straight ahead, the dining room adjoins the island kitchen, while offering a compact laundry closet and sliding glass doors to a large rear patio.
- Focusing on quality, the home also offers features such as a 10-ft. tray ceiling in the living room and a 9-ft. stepped ceiling in the dining room.
- The three bedrooms are well proportioned. The master bedroom includes a private bathroom, while the two smaller bedrooms share another full bath. Note that the fixtures are arranged to reduce plumbing runs.

Plan AX-91316

Bedrooms: 3	Baths: 2
Living Area:	
Main floor	1,097 sq. ft.
Total Living Area:	**1,097 sq. ft.**
Basement	1,097 sq. ft.
Garage	461 sq. ft.
Exterior Wall Framing:	2x4

Foundation Options:

Daylight basement
Standard basement
Slab

(All plans can be built with your choice of foundation and framing. A generic conversion diagram is available. See order form.)

BLUEPRINT PRICE CODE: A

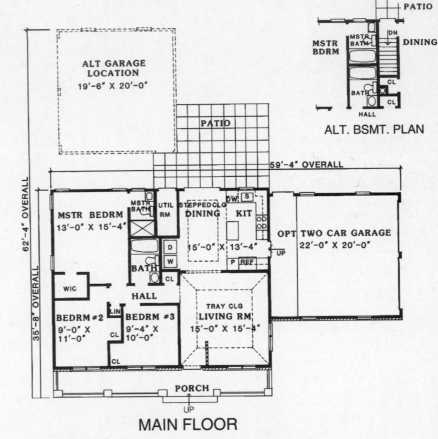

MAIN FLOOR

ALT. BSMT. PLAN

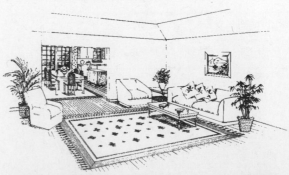

VIEW INTO LIVING ROOM AND DINING ROOM

TO ORDER THIS BLUEPRINT, CALL TOLL-FREE 1-800-820-1283

Plan AX-91316

PRICES AND DETAILS ON PAGES 12-15

Center of Attention

- Family togetherness is central to this home's appeal. Special attention was paid to create gathering areas where loved ones can meet and grow closer.
- Ornate posts adorn the porch, lending the facade a homey touch. You can almost hear the porch swing creak!
- Inside, the welcoming family room is immediately introduced. Its handsome fireplace basks in the glow from windows overlooking the side yard and front porch. Holidays and special events were meant to be enjoyed here.
- The joined kitchen and bayed dining room also provide ample opportunity for togetherness. Beautiful windows invite the angle of early morning sunlight, and a door allows you to step outside to enjoy the dwindling day.
- For privacy's sake, the master bedroom is removed from the two secondary bedrooms. Its bay window almost begs you to relax in your favorite chair with a good book. The private bath satisfies your need for practicality enveloped in simple beauty.

Plan L-1358

Bedrooms: 3	Baths: 2
Living Area:	
Main floor	1,358 sq. ft.
Total Living Area:	**1,358 sq. ft.**
Exterior Wall Framing:	2x4
Foundation Options:	

Slab
(All plans can be built with your choice of foundation and framing. A generic conversion diagram is available. See order form.)

BLUEPRINT PRICE CODE:	**A**

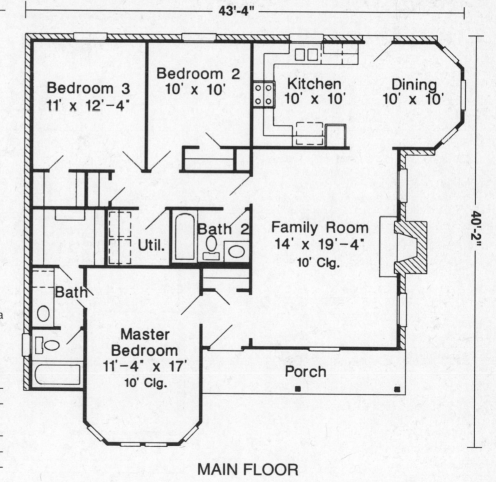

MAIN FLOOR

Cozy, Rustic Country Home

- This cozy, rustic home offers a modern, open interior that efficiently maximizes the square footage.
- The large living room features a 13-ft. sloped ceiling accented by rustic beams and an eye-catching corner fireplace.
- The living room flows into the adjoining dining room and the efficient U-shaped kitchen for a spacious, open feel.
- The master and secondary bedrooms are separated by the activity areas. The master suite includes a private bath and a separate dressing area with a dual-sink vanity.
- The secondary bedrooms share another full bath.

Plan E-1109

Bedrooms: 3	Baths: 2
Living Area:	
Main floor	1,191 sq. ft.
Total Living Area:	**1,191 sq. ft.**
Garage	462 sq. ft.
Storage	55 sq. ft.
Utility	55 sq. ft.
Exterior Wall Framing:	2x6

Foundation Options:

Crawlspace

Slab

(All plans can be built with your choice of foundation and framing. A generic conversion diagram is available. See order form.)

BLUEPRINT PRICE CODE: A

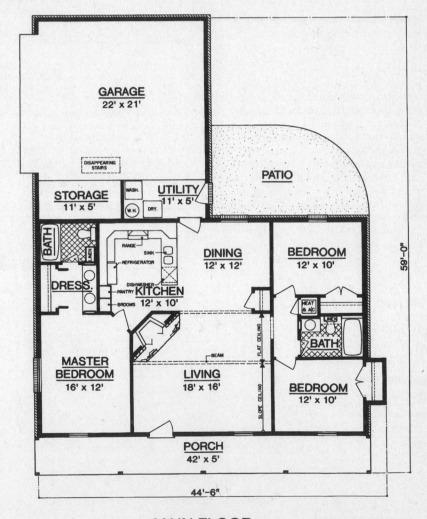

MAIN FLOOR

Plan E-1109

PRICES AND DETAILS ON PAGES 12-15

Appealing Farmhouse

- This appealing farmhouse design features a shady and inviting front porch with decorative railings.
- Inside, 14-ft. vaulted ceilings expand the living and dining rooms.
- This large area is brightened by bay windows and warmed by a unique two-way fireplace. Sliding glass doors lead to a sunny backyard patio.
- The functional kitchen includes a pantry closet, plenty of cabinet space and a serving bar to the dining room.
- The master bedroom boasts a mirrored dressing area, a private bath and abundant closet space.
- Two additional bedrooms share another full bath. The third bedroom includes a cozy window seat.

Plan NW-521

Bedrooms: 3	Baths: 2
Living Area:	
Main floor	1,187 sq. ft.
Total Living Area:	**1,187 sq. ft.**
Garage	448 sq. ft.
Exterior Wall Framing:	2x6

Foundation Options:

Crawlspace
(All plans can be built with your choice of foundation and framing. A generic conversion diagram is available. See order form.)

BLUEPRINT PRICE CODE: A

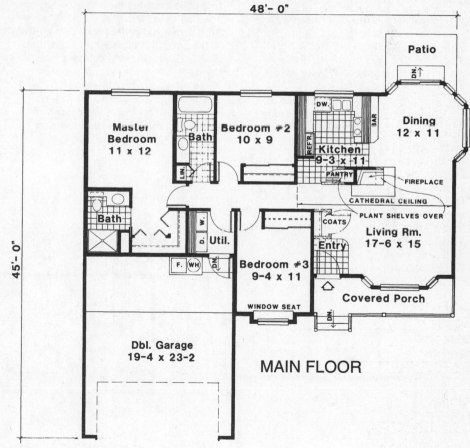

MAIN FLOOR

Tradition Updated

- The nostalgic exterior of this home gives way to dramatic cathedral ceilings and illuminating skylights inside.
- The covered front porch welcomes guests into the stone-tiled foyer, which flows into the living spaces.
- The living and dining rooms merge together, forming an open entertaining area under a 16-ft. cathedral ceiling.

- The family room shares the 16-ft. cathedral ceiling and a cozy three-sided fireplace with the living room. A sunny skylight and sliding glass doors to a patio brighten the room.
- The skylighted island kitchen offers a 16-ft. cathedral ceiling and easy access to the garage. A cheery breakfast nook with a 15-ft. cathedral ceiling serves as the perfect spot for everyday meals.
- The master suite boasts a walk-in closet and a skylighted bath with an 11-ft., 8-in. vaulted ceiling, a dual-sink vanity, a soaking tub and a separate shower.

Plan AX-90303-A

Bedrooms: 3	Baths: 2
Living Area:	
Main floor	1,615 sq. ft.
Total Living Area:	**1,615 sq. ft.**
Basement	1,615 sq. ft.
Garage	412 sq. ft.
Exterior Wall Framing:	2x4

Foundation Options:
Daylight basement
Standard basement
Crawlspace
Slab
(All plans can be built with your choice of foundation and framing. A generic conversion diagram is available. See order form.)

BLUEPRINT PRICE CODE: B

MAIN FLOOR

72'-4" OVERALL

32'-4" OVERALL

PATIO

SL GL DR

SKYLITE

CL W D

LAUN RM

UTIL RM

CATH CEIL
BRKFST RM
8'-6" x 11'-4"

DW S

CATH CEIL
KITCHEN
9'-6" x 13'-4"

SKYLITE

REF

CATH CEIL
FAMILY RM
15'-0" x 13'-4"

SKYLITE

FIREPLACE

MSTR BATH

BATH #2

WICL

MSTR BEDRM
15'-0" x 13'-4"

CL CL

TWO CAR GARAGE
20'-0" x 20'-0"

CATH CEIL
DINING RM
10'-2" x 12'-4"

CATH CEIL
LIVING RM
12'-6" x 13'-4"

LIN

CL

FOYER

BEDRM #3
10'-0" x 9'-8"

BEDRM #2
11'-4" x 11'-0"

PORCH

UP

Plan AX-90303-A

Details, Details!

- The wonderful Victorian details in this lovely one-story home create a stylish, yet practical, charm.
- Fishscale shingles, a railed wraparound porch and dual bay windows highlight the inviting exterior. You'll be tempted to stretch a hammock and spend the weekend relaxing on the cozy porch.
- Inside, the immense living room features a huge brick hearth and built in book shelves. Three large windows in front help to bring in the warmth of the sun.
- The galley-style kitchen comes equipped with a large walk-in pantry

and enough conveniences to make gourmet meals a breeze. The bayed dining room provides a sparkling setting for those culinary delights. Access to the backyard adds a pleasant and useful touch.
- A lavish bath awaits as just one of the alluring details in the master bedroom suite. A 12-ft.-high cathedral ceiling adds drama, while two walk-in closets, twin vanities, built-in bookshelves and its own linen closet make the suite smartly functional.
- Two more bedrooms, each with ample closet space and one with a gorgeous bay window, complete the design.

Plan L-1659	
Bedrooms: 3	**Baths:** 2
Living Area:	
Main floor	1,659 sq. ft.
Total Living Area:	**1,659 sq. ft.**
Exterior Wall Framing:	2x4
Foundation Options:	

Slab
(All plans can be built with your choice of foundation and framing. A generic conversion diagram is available. See order form.)

BLUEPRINT PRICE CODE:	B

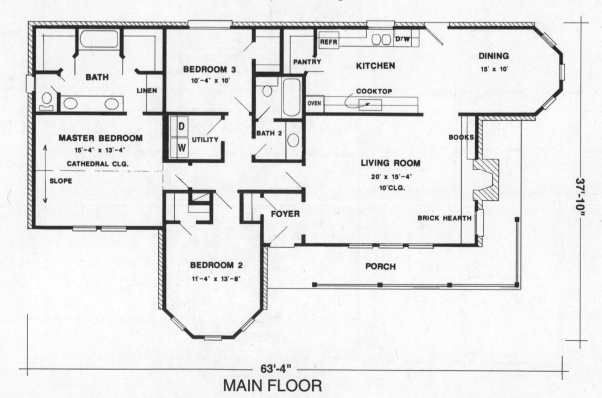

MAIN FLOOR

63'-4"

37'-10"

Charming Traditional

- The attractive facade of this traditional home features decorative fretwork and louvers in the gables, plus eye-catching window and door treatments.
- The entry area features a commanding view of the living room, which boasts a 12½-ft. ceiling and a corner fireplace. A rear porch and patio are visible through French doors.
- The bayed dining room shares an eating bar with the U-shaped kitchen. The nearby utility room includes a pantry and laundry facilities.
- The quiet master suite includes a big walk-in closet and a private bath with a dual-sink vanity.
- On the other side of the home, double doors close off the two secondary bedrooms from the living areas. A full bath services this wing.

Plan E-1428

Bedrooms: 3	Baths: 2

Living Area:

Main floor	1,415 sq. ft.
Total Living Area:	**1,415 sq. ft.**
Garage	484 sq. ft.
Storage	60 sq. ft.
Exterior Wall Framing:	**2x6**

Foundation Options:

Crawlspace
Slab

(All plans can be built with your choice of foundation and framing. A generic conversion diagram is available. See order form.)

BLUEPRINT PRICE CODE: **A**

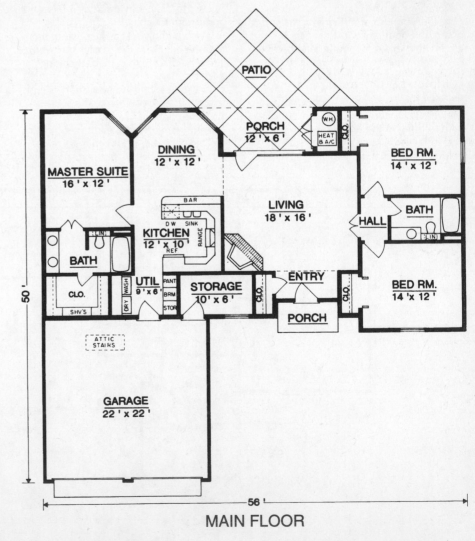

MAIN FLOOR

Open Invitation

- The wide front porch of this friendly country farmhouse presents an open invitation to all who visit.
- Highlighted by a round-topped transom, the home's entrance opens directly into the spacious living room, which features a warm fireplace flanked by windows.
- The adjoining dining area is enhanced by a lovely bay window and is easily serviced by the updated kitchen's angled snack bar.
- A bright sun room off the kitchen provides a great space for informal meals or relaxation. Access to a covered backyard porch is nearby.
- The good-sized master bedroom is secluded from the other sleeping areas. The lavish master bath includes a garden tub, a separate shower, a dual-sink vanity and a walk-in closet.
- Two more bedrooms share a second full bath. A laundry/utility room is nearby.
- An additional 1,007 sq. ft. of living space can be made available by finishing the upper floor.
- All ceilings are 9 ft. high for added spaciousness.

Plan J-91078

Bedrooms: 3	**Baths:** 2

Living Area:	
Main floor	1,846 sq. ft.
Total Living Area:	**1,846 sq. ft.**
Future upper floor	1,007 sq. ft.
Standard basement	1,846 sq. ft.
Garage	484 sq. ft.
Exterior Wall Framing:	2x6

Foundation Options:

Standard basement

Crawlspace

Slab

(All plans can be built with your choice of foundation and framing. A generic conversion diagram is available. See order form.)

BLUEPRINT PRICE CODE:	B

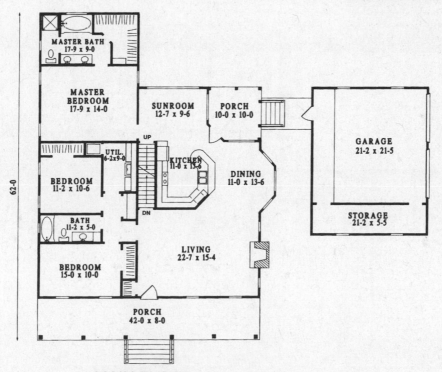

MAIN FLOOR

Family-Style Leisure Living

- This handsome ranch-style home features a floor plan that is great for family living and entertaining.
- In from the quaint covered porch, the spacious formal areas flow together for a dramatic impact. The living room is enhanced by a fireplace and a sloped ceiling. A patio door in the dining room extends activities to the outdoors.
- The efficient U-shaped kitchen opens to the dining room and offers a pantry, a

window above the sink and abundant counter space.
- A good-sized utility room with convenient laundry facilities opens to the carport. This area also includes a large storage room and disappearing stairs to even more storage space.
- Three bedrooms and two baths occupy the sleeping wing. The master suite features a large walk-in closet and a private bath.
- The two remaining bedrooms are well proportioned and share a hall bath. Storage space is well accounted for here as well, with two linen closets and a coat closet in the bedroom hall.

Plan E-1308	
Bedrooms: 3	**Baths: 2**
Living Area:	
Main floor	1,375 sq. ft.
Total Living Area:	**1,375 sq. ft.**
Carport	430 sq. ft.
Storage	95 sq. ft.
Exterior Wall Framing:	2x4

Foundation Options:

Crawlspace
Slab
(All plans can be built with your choice of foundation and framing. A generic conversion diagram is available. See order form.)

BLUEPRINT PRICE CODE: **A**

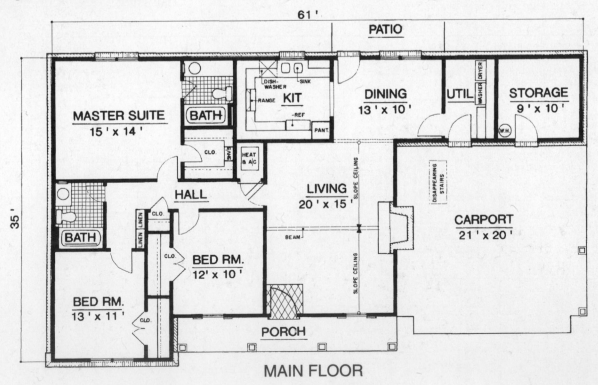

MAIN FLOOR

Quite a Cottage

- This cottage's inviting wraparound veranda is topped by an eye-catching metal roof that will draw admiring gazes from neighbors out for a stroll.
- Inside, the raised foyer ushers guests into your home in style. Straight ahead, built-in bookshelves line one wall in the living room, creating a look reminiscent of an old-fashioned library. A neat pass-through to the wet bar in the kitchen saves trips back and forth when you entertain friends.
- The family chef will love the gourmet kitchen, where an island cooktop frees counter space for other projects. For morning coffee and casual meals, the breakfast nook sets a cheery, relaxed tone. When appearances count, move out to the formal dining room.
- Across the home, the master suite serves as an oasis of peace and quiet. First thing in the morning, step out to the veranda to watch the rising sun soak up the mist. When you want a little extra special treatment, sink into the oversized garden tub for a long bath.
- The foremost bedroom boasts a large walk-in closet and built-in bookshelves for the student of the house.

Plan L-893-VSA

Bedrooms: 3	Baths: 2
Living Area:	
Main floor	1,891 sq. ft.
Total Living Area:	**1,891 sq. ft.**
Exterior Wall Framing:	2x4

Foundation Options:

Slab

(All plans can be built with your choice of foundation and framing. A generic conversion diagram is available. See order form.)

BLUEPRINT PRICE CODE:	**B**

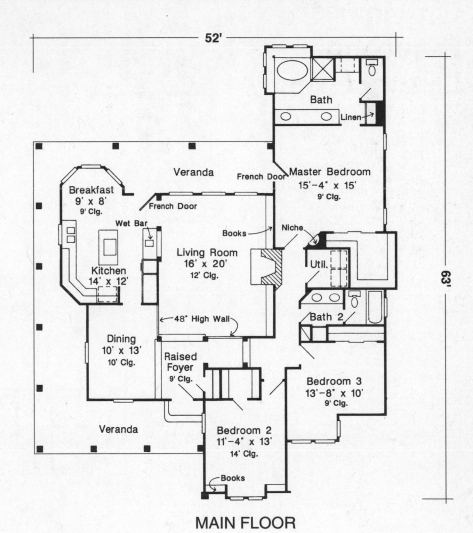

MAIN FLOOR

Gracious Demeanor

- Elegant windows and a covered porch adorn the facade of this country-style home, giving it a gracious demeanor.
- Directly ahead of the ornate foyer, the skylighted living room boasts a cozy fireplace flanked by shelves and cabinets. An impressive 12-ft., 5-in. vaulted ceiling rises overhead, while oversized windows provide great backyard views.
- The adjoining dining room is topped by an elaborate 10-ft. vaulted ceiling and offers a door to a skylighted porch. The porch unfolds to a large patio and accesses the huge garage.
- Behind double doors, the master bedroom presents a 12-ft., 5-in. vaulted ceiling. The master bath flaunts a garden tub and a private toilet.
- At the front of the home, two good-sized bedrooms share a full bath near the laundry room. The den or study may be used as an extra bedroom.

Plan J-9421

Bedrooms: 3+	Baths: 2
Living Area:	
Main floor	1,792 sq. ft.
Total Living Area:	**1,792 sq. ft.**
Standard basement	1,792 sq. ft.
Garage and storage	597 sq. ft.
Exterior Wall Framing:	2x4

Foundation Options:

Standard basement
Crawlspace
Slab
(All plans can be built with your choice of foundation and framing. A generic conversion diagram is available. See order form.)

BLUEPRINT PRICE CODE:	B

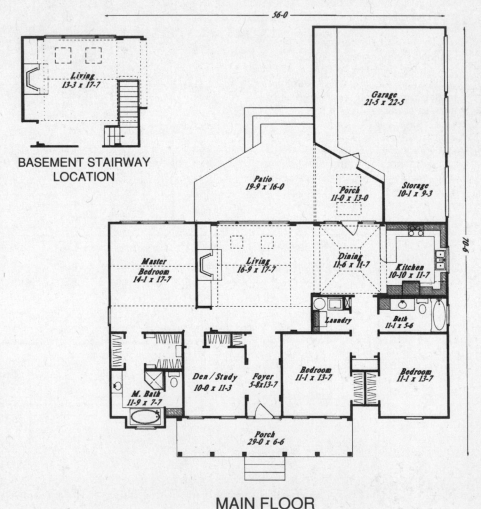

BASEMENT STAIRWAY LOCATION

MAIN FLOOR

Plan J-9421

PRICES AND DETAILS ON PAGES 12-15

Inviting Country Porch

- A columned porch with double doors invites you into the rustic living areas of this ranch-style home.
- Inside, the entry allows views back to the expansive, central living room and the backyard beyond.
- The living room boasts an exposed-beam ceiling and a massive fireplace with a wide stone hearth, a wood box and built-in bookshelves. A sunny patio offers additional entertaining space.
- The dining room and the efficient kitchen combine for easy meal service, with a serving bar separating the two.
- The main hallway leads to the sleeping wing, which offers a large master bedroom with a walk-in closet and a private bath.
- Two additional bedrooms share another full bath, and a laundry closet is easily accessible to the entire bedroom wing.

Plan E-1304	
Bedrooms: 3	**Baths:** 2
Living Area:	
Main floor	1,395 sq. ft.
Total Living Area:	**1,395 sq. ft.**
Garage and storage	481 sq. ft.
Exterior Wall Framing:	2x4
Foundation Options:	

Crawlspace
Slab
(All plans can be built with your choice of foundation and framing. A generic conversion diagram is available. See order form.)

BLUEPRINT PRICE CODE:	A

MAIN FLOOR

73'-0"

37'-0"

MASTER BEDROOM 14 x 13'

KNEE SPACE

DRESSING ROOM

CLOSET

LIVING 18' x 17'

BEAM

BEAM

STONE

PATIO

WOOD BOX

CLOSET · LINEN

WASH · DRY

HALL

STORAGE 7'-6" x 4'

REF. · RANGE

W.H.

DISAPPEARING STAIRS

BEDROOM 12' x 11'

BEDROOM 12' x 11'

HEAT & A.C.

CLOSET

CLOSET

ENTRY

DINING 12' x 11'

KITCHEN 12' x 10'

BAR

D.W. · SINK

GARAGE 21' x 21'

PORCH 42' x 7'

Plan E-1304

Indoor/Outdoor Delights

- A curved porch in the front and a garden sun room in the back make this home an indoor/outdoor delight.
- Inside, a roomy kitchen is open to a five-sided, glassed-in dining room that views out to the porch.
- The living room features a fireplace along a glass wall that adjoins the gloriously sunny garden room.

- Wrapped in windows, the garden room accesses the backyard as well as a large storage area in the unobtrusive, side-entry garage.
- The master suite is no less luxurious, featuring a a sumptuous master bath with a garden spa tub, a corner shower and a walk-in closet.
- Each of the two remaining bedrooms has a boxed-out window and a walk-in closet. A full bath with a corner shower and a dual-sink vanity is close by.
- A stairway leads to the attic, which provides more potential living space.

Plan DD-1852

Bedrooms: 3	Baths: 2
Living Area:	
Main floor	1,852 sq. ft.
Total Living Area:	**1,852 sq. ft.**
Standard basement	1,852 sq. ft.
Garage	528 sq. ft.
Exterior Wall Framing:	2x4

Foundation Options:

Standard basement
Crawlspace
Slab
(All plans can be built with your choice of foundation and framing. A generic conversion diagram is available. See order form.)

BLUEPRINT PRICE CODE: B

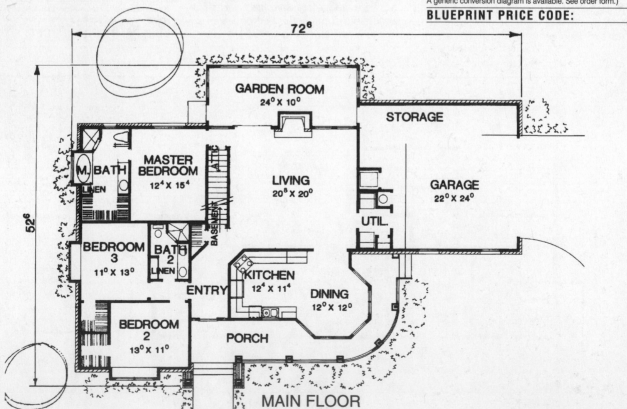

MAIN FLOOR

TO ORDER THIS BLUEPRINT, CALL TOLL-FREE 1-800-820-1283

Plan DD-1852

PRICES AND DETAILS ON PAGES 12-15

Tasteful Charm

- Columned covered porches lend warmth and charm to the front and rear of this tasteful traditional home.
- Sidelight and transom glass brightens the entry foyer, which shares a 10-ft. ceiling with the elegant dining room.
- The dining room provides a quiet spot for formal meals, while a Palladian window arrangement adds light and flair.
- The spacious living room offers a warm fireplace and an adjacent TV cabinet. The dramatic ceiling vaults to a height of 11 ft., 8 inches. French doors give way to the skylighted rear porch, which is finished with lovely brick pavers.

Two brick steps descend to the adjoining patio, which is also beautifully paved with brick.
- The gourmet kitchen offers a built-in oven/microwave cabinet, a separate cooktop and an island snack bar with a sink. Its 10-ft. ceiling extends into the sunny breakfast nook.
- The oversized laundry room includes a handy half-bath, a wall-to-wall storage cabinet, a hanging rod, a large sink and nearby porch access.
- The secluded master bedroom boasts a 12-ft. vaulted ceiling and a large walk-in closet. In the private master bath, a glass-block divider separates the whirlpool tub from the shower stall.

Plan J-9414

Bedrooms: 3	Baths: 2½
Living Area:	
Main floor	1,974 sq. ft.
Total Living Area:	**1,974 sq. ft.**
Standard basement	1,974 sq. ft.
Garage and storage	518 sq. ft.
Exterior Wall Framing:	2x4

Foundation Options:
Standard basement
Crawlspace
Slab
(All plans can be built with your choice of foundation and framing A generic conversion diagram is available. See order form.)

BLUEPRINT PRICE CODE:	B

BASEMENT STAIRWAY LOCATION

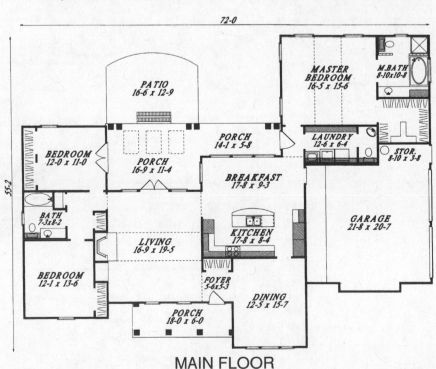

MAIN FLOOR

While Away an Afternoon

- The pretty porch that stretches along the front of this traditional home provides plenty of room for sitting and whiling away an afternoon. Try a porch swing on one end and a cluster of comfortable wicker furniture on the other.
- Inside, handsome columns introduce the living room and the dining room, on either side of the foyer. A 10-ft. tray ceiling lends a touch of elegance to the living room, while the open relationship to the dining room consolidates formal affairs in one impressive space.
- At the rear, the Great Room, the breakfast nook and the kitchen flow into one another, creating an easygoing, casual spot for family fun. In the Great Room, a neat media wall holds the TV, the VCR and the stereo. An angled fireplace adds a bit of rustic charm to the setting.
- Tucked away for privacy, the master bedroom provides a pleasant retreat. A stepped ceiling crowns the room, while a bay window serves as a sitting area.

Plan AX-5374	
Bedrooms: 3	**Baths: 2**
Living Area:	
Main floor	1,902 sq. ft.
Total Living Area:	**1,902 sq. ft.**
Standard basement	1,925 sq. ft.
Garage and storage	552 sq. ft.
Exterior Wall Framing:	2x4
Foundation Options:	
Standard basement	
Crawlspace	
Slab	

(All plans can be built with your choice of foundation and framing. A generic conversion diagram is available. See order form.)

BLUEPRINT PRICE CODE: **B**

VIEW INTO GREAT ROOM

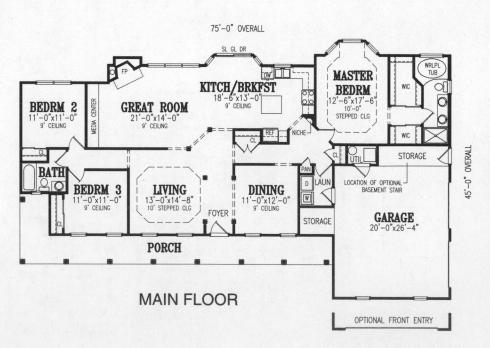

MAIN FLOOR

 Plan AX-5374

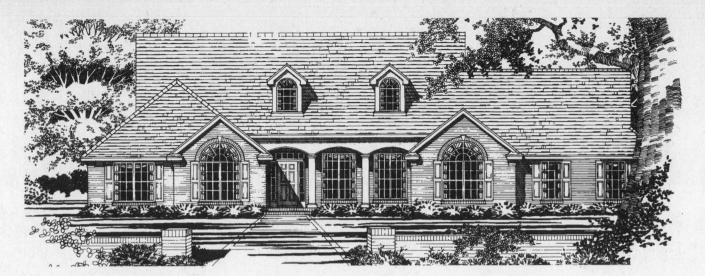

Country Road

- The pretty countenance of this one-story home makes it look as if it was plucked straight from a winding country road. Whether rocking on the front porch, or reading a book by a sunny window, you will love the home's peaceful nature.
- An elegant gallery welcomes guests inside and leads through four handsome columns into the impressive living room. When you want to roll out the red carpet, this is the room.
- On the right, the breakfast nook and the kitchen merge together, creating an efficient space for casual meals. A neat

serving counter between the two rooms holds dishes, platters and pitchers while serving dinner. In the kitchen, an island cooktop frees up counter space to chop vegetables for your stir-fry.
- The home's showstopper is the fantastic media room. Instead of driving to a crowded theater, settle into a comfortable easy chair for a night of entertainment in your own home.
- Across the home, the master bedroom boasts private access to a patio. As the day begins and ends, the amenity-packed bath offers luxurious treatment for the masters of the home. A large walk-in closet completes the suite.

Plan DD-2510

Bedrooms: 3+	Baths: 2
Living Area:	
Main floor	2,510 sq. ft.
Total Living Area:	**2,510 sq. ft.**
Standard basement	2,510 sq. ft.
Garage and workshop	508 sq. ft.
Exterior Wall Framing:	2x4

Foundation Options:
Standard basement
Crawlspace
Slab
(All plans can be built with your choice of foundation and framing. A generic conversion diagram is available. See order form.)

BLUEPRINT PRICE CODE:	D

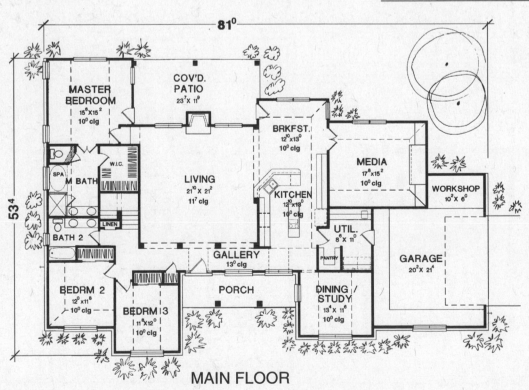

MAIN FLOOR

Believe It!

- For those who don't believe they can get all the bells and whistles in an affordable home, this one-story design will be a dream come true.
- Out front, the porch includes ample room for two favorite rocking chairs. Have a seat and enjoy the sunset!
- Inside, the sunken living room extends to the dining room, creating a consolidated space for special affairs.
- Located to provide easy service to the dining room and the breakfast nook, the kitchen will be a buzz of activity.

- In the skylighted family room, a 12-ft., 3-in. vaulted ceiling adds freshness. Serving as a rustic focal point, the brick fireplace and log storage area display decorative brick arches. Another arch frames the adjacent wet bar, which is sure to come in handy.
- The gem of the home, the screened patio, is also serviced by the wet bar. This area is ideal for a summer night of cocktails and conversation.
- A cozy window seat and private access to the patio make the master suite a peaceful retreat, while a 10-ft., 4-in. vaulted ceiling adds a bit of spice.

Plan HDS-99-270

Bedrooms: 4	**Baths:** 2

Living Area:	
Main floor	2,173 sq. ft.
Total Living Area:	**2,173 sq. ft.**
Screened patio	311 sq. ft.
Garage	462 sq. ft.

Exterior Wall Framing:

2x4 and 8-in. concrete block

Foundation Options:

Slab

(All plans can be built with your choice of foundation and framing. A generic conversion diagram is available. See order form.)

BLUEPRINT PRICE CODE:	**C**

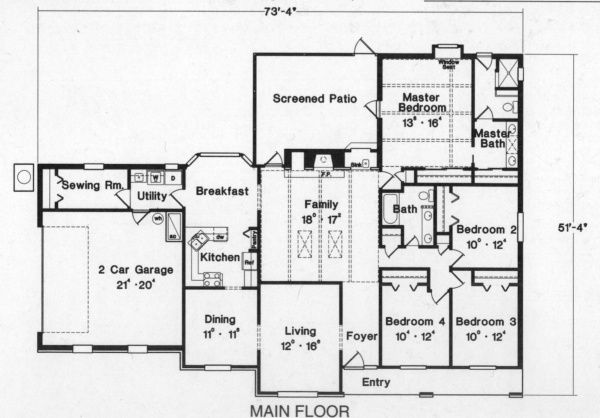

MAIN FLOOR

Plan HDS-99-270

PRICES AND DETAILS ON PAGES 12-15

Sweet Whisper of Nostalgia

- This home's covered porch, fishscale shingles and detailed columns bring a sweet whisper of nostalgia to any neighborhood. On steamy summer nights, the porch provides a front-row seat for watching thunderstorms.
- Inside, the family room will serve as the focal point of the home. When gathering to catch up on the day's events, family members will gravitate to this comfortable area. A 14½-ft. vaulted ceiling creates an added sense of space.
- Located off the family room, a second porch provides a more private spot for outdoor entertaining. What a lovely setting for visiting with friends!
- Near the kitchen, a serving bar provides a place for snacks during Friday night card games. Easy access between the garage and the kitchen saves steps when unloading heavy groceries.
- Across the home, highlights in the master suite include a walk-in closet and a private, split bath.
- Unless otherwise noted, all rooms include 9-ft. ceilings.

Plan VL-1463

Bedrooms: 3	Baths: 2
Living Area:	
Main floor	1,463 sq. ft.
Total Living Area:	**1,463 sq. ft.**
Garage and utility	468 sq. ft.
Exterior Wall Framing:	2x4

Foundation Options:

Crawlspace
Slab
(All plans can be built with your choice of foundation and framing. A generic conversion diagram is available. See order form.)

BLUEPRINT PRICE CODE:	A

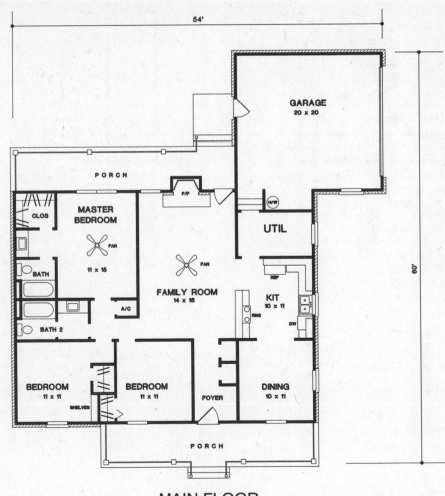

MAIN FLOOR

TO ORDER THIS BLUEPRINT, CALL TOLL-FREE 1-800-820-1283

Plan VL-1463

PRICES AND DETAILS ON PAGES 12-15

Breathtaking Open Space

- Soaring ceilings and an open floor plan add breathtaking volume to this charming country-style home.
- The inviting covered-porch entrance opens into the spacious living room, which boasts a spectacular 17-ft.-high cathedral ceiling. Two overhead dormers fill the area with natural light, while a fireplace adds warmth.
- Also under the cathedral ceiling, the kitchen and bayed breakfast room share an eating bar. Skylights brighten the convenient laundry room and the computer room, which provides access to a covered rear porch.
- The secluded master bedroom offers private access to another covered porch. The skylighted master bath has a walk-in closet and a 10-ft. sloped ceiling above a whirlpool tub.
- Optional upper-floor areas provide future expansion space for the needs of a growing family.

Plan J-9302

Bedrooms: 3+	Baths: 2
Living Area:	
Main floor	1,745 sq. ft.
Total Living Area:	**1,745 sq. ft.**
Upper floor (future area)	500 sq. ft.
Future area above garage	241 sq. ft.
Standard basement	1,745 sq. ft.
Garage and storage	559 sq. ft.
Exterior Wall Framing:	2x4

Foundation Options:

Standard basement

Crawlspace

Slab

(All plans can be built with your choice of foundation and framing. A generic conversion diagram is available. See order form.)

BLUEPRINT PRICE CODE: B

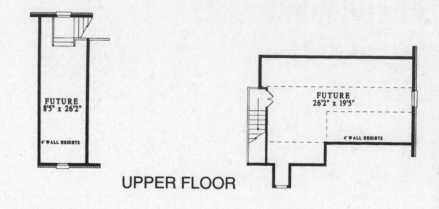

UPPER FLOOR

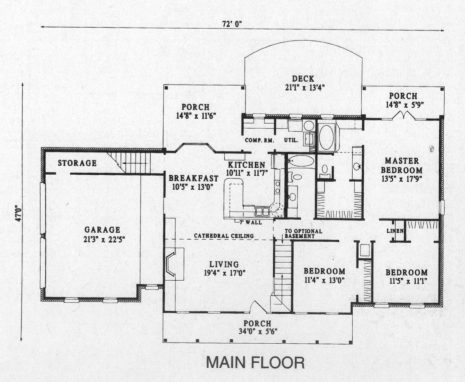

MAIN FLOOR

TO ORDER THIS BLUEPRINT, CALL TOLL-FREE 1-800-820-1283   Plan J-9302   *PRICES AND DETAILS ON PAGES 12-15*

Country Highlights

- This nice home has country highlights, with shuttered windows, lap siding and a quaint covered porch.
- The foyer flows into the spacious living room, which offers a 9-ft.-high ceiling, a warm fireplace and tall windows that give views to the front porch. French doors open from the adjoining dining room to a backyard terrace.
- The kitchen features a sunny dinette that accesses the terrace, plus an angled pass-through to the dining room. A nifty mudroom with laundry facilities accesses the garage and the terrace.
- The master bedroom boasts a large walk-in closet and a private bath with a dual-sink vanity, a whirlpool tub and a separate shower.
- Across the home, two secondary bedrooms share another full bath.
- Dormered windows brighten the unfinished upper floor, which provides for future expansion possibilities.

Plan HFL-1700-SR

Bedrooms: 3+	Baths: 2
Living Area:	
Main floor	1,567 sq. ft.
Total Living Area:	**1,567 sq. ft.**
Upper floor (unfinished)	338 sq. ft.
Standard basement	1,567 sq. ft.
Garage	504 sq. ft.
Exterior Wall Framing:	2x6

Foundation Options:

Standard basement

Slab

(All plans can be built with your choice of foundation and framing. A generic conversion diagram is available. See order form.)

BLUEPRINT PRICE CODE:	**B**

VIEW INTO LIVING ROOM

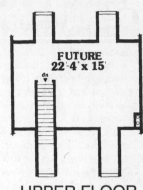

FUTURE
22'-4" x 15'

UPPER FLOOR

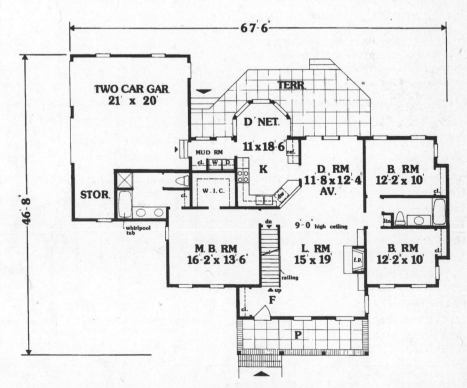

MAIN FLOOR

Shady Porches, Sunny Patio

- Designed with stylish country looks, this attractive one-story also has shady porches and a sunny patio for relaxed indoor/outdoor living.
- The inviting foyer flows into the spacious living room, which is warmed by a handsome fireplace.
- The adjoining dining room has a door to a screened-in porch, which opens to the

backyard and serves as a breezeway to the nearby garage
- The U-shaped kitchen has a pantry closet and plenty of counter space. Around the corner, a space-efficient laundry/utility room exits to a big backyard patio.
- The master bedroom is brightened by windows on two sides and includes a wardrobe closet. The compartmentalized master bath offers a separate dressing area and a walk-in closet.
- Another full bath serves two additional good-sized bedrooms.

Plan C-7557	
Bedrooms: 3	**Baths: 2**
Living Area:	
Main floor	1,688 sq. ft.
Total Living Area:	**1,688 sq. ft.**
Daylight basement	1,688 sq. ft.
Garage	400 sq. ft.
Exterior Wall Framing:	2x4

Foundation Options:
Daylight basement
Crawlspace
Slab
(All plans can be built with your choice of foundation and framing. A generic conversion diagram is available. See order form.)

BLUEPRINT PRICE CODE: **B**

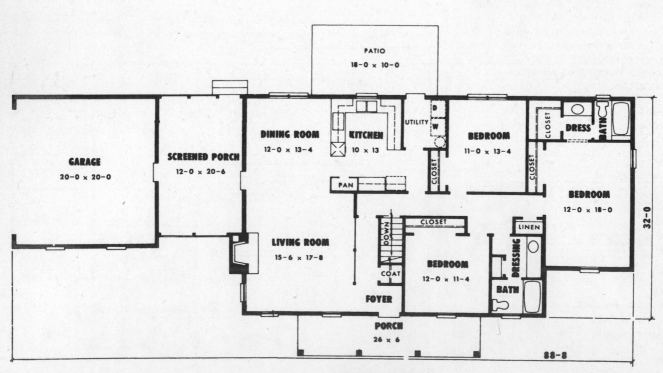

MAIN FLOOR

TO ORDER THIS BLUEPRINT, CALL TOLL-FREE 1-800-820-1283   Plan C-7557   *PRICES AND DETAILS ON PAGES 12-15*

Design Fits Narrow Lot

- This compact, cozy and dignified plan makes great use of a small lot, while also offering an exciting interior design.
- In from the covered front porch, the living room features a warm fireplace and a 13-ft., 6-in. cathedral ceiling.
- The bay-windowed dining room joins the living room to provide a spacious area for entertaining.
- The galley-style kitchen has easy access to a large pantry closet, the utility room and the carport.
- The master suite includes a deluxe bath and a roomy walk-in closet.
- Two secondary bedrooms share another bath off the hallway.
- A lockable storage area is located off the rear patio.

Plan J-86161

Bedrooms: 3	Baths: 2
Living Area:	
Main floor	1,626 sq. ft.
Total Living Area:	**1,626 sq. ft.**
Standard basement	1,626 sq. ft.
Carport	410 sq. ft.
Storage	104 sq. ft.
Exterior Wall Framing:	2x4

Foundation Options:

Standard basement
Crawlspace
Slab

(All plans can be built with your choice of foundation and framing. A generic conversion diagram is available. See order form.)

BLUEPRINT PRICE CODE: **B**

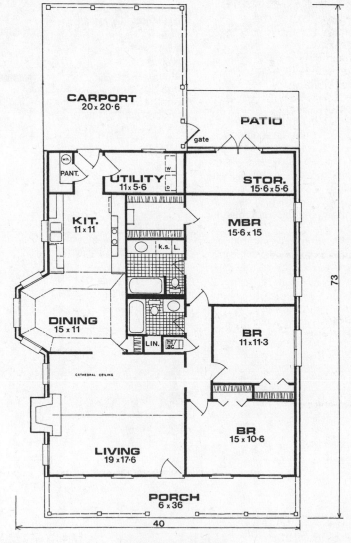

MAIN FLOOR

Captivating Showpiece

- This design is sure to be the showpiece of the neighborhood, with its captivating blend of traditional and contemporary features.
- The angled front porch creates an eye-catching look. Inside, the foyer, the dining room and the Great Room are expanded by 9-ft., 4-in. tray ceilings and separated by columns.
- The dining room features a spectacular arched window, while the spacious Great Room hosts a fireplace framed by windows overlooking the rear terrace.
- The glass-filled breakfast room is given added impact by a 9-ft., 4-in. tray ceiling. The adjoining kitchen offers an expansive island counter with an eating bar and a cooktop.
- A wonderful TV room or home office views out to the front porch.
- The master suite is highlighted by a 9-ft., 10-in. tray ceiling and a sunny sitting area with a large picture window topped by an arched transom.

Plan AX-92322

Bedrooms: 3+	Baths: 2
Living Area:	
Main floor	1,699 sq. ft.
Total Living Area:	**1,699 sq. ft.**
Standard basement	1,740 sq. ft.
Garage	480 sq. ft.
Exterior Wall Framing:	2x4

Foundation Options:

Standard basement
Crawlspace
Slab

(All plans can be built with your choice of foundation and framing. A generic conversion diagram is available. See order form.)

BLUEPRINT PRICE CODE: **B**

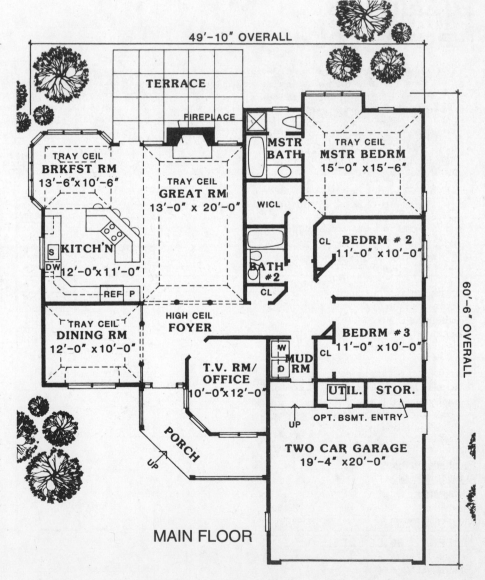

MAIN FLOOR

49'-10" OVERALL
60'-6" OVERALL

TERRACE
FIREPLACE
TRAY CEIL BRKFST RM 13'-6"x10'-6"
TRAY CEIL GREAT RM 13'-0" x 20'-0"
MSTR BATH
TRAY CEIL MSTR BEDRM 15'-0" x15'-6"
WICL
KITCH'N 12'-0"x11'-0"
S
DW
REF P
BATH #2
CL
CL BEDRM #2 11'-0" x10'-0"
TRAY CEIL DINING RM 12'-0" x 10'-0"
HIGH CEIL FOYER
BEDRM #3 11'-0" x 10'-0"
CL
W MUD D RM
T.V. RM/ OFFICE 10'-0"x12'-0"
UTIL. STOR.
UP OPT. BSMT. ENTRY
PORCH
UP
UP
TWO CAR GARAGE 19'-4" x20'-0"

Arranged for Family Living

- This distinguished ranch home has a neatly arranged floor plan with a large activity area at the center and a strategically placed master bedroom.
- The formal living room and dining room flank the entry. The dining room provides views out to the covered front porch and a decorative planter with brick veneer. The living room boasts corner windows and a display niche with shelves.
- The double-doored entry also opens to a large sunken family room with a 13-ft. cathedral ceiling, a handsome fireplace, a patio view and a 10-ft-high decorative bridge.
- The huge modern kitchen offers a handy snack counter to the adjacent family room. The bayed breakfast room has French-door access to an expansive covered patio.
- Secluded to one end of the home is the deluxe master bedroom, which offers an 11-ft. cathedral ceiling, a spacious walk-in closet and French-door patio access. The master bath has a dual-sink vanity and outdoor access.
- Three additional bedrooms and two more baths are located at the opposite end of the home.

Plan Q-2266-1A

Bedrooms: 4	Baths: 3
Living Area:	
Main floor	2,266 sq. ft.
Total Living Area:	**2,266 sq. ft.**
Garage	592 sq. ft.
Exterior Wall Framing:	2x4

Foundation Options:

Slab

(All plans can be built with your choice of foundation and framing. A generic conversion diagram is available. See order form.)

BLUEPRINT PRICE CODE: C

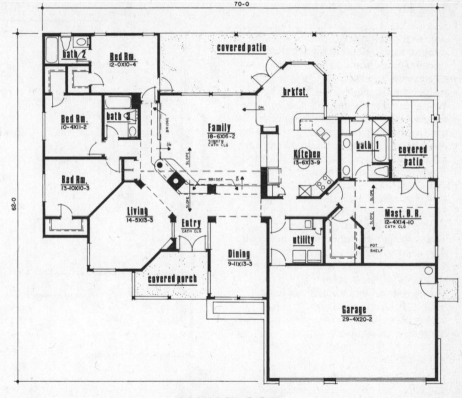

MAIN FLOOR

Morning Room with a View

- This modern-looking ranch is stylishly decorated with a pair of arched-window dormers, handsome brick trim and a covered front porch.
- Inside, the dining room is set off by columns, as it merges with the entry.
- The main living areas are oriented to the rear, where a huge central family room offers a patio view and a fireplace that may also be enjoyed from the bayed morning room and adjoining kitchen.
- The walk-through kitchen features a pantry, a snack bar to the family room and easy service to the formal dining room across the hall.
- The secluded master suite boasts a wide window seat and a private bath with a walk-in closet, a corner garden tub and a separate shower.
- Across the home, the three secondary bedrooms share another full bath. The fourth bedroom may double as a study.
- High 10-ft. ceilings are found throughout the home, except in the secondary bedrooms.

Plan DD-1962-1

Bedrooms: 3+	Baths: 2
Living Area:	
Main floor	1,962 sq. ft.
Total Living Area:	**1,962 sq. ft.**
Standard basement	1,962 sq. ft.
Garage	386 sq. ft.
Exterior Wall Framing:	2x4

Foundation Options:

Standard basement

Crawlspace

Slab

(All plans can be built with your choice of foundation and framing. A generic conversion diagram is available. See order form.)

BLUEPRINT PRICE CODE: **B**

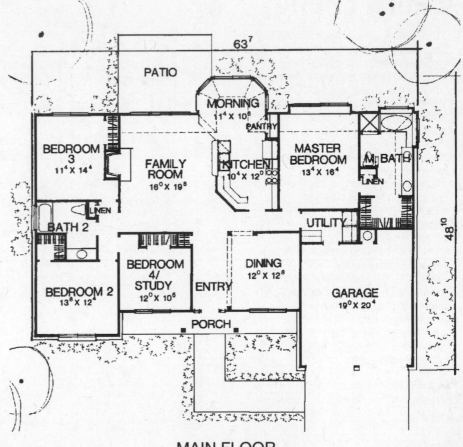

MAIN FLOOR

A Perfect Fit

- This country-style home will fit anywhere. Its charming character and narrow width make it ideal for those who value vintage styling along with plenty of yard space.
- The quaint covered front porch opens into the living room, which boasts a 12-ft., 8-in. cathedral ceiling and an inviting fireplace.
- The adjacent bay-windowed dining area features a 9-ft.-high vaulted ceiling and easy access to the efficient, galley-style kitchen.
- Off the kitchen, a handy laundry/utility room is convenient to the back entrance. The carport can accommodate two cars and includes a lockable storage area.
- The master bedroom suite offers a roomy walk-in closet, a private bath and sliding glass doors to a rear patio.
- Another full bath is centrally located for easy service to the rest of the home. Two more nice-sized bedrooms complete the plan.

Plan J-86119

Bedrooms: 3	Baths: 2
Living Area:	
Main floor	1,346 sq. ft.
Total Living Area:	**1,346 sq. ft.**
Standard basement	1,346 sq. ft.
Carport	400 sq. ft.
Exterior Wall Framing:	2x4

Foundation Options:

Standard basement

Crawlspace

Slab

(All plans can be built with your choice of foundation and framing. A generic conversion diagram is available. See order form.)

BLUEPRINT PRICE CODE:	A

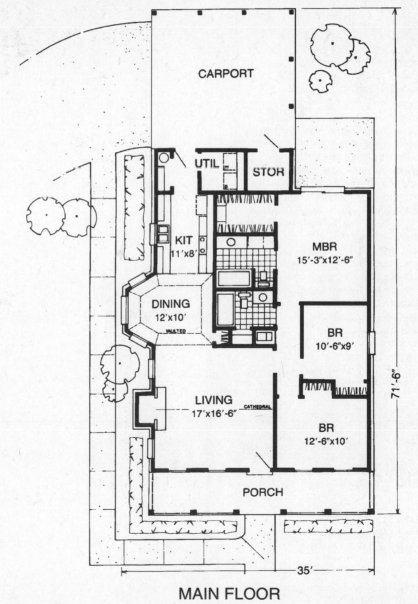

MAIN FLOOR

Attainable Luxury

- This traditional ranch home offers a large, central living room with a 12-ft. ceiling, a corner fireplace and an adjoining patio.
- The U-shaped kitchen easily services both the formal dining room and the bayed eating area.
- The luxurious master suite features a large bath with separate vanities and dressing areas.
- Two secondary bedrooms share a second full bath.
- A covered carport boasts a decorative brick wall and attic space above. Two additional storage areas provide plenty of room for gardening supplies and sports equipment.

Plan E-1812

Bedrooms: 3	Baths: 2
Living Area:	
Main floor	1,860 sq. ft.
Total Living Area:	**1,860 sq. ft.**
Carport	484 sq. ft.
Storage	132 sq. ft.
Exterior Wall Framing:	2x6

Foundation Options:

Crawlspace

Slab

(All plans can be built with your choice of foundation and framing. A generic conversion diagram is available. See order form.)

BLUEPRINT PRICE CODE: B

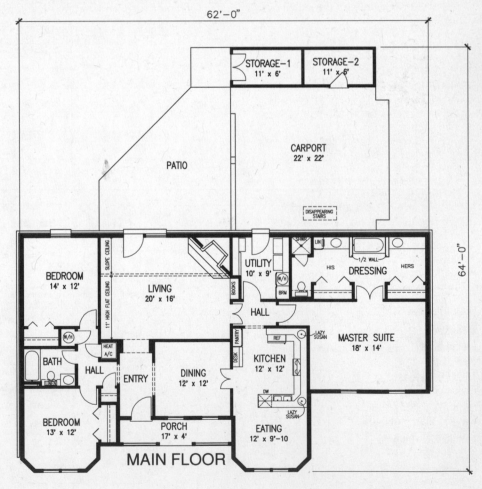

MAIN FLOOR

TO ORDER THIS BLUEPRINT, CALL TOLL-FREE 1-800-820-1283

Plan E-1812

PRICES AND DETAILS ON PAGES 12-15

Elegant Facade

- Eye-catching windows and columns add elegance to both the front and rear of this appealing ranch-style home.
- The columns of the covered front porch are repeated inside, defining the spacious gallery. The central section soars to a height of 20 ft., 4 in., basking in sunlight from a windowed dormer.
- The gorgeous Great Room features a cozy fireplace flanked by built-ins. Two sets of sliding glass doors with elliptical transoms open to a backyard terrace.
- The gourmet kitchen offers a handy snack bar, while the breakfast room expands to a columned rear porch.
- The peaceful dining room boasts a stepped ceiling that rises to 10 ft. at the stunning front window.
- The secluded master suite provides a sitting area, porch access and a private whirlpool bath with dual sinks and wardrobe closets.
- The second bedroom is brightened by an arched window arrangement under a 12½-ft.-high vaulted area.
- Ceilings are at least 9½ ft. high throughout the home.

Plan AX-4315

Bedrooms: 3	Baths: 2
Living Area:	
Main floor	2,018 sq. ft.
Total Living Area:	**2,018 sq. ft.**
Basement	2,018 sq. ft.
Garage/storage/utility	474 sq. ft.
Exterior Wall Framing:	2x4

Foundation Options:

Daylight basement
Standard basement
Crawlspace
Slab

(All plans can be built with your choice of foundation and framing. A generic conversion diagram is available. See order form.)

BLUEPRINT PRICE CODE: C

VIEW INTO GREAT ROOM

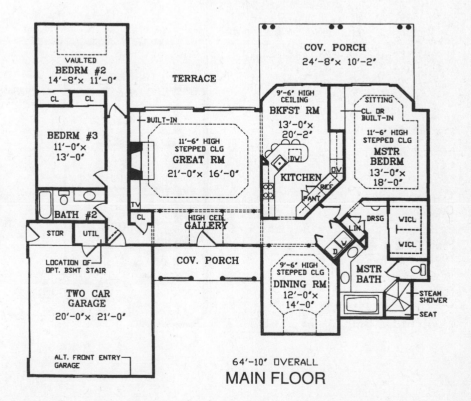

MAIN FLOOR

Classic Country-Style

- The classic covered front porch with decorative railings and columns make this home reminiscent of an early 20th-century farmhouse.
- Dormers give the home the appearance of a two-story, even though it is designed for single-level living.
- The huge living room features a ceiling that slopes up to 13 feet. A corner fireplace radiates warmth to both the living room and the dining room.
- The dining room overlooks a backyard patio and shares a versatile serving bar with the open kitchen. A large utility room is just steps away.
- The master bedroom boasts a roomy bath with a dual-sink vanity. The two smaller bedrooms at the other end of the home share a full bath.

Plan E-1412

Bedrooms: 3	Baths: 2
Living Area:	
Main floor	1,484 sq. ft.
Total Living Area:	**1,484 sq. ft.**
Garage	440 sq. ft.
Exterior Wall Framing:	2x6

Foundation Options:

Crawlspace

Slab

(All plans can be built with your choice of foundation and framing. A generic conversion diagram is available. See order form.)

BLUEPRINT PRICE CODE: A

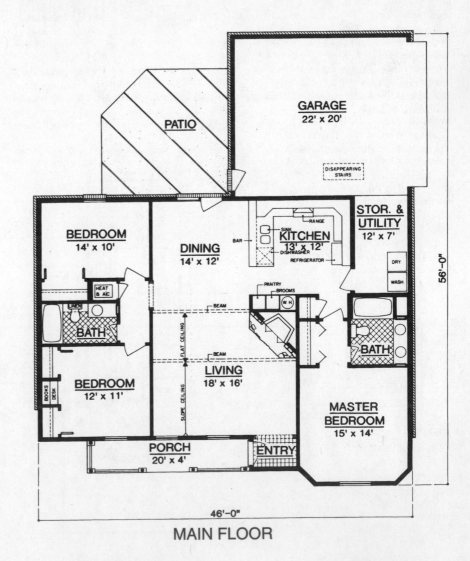

MAIN FLOOR

Plan E-1412

PRICES AND DETAILS ON PAGES 12-15

Still Life with Potential

- Imagine the possibilities waiting to be discovered in this quiet, unassuming country home!
- Its nostalgic porch begs to be enjoyed; a sultry summer night and a cedar porch swing would complete the scene nicely.
- A family favorite, the vaulted Great Room beckons all to relax in front of its fireplace. The French doors flanking the fireplace open to a skylighted porch that spills onto a backyard patio.

- An oversized breakfast nook unfolds to the island kitchen, where the family chef will have plenty of room to move about. If Easter is a favorite holiday, you'll have plenty of room to decorate those eggs! Close by, the utility room lets you perform other tasks while spending quality time with the kids.
- Any budding entrepreneurs in your family? Have them set up shop in the handy office space near the master bedroom. Two doors close off noise.
- The master bedroom is fit for royalty, and flaunts a private bath with a lovely raised tub and a separate shower. Twin walk-in closets separate your clothes.

Plan J-9306	
Bedrooms: 3+	**Baths:** 2½
Living Area:	
Upper floor (optional balcony)	118 sq. ft.
Main floor	2,310 sq. ft.
Total Living Area:	**2,428 sq. ft.**
Upper floor (future areas)	982 sq. ft.
Standard basement	2,310 sq. ft.
Garage	518 sq. ft.
Storage	180 sq. ft.
Exterior Wall Framing:	2x4
Foundation Options:	

Standard basement
Crawlspace
Slab
(All plans can be built with your choice of foundation and framing. A generic conversion diagram is available. See order form.)

BLUEPRINT PRICE CODE:	C

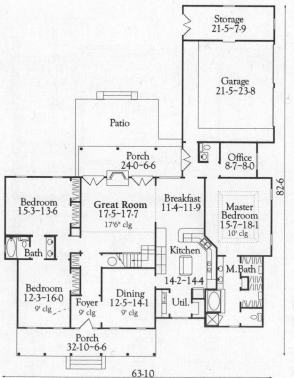

MAIN FLOOR

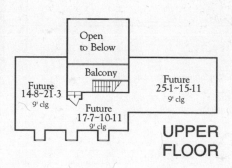

UPPER FLOOR

Traditional Heritage

- A distinctive roofline and a covered wraparound porch reflect this charming home's traditional heritage.
- The roomy entry flows directly into the spacious, open living area. Enhanced by a cathedral ceiling, the living room is warmed by a fireplace and offers a French door to a backyard patio. A good-sized laundry room is nearby.

- The adjoining dining area shares porch access with the stylish gourmet kitchen, which includes an eating bar and a garden window over the sink.
- The master bedroom suite features a lavish private bath with a garden spa tub, a separate shower, a dual-sink vanity and a big walk-in closet.
- A second full bath, located at the end of the bedroom hallway, is convenient to the two remaining bedrooms.
- The double carport includes a separate lockable storage area.

Plan J-86142

Bedrooms: 3	**Baths:** 2

Living Area:	
Main floor	1,536 sq. ft.
Total Living Area:	**1,536 sq. ft.**
Standard basement	1,536 sq. ft.
Carport and storage	520 sq. ft.
Exterior Wall Framing:	2x4

Foundation Options:

Standard basement
Crawlspace
Slab

(All plans can be built with your choice of foundation and framing. A generic conversion diagram is available. See order form.)

BLUEPRINT PRICE CODE:	B

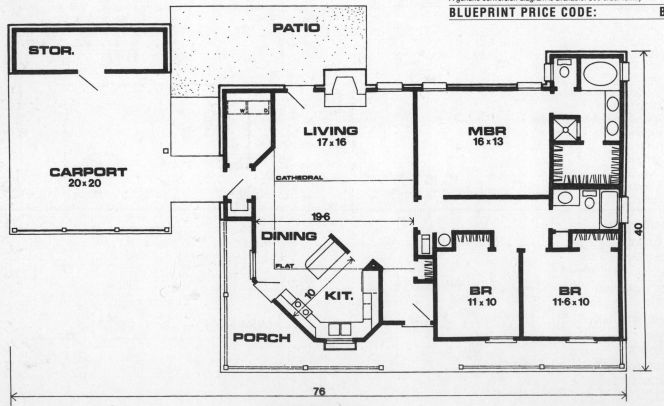

MAIN FLOOR

Plan J-86142

PRICES AND DETAILS ON PAGES 12-15

A Real Original

- This home's round window, elegant entry and transom windows create an eye-catching, original look.
- Inside, high ceilings and tremendous views let the eyes wander. The foyer provides an exciting look at an expansive deck and inviting spa through the living room's tall windows. The windows frame a handsome fireplace, while a 10-ft. ceiling adds volume and interest.
- To the right of the foyer is a cozy den or home office with its own fireplace, 10-ft. ceiling and dramatic windows.
- The spacious kitchen/breakfast area features an oversized snack bar island and opens to a large screen porch. Within easy reach are the laundry room and the entrance to the garage.
- The bright formal dining room overlooks the deck and boasts a ceiling that vaults up to 10 feet.
- The secluded master suite looks out to the deck as well, with access through a patio door. The private bath features a dynamite corner spa tub, a separate shower and a large walk-in closet.
- A second bedroom and bath complete the main floor.

Plan B-90065

Bedrooms: 2+	Baths: 2
Living Area:	
Main floor	1,889 sq. ft.
Total Living Area:	**1,889 sq. ft.**
Screen porch	136 sq. ft.
Standard basement	1,889 sq. ft.
Garage	406 sq. ft.
Exterior Wall Framing:	2x6

Foundation Options:

Standard basement

(All plans can be built with your choice of foundation and framing. A generic conversion diagram is available. See order form.)

BLUEPRINT PRICE CODE: B

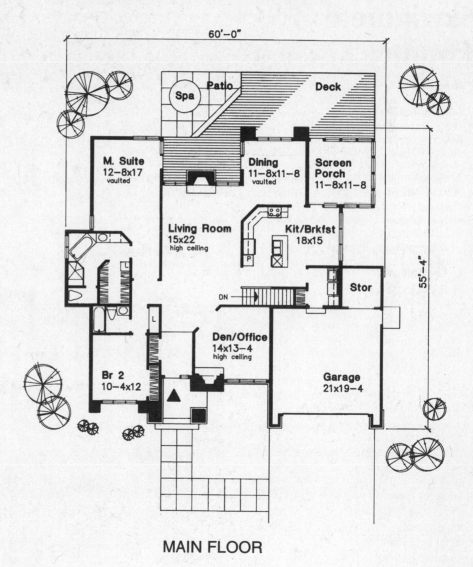

MAIN FLOOR

Skylighted Country Kitchen

- This country ranch-style home combines rustic wood posts and shutters with stylish curved glass.
- The tiled foyer unfolds to the dramatic, flowing formal areas. The living room and the bayed dining room each offer a 9-ft. stepped ceiling and a view of one of the two covered porches.
- The skylighted country kitchen shares the family room's warm fireplace. The kitchen's central island cooktop and snack bar make serving a breeze!
- In addition to the fireplace, the family room also boasts an 11-ft. vaulted ceiling and gliding French doors to the adjacent porch.
- The bedroom wing houses three bedrooms and two full baths. The master bedroom shows off a relaxing sitting bay and a 9-ft., 9-in. tray ceiling. The skylighted master bath flaunts a whirlpool tub and a dual-sink vanity.
- Each of the secondary bedrooms has a 10-ft., 9-in. ceiling area above its lovely arched window.

Plan AX-92321

Bedrooms: 3	Baths: 2
Living Area:	
Main floor	1,735 sq. ft.
Total Living Area:	**1,735 sq. ft.**
Standard basement	1,735 sq. ft.
Garage, storage and utility	505 sq. ft.
Exterior Wall Framing:	2x4

Foundation Options:

Standard basement
Crawlspace
Slab

(All plans can be built with your choice of foundation and framing. A generic conversion diagram is available. See order form.)

BLUEPRINT PRICE CODE:	**B**

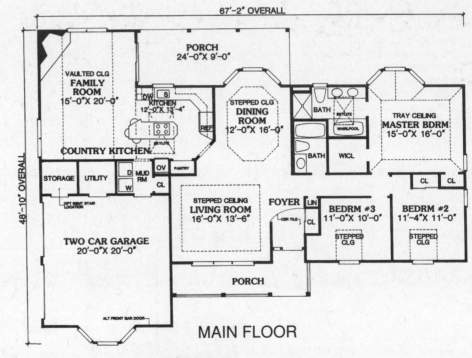

MAIN FLOOR

REAR VIEW

TO ORDER THIS BLUEPRINT, CALL TOLL-FREE 1-800-820-1283   Plan AX-92321   **PRICES AND DETAILS ON PAGES 12-15**

Classic Styling

- This handsome one-story traditional would look great in town or in the country. The shuttered and paned windows, narrow lap siding and brick accents make it a classic.
- The sprawling design begins with the spacious, central living room, featuring a beamed ceiling that slopes up to 14 feet. A window wall overlooks the covered backyard porch, and an

inviting fireplace includes an extra-wide hearth and built-in bookshelves.
- The galley-style kitchen features a snack bar to the sunny eating area and a raised-panel door to the dining room.
- The isolated master suite is a quiet haven offering a large walk-in closet, a dressing room and a spacious bath.
- Three more bedrooms, two with walk-in closets, and a compartmentalized bath are located at the opposite side of the home.

Plan E-2206	
Bedrooms: 4	**Baths:** 2
Living Area:	
Main floor	2,200 sq. ft.
Total Living Area:	**2,200 sq. ft.**
Standard basement	2,200 sq. ft.
Garage and storage	624 sq. ft.
Exterior Wall Framing:	2x6

Foundation Options:
Standard basement
Crawlspace
Slab
(All plans can be built with your choice of foundation and framing. A generic conversion diagram is available. See order form.)

BLUEPRINT PRICE CODE: C

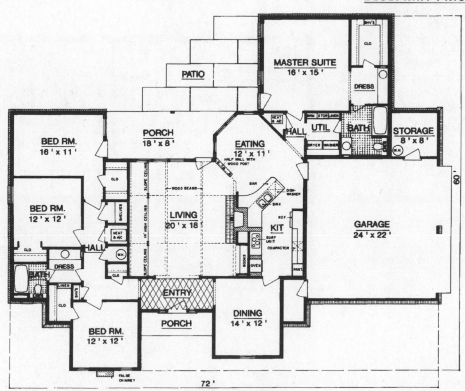

MAIN FLOOR

Friendly Farmhouse

- Reminiscent of a turn-of-the-century farmhouse, this warm, friendly home is characterized by an authentic front porch with fine post-and-rail detailing.
- The open entry provides a sweeping view of the dining room and the adjoining living room. Three columns function as an elegant divider between the two rooms. The living room features a 12-ft.-high sloped ceiling with exposed beams, an inviting fireplace, built-in bookshelves and windows overlooking the rear patio.
- A nice-sized eating area opens to the airy kitchen, which offers a snack bar, a pantry and a lazy Susan. Double doors conceal a utility room with extra storage space.
- Another set of double doors opens to the bedroom wing, where all three bedrooms have walk-in closets. The master bedroom has a private bath with a dual-sink vanity. The secondary bedrooms share another full bath.

Plan E-1813

Bedrooms: 3	Baths: 2
Living Area:	
Main floor	1,892 sq. ft.
Total Living Area:	**1,892 sq. ft.**
Carport	440 sq. ft.
Storage	120 sq. ft.
Exterior Wall Framing:	2x6

Foundation Options:

Crawlspace
Slab

(All plans can be built with your choice of foundation and framing. A generic conversion diagram is available. See order form.)

BLUEPRINT PRICE CODE:	B

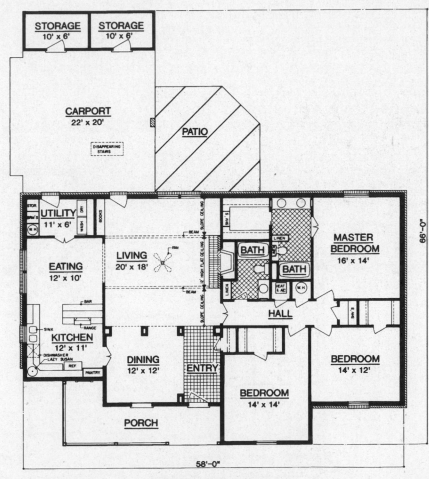

MAIN FLOOR

Plan E-1813

PRICES AND DETAILS
ON PAGES 12-15

Extraordinary Split-Level

- This design boasts a striking arched window in an inviting facade that introduces an extraordinary split-level floor plan.
- The recessed entry opens into the expansive living room, with its fabulous windows, nice fireplace and breathtaking 12-ft. vaulted ceiling.
- The dining room, which features a 14-ft. vaulted ceiling, expands the open living area and lends an air of spaciousness to the entire main floor.
- The kitchen is a gourmet's dream, offering a wraparound counter, a double sink and a pass-through to the dining room. A 12-ft. vaulted ceiling is shared with the sunny breakfast room, which shows off a built-in desk and sliding-door access to a backyard deck.
- The sizable master bedroom, a second bedroom and a shared bath are several steps up from the main level, creating a sense of privacy.
- The third bedroom makes a great den, playroom, office or guest room.

Plan B-87112

Bedrooms: 2+	Baths: 2
Living Area:	
Main floor	1,452 sq. ft.
Total Living Area:	**1,452 sq. ft.**
Standard basement	1,452 sq. ft.
Garage	448 sq. ft.
Exterior Wall Framing:	2x4

Foundation Options:

Standard basement
(All plans can be built with your choice of foundation and framing. A generic conversion diagram is available. See order form.)

BLUEPRINT PRICE CODE: A

MAIN FLOOR

64'-8"

40'-4"

MBr 15-4x11-8
Br 2 11-6x11-8
Deck
Desk
Brkfst 12-8x7 vaulted
Kit vaulted
DN UP
Dining 9x12 vaulted
Garage 21-4x21
Br 3/ Den 13x11-6
Entry
Living Rm 20x13 vaulted

Plan B-87112

Country Sophistication

- Arched windows, high ceilings and a luxurious master suite lend a certain sophistication to this inviting country-style home.
- A wraparound porch reminds you of years gone by as it welcomes guests.
- Inside, the entry foyer offers views of the living den and the patio beyond. A fireplace and a 10-ft. ceiling enhance the living den, making it a great place to gather. A French door opens to the covered patio, for summer entertaining.

- The walk-through kitchen includes a handy pantry and an L-shaped breakfast bar. Place your favorite hors d'oeuvres here and watch them disappear!
- Enjoy a quiet cup of coffee in the bay-windowed breakfast room before beginning your day.
- Brightened by a tall, arched window arrangement under a 10-ft. ceiling, the elegant dining room will host your holiday meals in style!
- A 10-ft. ceiling presides over the secluded master bedroom, which boasts direct access to the patio. The master bath is second to none, with its step-up garden tub, sit-down shower and two walk-in closets.

Plan KD-1805	
Bedrooms: 3	Baths: 2
Living Area:	
Main floor	1,805 sq. ft.
Total Living Area:	1,805 sq. ft.
Garage and storage	431 sq. ft.
Exterior Wall Framing:	2x4
Foundation Options:	

Slab

(All plans can be built with your choice of foundation and framing. A generic conversion diagram is available. See order form.)

BLUEPRINT PRICE CODE: B

MAIN FLOOR

Plan KD-1805

PRICES AND DETAILS ON PAGES 12-15

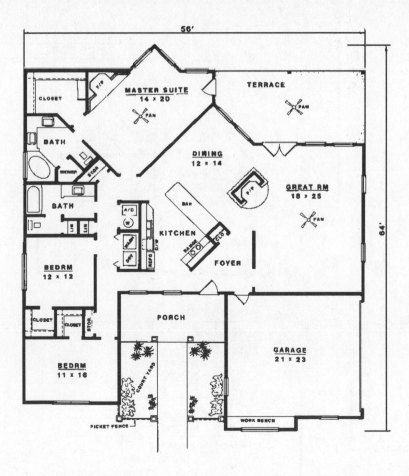

Attractive Angles

- Unique angles and open circulation is the theme for this traditional Early American styled home.
- Centered around a stone fireplace are the foyer, Great Room, dining room and angled kitchen with counter bar, all with a rear view to the terrace and backyard.
- The unique angles carry through to the exciting master suite, which offers its own cozy fireplace, panoramic rear view and private access to the terrace; the colorful master bath offers a garden tub, twin vanities and separate shower.
- A nice hall bath, convenient laundry facilities and two more bedrooms complete the floor plan.

Plan VL-2121	
Bedrooms: 3	**Baths: 2**
Space:	
Main floor	2,121 sq. ft.
Total Living Area	**2,121 sq. ft.**
Garage	483 sq. ft.
Exterior Wall Framing	2x4
Foundation options:	
Crawlspace	
Slab	
(Foundation & framing conversion diagram available—see order form.)	
Blueprint Price Code	C

Traditional Design for Hillside Home

- Window walls and solarium glass capture the view and fill this home with light.
- Traditional exterior is at home in any neighborhood.
- Deluxe master bedroom suite opens onto private deck.
- Lower level features huge recreation room with abundant window space.
- Deck off kitchen/nook provides delightful outdoor dining area.

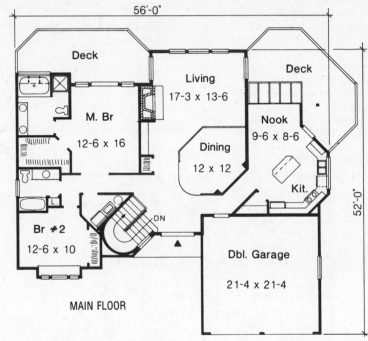

MAIN FLOOR

56'-0"

Deck

M. Br 12-6 x 16

Br #2 12-6 x 10

Living 17-3 x 13-6

Deck

Dining 12 x 12

Nook 9-6 x 8-6

Kit.

DN

Dbl. Garage 21-4 x 21-4

52'-0"

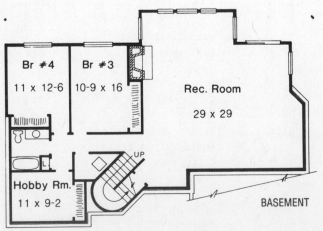

Br #4 11 x 12-6

Br #3 10-9 x 16

Rec. Room 29 x 29

Hobby Rm. 11 x 9-2

UP

BASEMENT

Plan NW-812

Bedrooms: 4	Baths: 3

Space:	
Main floor:	1,685 sq. ft.
Lower floor:	1,611 sq. ft.
Total living area:	**3,296 sq. ft.**
Garage:	460 sq. ft.

Exterior Wall Framing:	2x6

Foundation options:
Daylight basement only.
(Foundation & framing conversion diagram available — see order form.)

Blueprint Price Code:	E

TO ORDER THIS BLUEPRINT, CALL TOLL-FREE 1-800-820-1283

Plan NW-812

PRICES AND DETAILS ON PAGES 12-15

Welcome Home

- An inviting covered porch welcomes you home to this country-kissed ranch.
- Inside, a 16-ft. cathedral ceiling soars over the expansive living room, which boasts a fireplace flanked by windows.
- Bathed in sunlight from more windows, the dining room flaunts an elegant French door that opens to a delightful backyard porch.
- The gourmet kitchen features a planning desk, a pantry and a unique, angled bar—a great place to settle for an afternoon snack. Garage access is conveniently nearby.

- Smartly secluded in one corner of the home is the lovely and spacious master bedroom, crowned by a 10-ft. tray ceiling. Other amenities include huge his-and-hers walk-in closets and a private bath with a garden tub and a dual-sink vanity.
- A neat laundry closet near the master bedroom is handy for last-minute loads.
- Two secondary bedrooms round out this wonderful design. The front-facing bedroom is complemented by a 10-ft. vaulted ceiling, while the rear bedroom offers a sunny window seat. A full bath accented by a stylish round window is shared by both rooms.

Plan J-91085

Bedrooms: 3	Baths: 2

Living Area:	
Main floor	1,643 sq. ft.
Total Living Area:	**1,643 sq. ft.**
Standard basement	1,643 sq. ft.
Garage and storage	480 sq. ft.
Exterior Wall Framing:	2x4

Foundation Options:

Standard basement
Crawlspace
Slab
(All plans can be built with your choice of foundation and framing. A generic conversion diagram is available. See order form.)

BLUEPRINT PRICE CODE:	B

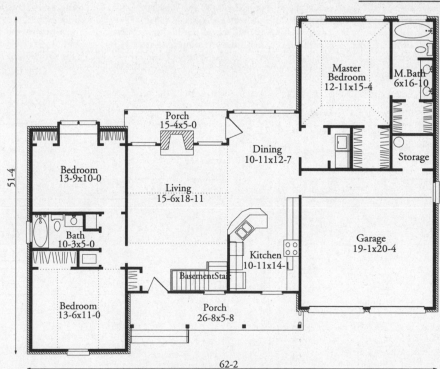

MAIN FLOOR

Traditional One-Story Cottage

Shuttered windows, covered porch trimmed with Colonial style posts and fascia, small window panes that match the paneling of the garage doors, clapboard siding with corner board trim, and other Colonial touches combine to imbue this cottage with Early American charm.

An attractive and functional entrance hall with convenient closet space acts as a buffer between the casual and formal activity areas. At the rear of the house, the kitchen with dining space has sliding glass doors leading to a rear garden terrace.

Designed for family living, the plan features three bedrooms and two full baths, one of which serves the master bedroom privately. You will also note the master bedroom has an oversized walk-in closet. The central walkway that serves the bedroom wing is flanked on both sides by numerous storage and linen closets. Both bathrooms have built-in vanities.

Another interesting feature is the play room located at the rear of the attached garage. A utility room of generous proportions is also found in both versions of the plan. The plan with a basement provides for a family room that measures 17' x 11'. A convenient access to the garage connects with the hallway leading to the family room. A corner fireplace with a raised hearth opening is featured in both plans.

Overall width of the home measures 60' and the greatest depth including front and rear projections is 40'.

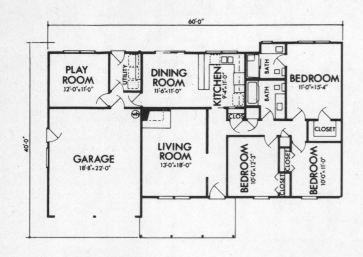

PLAN H-3707-1A
WITHOUT BASEMENT
(CRAWLSPACE FOUNDATION)

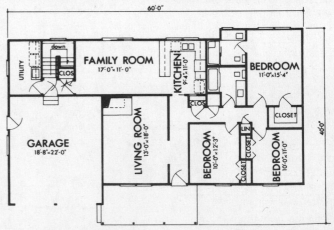

PLAN H-3707-1
WITH BASEMENT

Total living area: 1,486 sq. ft.
(Not counting garage)

Blueprint Price Code A

Plans H-3707-1 & -1A

TO ORDER THIS BLUEPRINT, CALL TOLL-FREE 1-800-820-1283

PRICES AND DETAILS ON PAGES 12-15

Taste of the Sea

- This stylish home recalls the roar of the sea with its distinct Cape Cod flavor.
- A wide, covered porch introduces the entry, which empties directly into the massive living room, with its handsome fireplace.
- From the efficient island kitchen and its neighboring breakfast nook, French doors open to a dazzling sun room. Beyond a dramatic wall of windows is a curved patio.
- Striking columns add style to the formal dining room, which also leads to the sun room.
- While housing the laundry facilities, a spacious hobby room provides a great space for relaxing pastimes.
- The master bedroom's private bath includes a garden tub a separate shower and a dressing area with knee space.
- In the opposite wing, two more bedrooms with walk-in closets share a compartmentalized bath.
- Expansion space is available on the upper floor for recreation or extra bedrooms.

Plan J-9506

Bedrooms: 3+	**Baths:** 2½
Living Area:	
Main floor	2,597 sq. ft.
Total Living Area:	**2,597 sq. ft.**
Future upper floor	735 sq. ft.
Standard basement	2,597 sq. ft.
Garage and storage	487 sq. ft.
Exterior Wall Framing:	2x6

Foundation Options:

Standard basement
Crawlspace
Slab

(All plans can be built with your choice of foundation and framing. A generic conversion diagram is available. See order form.)

BLUEPRINT PRICE CODE:	D

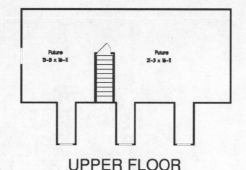

UPPER FLOOR

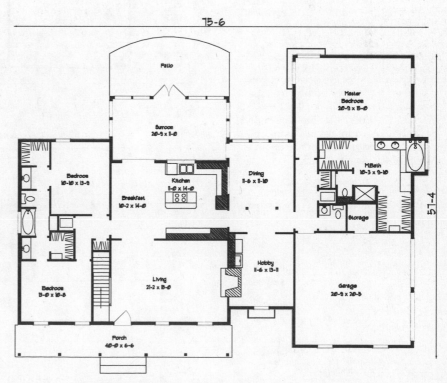

MAIN FLOOR

Well-Appointed Walk-Out Design

- The hipped roof and covered entry give this well-appointed home a look of distinction.
- Inside, the foyer leads directly into the expansive Great Room, which boasts a 13-ft. vaulted ceiling, an inviting fireplace, a built-in entertainment center and a dramatic window wall that overlooks an exciting full-width deck with a hot tub!
- A half-wall separates the Great Room from the nook, which is open to the U-shaped kitchen. The impressive kitchen includes a snack bar, a walk-in pantry and a greenhouse window.
- The isolated master suite offers a vaulted ceiling that slopes up to 9 feet. A French door opens to the deck and hot tub, while a pocket door accesses the sumptuous master bath with a spa tub under a glass-block wall.
- Two more bedrooms in the walk-out basement share another full bath. The optional expansion areas provide an additional 730 sq. ft. of space.

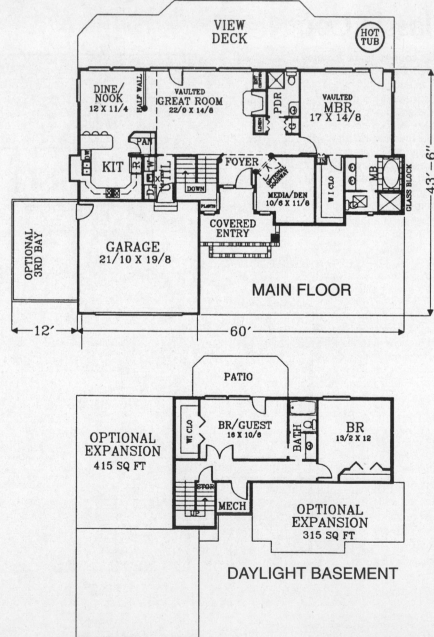

MAIN FLOOR

DAYLIGHT BASEMENT

Plan S-41792

Bedrooms: 3	Baths: 3
Living Area:	
Main floor	1,450 sq. ft.
Partial daylight basement	590 sq. ft.
Total Living Area:	**2,040 sq. ft.**
Garage	429 sq. ft.
Unfinished expansion areas	730 sq. ft.
Exterior Wall Framing:	2x6

Foundation Options:

Partial daylight basement
(All plans can be built with your choice of foundation and framing. A generic conversion diagram is available. See order form.)

BLUEPRINT PRICE CODE: C

TO ORDER THIS BLUEPRINT,
CALL TOLL-FREE 1-800-820-1283

Plan S-41792

PRICES AND DETAILS
ON PAGES 12-15

Classic Country

- This country home features a classic exterior and a luxurious interior design in an economical floor plan.
- A covered front porch leads through a sidelighted entry directly to the living room. A coat closet is close by.
- Stylish windows brighten the spacious living room, where a handsome recessed fireplace crackles. A marvelous 12-ft., 3-in. vaulted ceiling soars overhead and extends to the dining room and kitchen.

- Stately columns set off the entry to the dining room, which offers French-door access to a backyard terrace that is perfect for summertime entertainment.
- The dining room and the efficient kitchen share a stylish serving bar.
- The secluded master suite is graced by a 12-ft. cathedral ceiling. A French door opens to a private terrace.
- The master bath flaunts a refreshing whirlpool tub and a separate shower.
- Lovely windows bring natural light into two more bedrooms. A hall bath easily services both rooms.

Plan AHP-9507

Bedrooms: 3	**Baths: 2**

Living Area:

Main floor	1,232 sq. ft.
Total Living Area:	**1,232 sq. ft.**
Standard basement	1,183 sq. ft.
Garage and storage	324 sq. ft.
Exterior Wall Framing:	2x4 or 2x6

Foundation Options:

Standard basement
Crawlspace
Slab
(All plans can be built with your choice of foundation and framing. A generic conversion diagram is available. See order form.)

BLUEPRINT PRICE CODE:	**A**

MAIN FLOOR

60'-4"
35'-2"

TERRACE

TERRACE

shr. whirlpool tub

MASTER SUITE
15 x 12
high ceiling

w.i.c.

cl. shr.

DINING
19 x 11
high ceiling

bar dw

KITCH

MUD RM

d
w

STORAGE

HALL

lin

high ceiling

ref. ptr.

dn.

GARAGE
11'-8" x 23'-8"

BED RM
10 x 10

BED RM
12'-4" x 10'

cl.

cl.

LIVING RM
19 x 13'-4"
fireplace

cl.

PORCH

railing

Modern Masterpiece

- This home's clean, modern lines, expansive windows and distinguished columns set the tone for the exciting floor plan found within.
- High ceilings and bright, open spaces are the hallmarks of the home. The impressive foyer, the dining room and the adjoining living room all have 12-ft.-high ceilings. Elegant archways lead from the hall to the dining room and from the living room to the nook.
- The sunny nook and adjoining family room are filled with glass. The adjacent kitchen includes a generous snack counter and a high opening above the stove. The family room features a 10-ft. ceiling, a fireplace and built-in shelves.
- Double doors lead to the roomy den and the dynamite master suite, each with a 10-ft. ceiling. The master suite features a superb bath with a spa tub and an oversized shower area.
- The cleverly designed hall bath serves guests from both indoors and out, while the two remaining bedrooms enjoy private access to another full bath.

Plan HDS-99-149

Bedrooms: 3+	Baths: 3
Living Area:	
Main floor	2,149 sq. ft.
Total Living Area:	**2,149 sq. ft.**
Garage	400 sq. ft.
Exterior Wall Framing:	2x4

Foundation Options:

Slab
(All plans can be built with your choice of foundation and framing. A generic conversion diagram is available. See order form.)

BLUEPRINT PRICE CODE: C

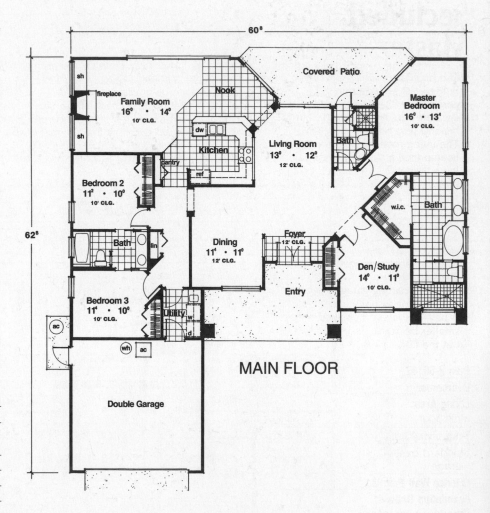

MAIN FLOOR

TO ORDER THIS BLUEPRINT, CALL TOLL-FREE 1-800-820-1283

Plan HDS-99-149

PRICES AND DETAILS ON PAGES 12-15

Secluded Master Suite

- The highlight of this cozy country home is its secluded master suite, complete with step-up garden tub, separate shower, dual vanities and his-and-hers walk-in closets.
- The living room is also stunning, with its impressive cathedral ceiling and large fireplace. The adjacent dining room is defined by striking columns and 36-in.-high cabinets. Dining guests will enjoy the lovely view of the rear porch and yard.
- The roomy kitchen features a pantry, a snack bar and plenty of counter space. A remarkable oversized utility area is just steps away.
- The side-loading garage keeps the front of the home visually appealing.
- A bay-windowed front bedroom, a smaller bedroom and a full bath round out the floor plan.

Plan J-86167

Bedrooms: 3	Baths: 2
Living Area:	
Main floor	1,880 sq. ft.
Total Living Area:	**1,880 sq. ft.**
Standard basement	1,880 sq. ft.
Garage	460 sq. ft.
Exterior Wall Framing:	2x4

Foundation Options:
Standard basement
Crawlspace
Slab
(Typical foundation & framing conversion diagram available—see order form.)

BLUEPRINT PRICE CODE:	B

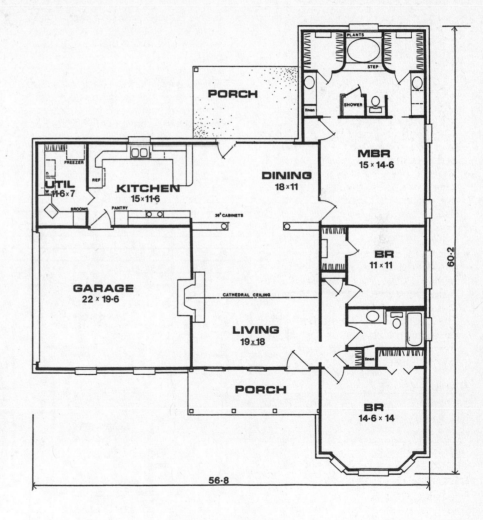

MAIN FLOOR

Compact Colonial

- This Colonial-style farmhouse ranch projects a warm feeling with its characteristic front porch and stone accents.
- The interior offers three distinct living spaces.
- The formal living and dining areas overlook the porch and the front yard.
- The informal family room and U-shaped kitchen combine at the rear of the home. Features include a decorative stone wall with fireplace, a sunny bay window and sliders that open to the patio.
- The sleeping wing is compactly arranged around three bedrooms. The master bedroom has a private bath, and the two additional bedrooms share a second bath, conveniently located near the foyer as well.

Plan HFL-1490-DV	
Bedrooms: 3	**Baths:** 2 ½
Space:	
Main floor	1,591 sq. ft.
Total Living Area	**1,591 sq. ft.**
Basement	875 sq. ft.
Garage	390 sq. ft.
Exterior Wall Framing	2x4
Foundation options:	
Partial Basement	
Slab	
(Foundation & framing conversion diagram available—see order form.)	
Blueprint Price Code	**B**

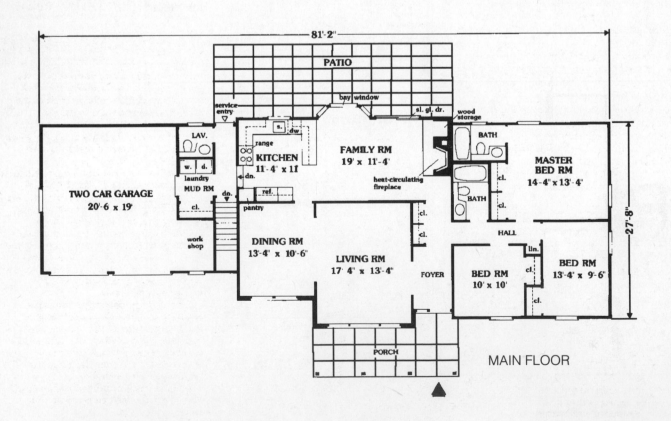

MAIN FLOOR

TO ORDER THIS BLUEPRINT,
CALL TOLL-FREE 1-800-820-1283

Plan HFL-1490-DV

PRICES AND DETAILS
ON PAGES 12-15

Simple Roofline Characterizes Country Home

55'-0"

54'-0"

Nook
11/0x10/6

pantry

Family
13/6x17/6

Master
12/0x16/0

walk in wardrobe

Dining
10/0x10/0

Kit.

ref.

linen

built in

Bdrm. 2
11/0x11/0

Living
17/0x13/6

Entry

w.

d.

f.

w.h.

Bdrm. 3
11/0x10/6

Garage
19/0x22/0

PLAN R-1030
WITHOUT BASEMENT
(CRAWLSPACE FOUNDATION)

Total living area:
(Not counting garage)

1,801 sq. ft.

Characterized by a simple roof line, the country-style home is among the most popular categories in today's real estate market. The brick masonry facade accented by shutters and an expansive bow window at the living room add to the comfortable country character of this three-bedroom design.

Inside, an informal family gathering area is carefully separated from the formal living/dining portion by a double door off the entry and a versatile pocket door to the dining room. The kitchen island counter is large enough to accommodate a family of six. A French door opens off the nook to a covered patio. The octagonal projection of the nook adds interest to the rear exterior wall as well as visually enhancing the interior.

Double doors open to an expansive master bedroom area characteristic of much larger homes. The third bedroom is conveniently located for the independent resident or guest, or may effectively serve as a secluded den/study for those not requiring a third bedroom.

Whether rural or urban, this home will blend well and look comfortable in a variety of settings.

TO ORDER THIS BLUEPRINT,
CALL TOLL-FREE 1-800-820-1283

Blueprint Price Code B
Plan R-1030

PRICES AND DETAILS
ON PAGES 12-15

63

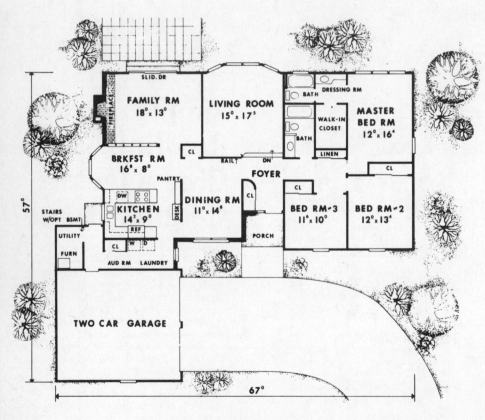

Country Classic

- A variety of siding materials blend together for a classic country exterior look.
- A dramatic sunken living room with bay window-wall is the view that greets arriving guests.
- A front-facing dining room completes the formal living area.
- The family room with fireplace is open to the kitchen and breakfast bay for informal family shared time.
- Three bedrooms and two full baths make up the sleeping wing of the home.

Plan AX-9762	
Bedrooms: 3	**Baths:** 2

Space:

Total living area:	2,003 sq. ft.
Basement:	2,003 sq. ft.
Garage:	485 sq. ft.
Exterior Wall Framing:	2x4

Foundation options:
Standard basement.
Slab.
(Foundation & framing conversion diagram available — see order form.)

Blueprint Price Code: C

TO ORDER THIS BLUEPRINT, CALL TOLL-FREE 1-800-820-1283

Plan AX-9762

PRICES AND DETAILS ON PAGES 12-15

Updated Traditional

- "Updated traditional," is how you might describe this 1,571 sq. ft. home. The exterior combines traditional materials, such as lap siding, divided light windows and an inviting entry with flanking side lights.
- Inside, the home has the design features the move-up or empty nesters markets desire. From the vaulted entry, there is a long view over the open railed stairs to the Great Room with fireplace and sliders to a deck.
- The island kitchen overlooks a breakfast eating area and has a pass-through to the Great Room eating area.
- The master bedroom has a vaulted ceiling, walk-in closet, and private bath with additional vanity in the dressing area.
- The third bedroom can be used as a den or study.

Plan B-88039

Bedrooms: 2-3	Baths: 2
Space:	
Total living area:	1,571 sq. ft.
Basement:	1,571 sq. ft.
Garage:	440 sq. ft.
Exterior Wall Framing:	2x4
Foundation options:	
Standard basement.	
(Foundation & framing conversion diagram available — see order form.)	
Blueprint Price Code:	B

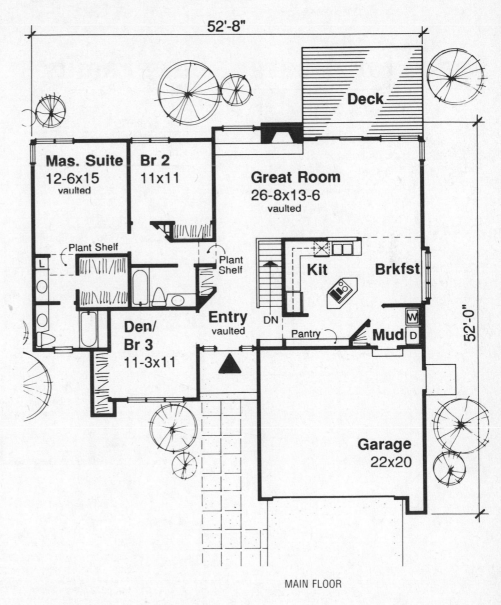

MAIN FLOOR

Space for A Large, Busy Family

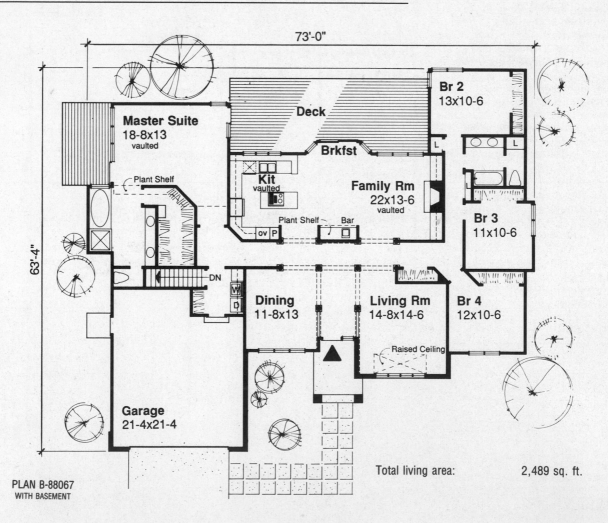

73'-0"

63'-4"

Master Suite
18-8x13
vaulted

Plant Shelf

Deck

Brkfst

Br 2
13x10-6

Kit
vaulted

Plant Shelf Bar

Family Rm
22x13-6
vaulted

Br 3
11x10-6

DN

Dining
11-8x13

Living Rm
14-8x14-6

Br 4
12x10-6

Raised Ceiling

Garage
21-4x21-4

PLAN B-88067
WITH BASEMENT

Total living area: 2,489 sq. ft.

**TO ORDER THIS BLUEPRINT,
CALL TOLL-FREE 1-800-820-1283**

Blueprint Price Code C
Plan B-88067

*PRICES AND DETAILS
ON PAGES 12-15*

Rustic and Accessible

- This rustic cedar home features great style and comfort, in addition to a handicap-accessible design.
- A convenient ramp leads up to the covered porch, which opens into a spacious and welcoming entry.
- Just ahead, a 13-ft., 8-in. ceiling soars over the Great Room, the adjacent dining room and the efficient kitchen.
- A unique angled wall between the Great Room and the sunny dining room provides French-door access to a fun backyard deck or patio.
- A neat island in the kitchen includes a counter that serves the dining room. The kitchen also boasts ample counter space and a window above the sink.
- The master suite features French doors to a private deck and two designs for the bath—one includes a dressing area and a walk-in closet, while the other boasts a tub with a bench, a dual-sink vanity and extra space to maneuver.
- Another bedroom nearby is serviced by a centrally located hall bath.
- Double doors off the entry open to a den or third bedroom.

Plan LMB-3716-CD

Bedrooms: 2+	Baths: 2
Living Area:	
Main floor	1,345 sq. ft.
Total Living Area:	**1,345 sq. ft.**
Carport and storage	480 sq. ft.
Exterior Wall Framing:	2x4

Foundation Options:

Crawlspace

Slab

(All plans can be built with your choice of foundation and framing. A generic conversion diagram is available. See order form.)

BLUEPRINT PRICE CODE: A

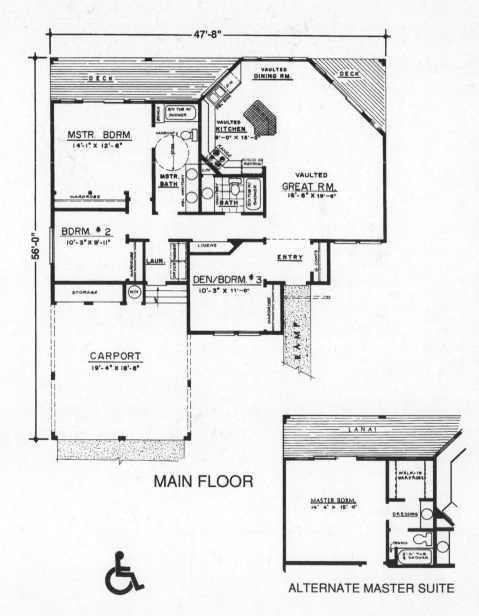

MAIN FLOOR

ALTERNATE MASTER SUITE

Dynamic Three-Bedroom Home

- The gabled roof, arched windows and design details such as the window planter make this a hot, new design.
- The covered front entry is highlighted by exposed beams that echo the shape of the arched window above the door.
- The foyer opens to the den on the left, which features an overhead plant shelf, and the vaulted Great Room straight ahead.
- The Great Room offers a corner fireplace and adjoins the rear deck and the vaulted dining room.
- The spacious kitchen has an island cooktop and a tucked-away laundry area. Note the convenient access to both a sheltered deck and patio and the two-car garage.
- The luxurious master suite includes a romantic window seat, vaulted ceilings and a walk-in closet. The private bath includes an elegant spa tub.
- Another full bath is adjacent to the second bedroom.

Plan B-87153

Bedrooms: 2-3	Baths: 2
Space:	
Main floor	1,709 sq. ft.
Total Living Area	**1,709 sq. ft.**
Basement	1,709 sq. ft.
Garage	462 sq. ft.
Exterior Wall Framing	2x4

Foundation options:

Standard Basement

(Foundation & framing conversion diagram available—see order form.)

Blueprint Price Code	B

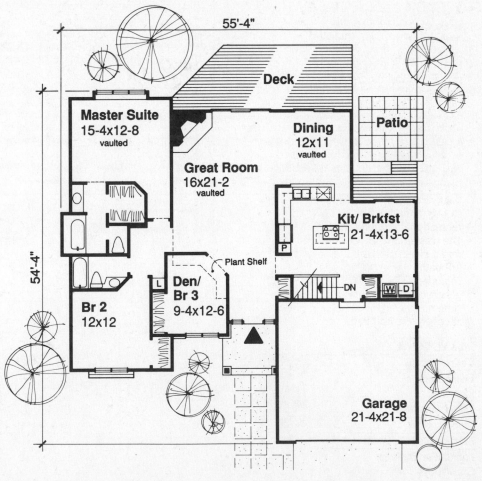

TO ORDER THIS BLUEPRINT, CALL TOLL-FREE 1-800-820-1283

Plan B-87153

PRICES AND DETAILS ON PAGES 12-15

Versatile Victorian

- An oval-glassed door, rounded cedar shakes and elaborate fretwork and lattice give this versatile home an impressive Victorian look.
- Its simple and economical design makes this a great starter, retirement or vacation home.
- Off the raised front porch, the sidelighted foyer opens immediately to the spacious living room with front views and built-in book storage.
- The living room unfolds to the dining and kitchen area, which is roomy and bright. A patio door accesses the backyard porch and the functional storage area that houses lawn tools or recreational equipment.
- The washer and dryer are neatly tucked into a closet off the main hall. The large full bath is centrally located as well.
- Secluded to the end of the hall are two generous-sized bedrooms. The master suite has a walk-in closet and direct access to the hall bath.

Plan VL-947

Bedrooms: 2	Baths: 1
Living Area:	
Main floor	947 sq. ft.
Total Living Area:	**947 sq. ft.**
Storage room	49 sq. ft.
Exterior Wall Framing:	2x4

Foundation Options:

Crawlspace

Slab

(All plans can be built with your choice of foundation and framing. A generic conversion diagram is available. See order form.)

BLUEPRINT PRICE CODE: **AA**

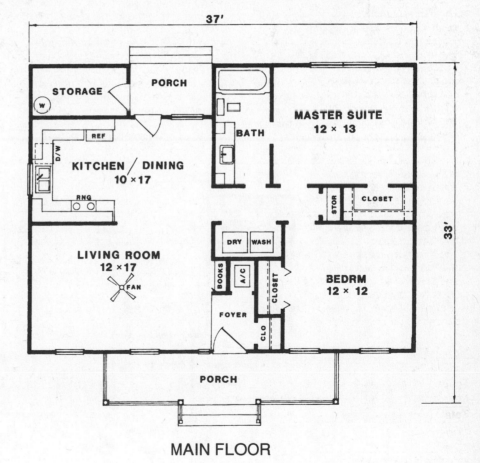

MAIN FLOOR

Morning Glory

- This melodious country-style home opens itself to the sights and sounds of nature with front and rear porches, and dazzling window treatments.
- From the sidelighted entry, a long hall leads to the right, introducing three secondary bedrooms. Along the way, you'll find plenty of closet space for coats and board games.
- There's plenty of gathering room in the family room, where a solid fireplace warms the spirit. The bird-watcher in your family can set up camp at the large boxed-out window to the rear.

- The cheery breakfast nook flaunts its own boxed-out window and a glassy door to the backyard porch.
- A raised bar joins the nook to the kitchen, which incorporates cabinets into its center island. Just a few steps brings you to the formal dining room for an exquisite meal.
- On the other side of the home, the master suite is enhanced by a charming window seat. The private bath is packed with essentials, including twin walk-in closets, a whirlpool tub beneath a radiant window, and a dual-sink vanity. The sit-down shower is sure to be a morning eye-opener!

Plan RD-1944	
Bedrooms: 4	**Baths:** 2
Living Area:	
Main floor	1,944 sq. ft.
Total Living Area:	**1,944 sq. ft.**
Standard basement	1,750 sq. ft.
Garage and storage	538 sq. ft.
Exterior Wall Framing:	2x4
Foundation Options:	

Standard basement
Crawlspace
Slab
(All plans can be built with your choice of foundation and framing. A generic conversion diagram is available. See order form.)

BLUEPRINT PRICE CODE:	B

MAIN FLOOR

Plan RD-1944

PRICES AND DETAILS ON PAGES 12-15

Plantation Home Ideal for Several Markets

- An efficient square footage appeals to many different buyers, from first-time, to second-home, to retirement.
- Compact building envelope of 65 x 55 is ideal for a smaller lot.
- A walk-up front porch, lap siding, and Palladian windows convey traditional charm.
- The Grand room features an ale bar, fireplace, and French doors to the rear deck.
- The gourmet kitchen features an island, greenhouse window, and sunny good morning room, and serves the private, formal dining room.
- The master suite features a luxury bath with separate his and her closets.

Plan EOF-25

Bedrooms: 2-3	Baths: 2½
Space:	
Total living area:	1,758 sq. ft.
Garage:	400 sq. ft.
Ceiling Heights:	
Main floor:	9'
Exterior Wall Framing:	2x6
Foundation options:	
Slab.	
(Foundation & framing conversion diagram available — see order form.)	
Blueprint Price Code:	B

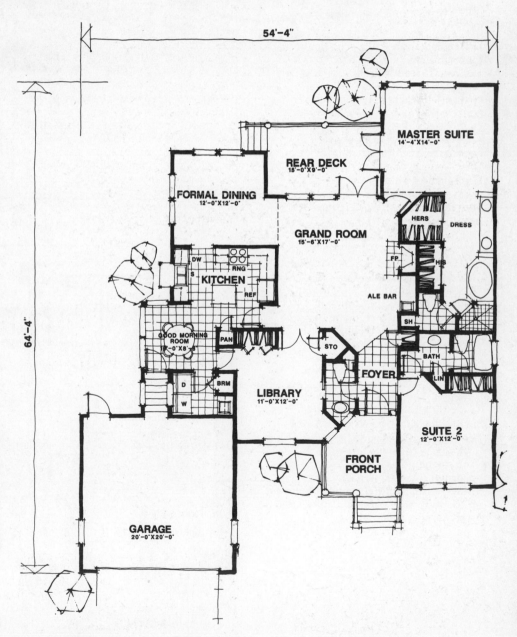

Three-Tiered Ranch

- A three-tiered roof externally defines the various internal areas of this traditional-styled ranch.
- An arched front portico and colonial details preview the inviting features you'll find inside, such as the large, dramatic living room; a cathedral ceiling, built-in bookshelves and a stunning two-way brick fireplace are highlights here.
- Opposite, the rear family room reveals a corner wet bar, sliders that access a backyard patio and the other side of the fireplace.
- A wraparound bay window creates an "alfresco" dining experience; across the snack bar is a U-shaped kitchen with pantry and view to the adjoining family room.
- The sleeping tier offers three bedrooms, the master with a walk-in closet and convenient half bath, and two additional bedrooms which share a full bath.

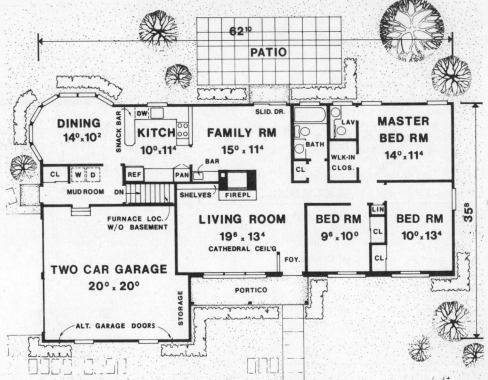

Plan AX-97624-A	
Bedrooms: 3	**Baths:** 1½
Space:	
Total living area:	1,396 sq. ft.
Partial basement:	900 sq. ft.
Full basement:	1,396 sq. ft.
Garage:	400 sq. ft.
Exterior Wall Framing:	2x4

Foundation options:
Partial basement.
Standard basement.
Slab.
(Foundation & framing conversion diagram available — see order form.)

Blueprint Price Code: A

Large and Livable Spaces

- With a 13-ft. sloped ceiling soaring above the entry and main living areas, a feeling of vastness lingers throughout this appealing home.
- Decorative plant shelves adorn the sidelighted entry and continue into the formal dining room.
- A toasty fireplace warms the airy living room straight ahead. A charming French door opens to a quaint backyard patio.
- The flow-through kitchen with fluorescent lighting is located for both formal and informal meal serving. The breakfast nook to the rear is brightened by a bay window.
- Around the corner, the master bedroom and bath share a 9-ft. ceiling. A restful window seat graces the bedroom, while the bath is enhanced by his-and-hers walk-in closets and a nice garden tub.
- Two good-sized secondary bedrooms share another full bath at the opposite end of the home.

Plan DD-1628

Bedrooms: 3	Baths: 2
Living Area:	
Main floor	1,628 sq. ft.
Total Living Area:	**1,628 sq. ft.**
Standard basement	1,628 sq. ft.
Garage	464 sq. ft.
Exterior Wall Framing:	2x4

Foundation Options:

Standard basement

Crawlspace

Slab

(All plans can be built with your choice of foundation and framing. A generic conversion diagram is available. See order form.)

BLUEPRINT PRICE CODE: B

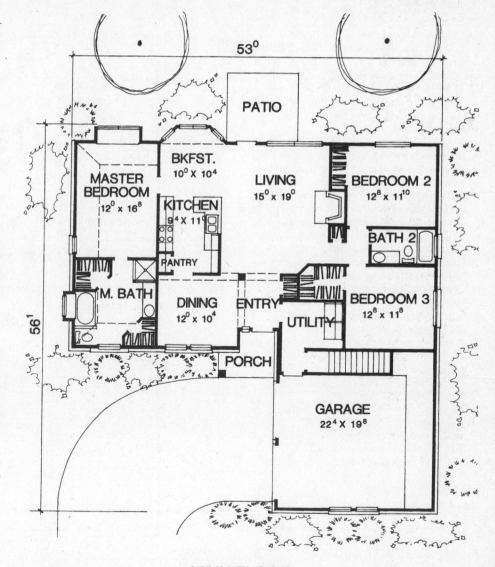

MAIN FLOOR

Free-Soaring Ceilings

- Soaring vaulted ceilings lend an air of freedom to every room in this appealing one-story home.
- French doors open from the covered front porch to the foyer, which flows smoothly into the formal living and dining areas. A high plant shelf adds vibrant color.
- This open space gives way to the family room, where sliding glass doors access the backyard. A warm fireplace exudes comfort and cheer.
- Nestled between the family and living rooms, the wonderful walk-through kitchen features a serving bar and a delightful plant shelf. A spacious bayed nook promises cheery breakfasts.
- The secluded master bedroom sports a quiet bayed sitting area and an attractive plant shelf. The sumptuous master bath is enhanced by a garden tub, a separate shower and a 12-ft., 8-in. ceiling.
- Two more good-sized bedrooms share a hall bath with an 11-ft. ceiling. Exotic plant shelves adorn each room.

Plan HDS-99-223

Bedrooms: 3	Baths: 2
Living Area:	
Main floor	1,571 sq. ft.
Total Living Area:	**1,571 sq. ft.**
Garage	381 sq. ft.
Exterior Wall Framing:	2x4

Foundation Options:

Slab

(All plans can be built with your choice of foundation and framing. A generic conversion diagram is available. See order form.)

BLUEPRINT PRICE CODE: B

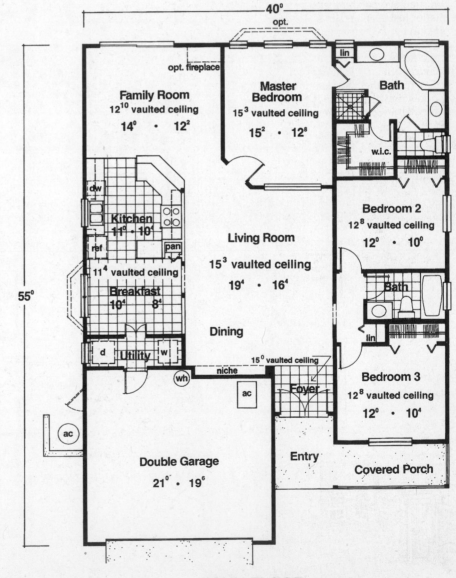

MAIN FLOOR

Plan HDS-99-223

PRICES AND DETAILS ON PAGES 12-15

Special Effects

- Arched windows set off by the raised center roof and the columned porch give this home plenty of personality.
- Unusual, eye-catching effects make the interior just as interesting. The foyer is open to the living room, which has a high, angled ceiling that draws the eye to the fireplace on the end wall.
- Columns outline the living room and the dining room, the latter featuring a bow window overlooking the huge deck. Sliding glass doors in the adjacent

kitchen/nook combination provide access to the deck.
- The deck is cleverly designed to offer a private outdoor retreat, complete with a hot tub, off the master suite. The master suite also includes extra closet space and a private bath with a spa tub. Two more bedrooms and a full bath complete the sleeping wing.
- The oversized garage provides extra storage space or an area for a workshop. The garage entrance leads to the mud room, laundry and pantry area on the left or to the optional basement straight ahead.

Plan HFL-1390-CH

Bedrooms: 3	Baths: 2
Living Area:	
Main floor	1,476 sq. ft.
Total Living Area:	**1,476 sq. ft.**
Standard basement	1,361 sq. ft.
Garage	548 sq. ft.
Exterior Wall Framing:	2x6

Foundation Options:
Standard basement
Slab
(Typical foundation & framing conversion diagram available—see order form.)

BLUEPRINT PRICE CODE: **A**

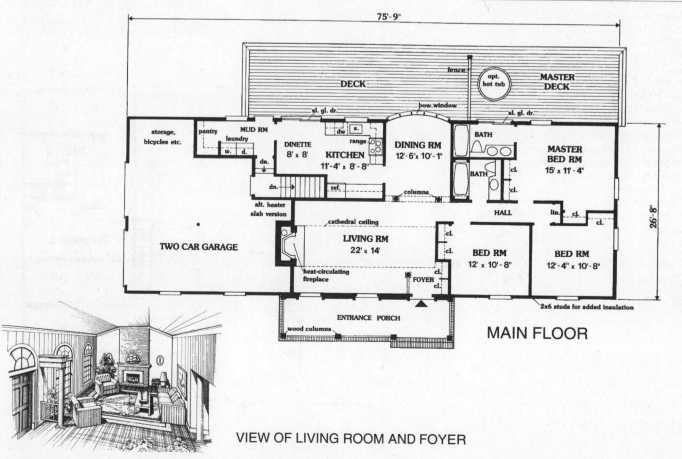

MAIN FLOOR

VIEW OF LIVING ROOM AND FOYER

Warm Country Welcome

- This sprawling country home has a warm, welcoming flavor. The rooflines build up pleasantly to the center, where dormer windows and a covered front porch provide the focal point.
- A roomy foyer opens to the living room, which offers a 10-ft.-high ceiling and flows into the adjacent dining room for expandable entertaining space.
- For casual get-togethers, the family room and dinette offer a media center, a nice fireplace and a bay window with views of an expansive terrace.
- The U-shaped kitchen boasts a handy pantry and is only steps away from laundry facilities and a half-bath.
- At the right side of the home is the bedroom wing. The master bedroom has a private bath with a whirlpool tub and a separate shower. Two additional bedrooms share a full bath.

Plan HFL-1650-TR

Bedrooms: 3	Baths: 2½
Living Area:	
Main floor	1,650 sq. ft.
Total Living Area:	**1,650 sq. ft.**
Standard basement	1,718 sq. ft.
Garage and storage	491 sq. ft.
Exterior Wall Framing:	2x6

Foundation Options:
Standard basement
Slab
(Typical foundation & framing conversion diagram available—see order form.)

BLUEPRINT PRICE CODE:	B

VIEW INTO DINETTE AND FAMILY ROOM

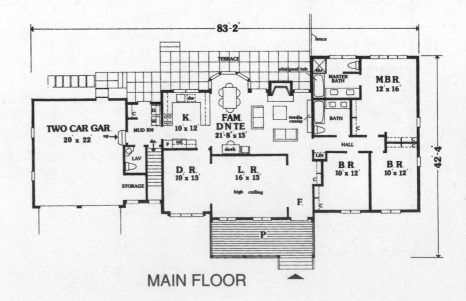

MAIN FLOOR

Relaxing Country Home

- This comfortable plan offers a relaxing country-style front porch, a gable roof, tall windows and rustic wood siding.
- Double doors lead to a welcoming foyer, which flows into the spacious Great Room. A 12-ft., 6-in. cathedral ceiling hovers above a handsome fireplace flanked by windows. The cozy screen porch is a nice accessory.
- The efficient kitchen offers ample counter space and easy access to both the dining room and the breakfast area.

- The dining room, which offers a view of the front porch, is easily converted into a game room or den.
- The master suite is isolated to the back of the home and boasts a spacious walk-in closet, twin sinks and a nice-sized sleeping area.
- The two secondary bedrooms have generous closet space and share another full bath.
- Two separate storage spaces are located behind the garage, one accessible from the garage and the other from the breakfast area.
- Stairs to the optional basement replace the hot-water heater in the foyer and reduce the size of the dining room.

Plan J-78105

Bedrooms: 3+	**Baths:** 2

Living Area:	
Main floor	1,816 sq. ft.
Total Living Area:	**1,816 sq. ft.**
Standard basement	1,816 sq. ft.
Garage	484 sq. ft.
Storage	132 sq. ft.
Exterior Wall Framing:	2x4

Foundation Options:
Standard basement
Crawlspace
Slab
(All plans can be built with your choice of foundation and framing. A generic conversion diagram is available. See order form.)

BLUEPRINT PRICE CODE:	B

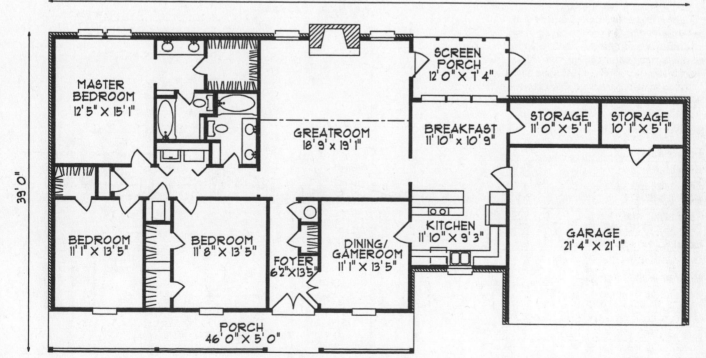

MAIN FLOOR

Look to the Future!

- Above this home's main floor is space for three rooms that may be finished to suit your taste. Imagine the games to be enjoyed in the skylighted spaces!
- Your life will flow smoothly on the main floor. The living and dining rooms are connected by nothing but air for an expansive, relaxed feel.
- Front and rear porches will complement your casual lifestyle.
- When you need time alone, slip away to the master bedroom, where radiant windows exist only to refresh you.
- When it's time to stock up on food, you'll appreciate the kitchen's close proximity to the garage.
- The laundry room is just a skip from the kitchen, so you can juggle chores!
- The kids will appreciate the seclusion of their bedrooms, where they'll have ample room to study or visit with pals.

Plan J-9316

Bedrooms: 3+	Baths: 2
Living Area:	
Main floor	1,709 sq. ft.
Total Living Area:	**1,709 sq. ft.**
Future upper floor	710 sq. ft.
Standard basement	1,709 sq. ft.
Garage and storage	526 sq. ft.
Exterior Wall Framing:	**2x4**

Foundation Options:

Standard basement
Crawlspace
Slab

(All plans can be built with your choice of foundation and framing. A generic conversion diagram is available. See order form.)

BLUEPRINT PRICE CODE:	B

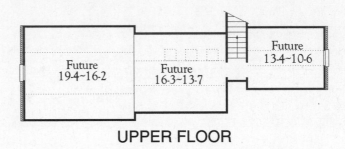

UPPER FLOOR

MAIN FLOOR

TO ORDER THIS BLUEPRINT, CALL TOLL-FREE 1-800-820-1283

Plan J-9316

PRICES AND DETAILS ON PAGES 12-15

Cottage with Country Charm

- This charming country cottage makes the most of its living space, with an open room arrangement, vaulted ceilings and modern window treatments.
- The covered front porch is 7 ft. deep, providing plenty of room for outdoor relaxation.
- Once inside the entry, guests are greeted by a dynamite Great Room with a 12-ft. vaulted ceiling and a warm

energy-efficient woodstove. Lots of windows, plus sliding glass doors to the side yard, brighten the room.
- Expanding the area is a spacious dining room, which has easy access to the uniquely shaped kitchen. A breakfast bar, a garden window above the sink and a pantry closet are highlights here.
- The master bedroom is enhanced by a 12-ft.-high vaulted ceiling and a large picture window. The master bath offers a spa tub, a skylighted dressing area and a walk-in closet.
- The secondary bedroom is enviable in its own right, boasting a beautiful bay window and a roomy wardrobe closet.

Plan LMB-1211	
Bedrooms: 2	**Baths:** 2
Living Area:	
Main floor	1,186 sq. ft.
Total Living Area:	**1,186 sq. ft.**
Garage	494 sq. ft.
Exterior Wall Framing:	2x6
Foundation Options:	

Crawlspace
(All plans can be built with your choice of foundation and framing. A generic conversion diagram is available. See order form.)

BLUEPRINT PRICE CODE:	**A**

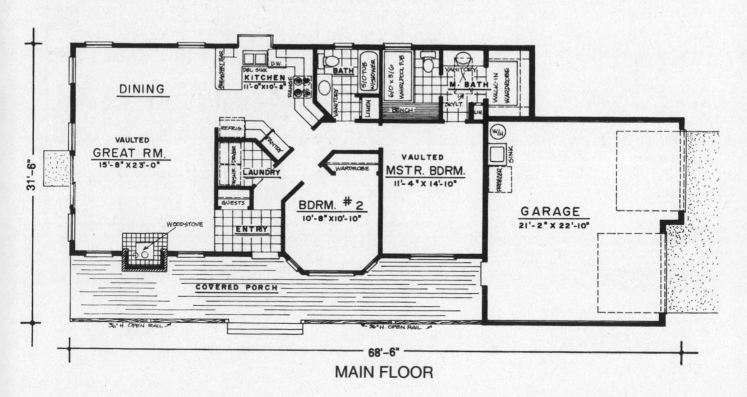

MAIN FLOOR

Plan LMB-1211

PRICES AND DETAILS ON PAGES 12-15

Country Welcome

- A broad porch extends a hearty country welcome to visitors of this compact yet very convenient home.
- The cathedral-ceilinged foyer provides access to a large unfinished upper level, which will allow a family plenty of room to grow.
- The foyer leads into the central living room, which features a fireplace, French doors and a cathedral ceiling.
- The bayed dining room provides views of the rear yard.
- The island kitchen, big enough for the largest family, boasts a generous pantry, a wall oven, a corner window sink and plenty of counter space.
- The master suite features double doors, twin walk-in closets and a private bath with high windows illuminating a whirlpool tub and a separate shower.

Plan OH-151

Bedrooms: 3	Baths: 2
Living Area:	
Main floor	1,578 sq. ft.
Total Living Area:	**1,578 sq. ft.**
Standard basement	1,578 sq. ft.
Garage	420 sq. ft.
Exterior Wall Framing:	2x4

Foundation Options:
Standard basement
(Typical foundation & framing conversion diagram available—see order form.)

BLUEPRINT PRICE CODE:	B

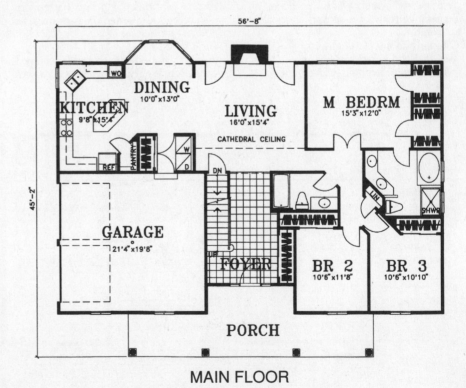

MAIN FLOOR

TO ORDER THIS BLUEPRINT, CALL TOLL-FREE 1-800-820-1283

Plan OH-151

PRICES AND DETAILS ON PAGES 12-15

Extra Sparkle

- A lovely front porch with a cameo front door, decorative posts, bay windows and dormers give this country-style home extra sparkle.
- The Great Room is at the center of the floor plan, where it merges with the dining room and the screened porch. The Great Room features a 10-ft. tray ceiling, a fireplace, a built-in wet bar and a wall of windows to the patio.
- The eat-in kitchen has a half-wall that keeps it open to the Great Room and hallway. The dining room offers a half-wall facing the foyer and a bay window overlooking the front porch.
- The delectable master suite is isolated from the other bedrooms and includes a charming bay window, a 10-ft. tray ceiling and a luxurious private bath.
- The two smaller bedrooms are off the main foyer and separated by a full bath.
- A mudroom with a washer and dryer is accessible from the two-car garage.

Plan AX-91312

Bedrooms: 3	Baths: 2
Space:	
Main floor	1,595 sq. ft.
Total Living Area	**1,595 sq. ft.**
Screened Porch	178 sq. ft.
Basement	1,595 sq. ft.
Garage, Storage and Utility	508 sq. ft.
Exterior Wall Framing	2x4

Foundation Options:
Daylight basement
Standard basement
Slab
(All plans can be built with your choice of foundation and framing. A generic conversion diagram is available. See order form.)

Blueprint Price Code	B

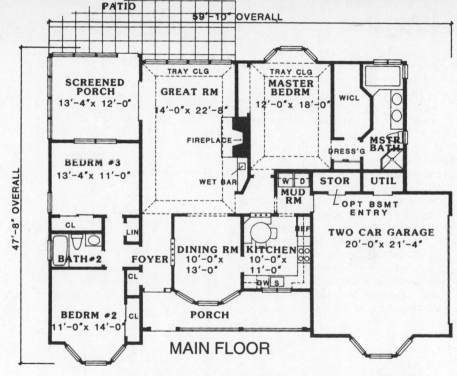

MAIN FLOOR

VIEW INTO GREAT ROOM

Modern Charmer

- This attractive plan combines country-style charm with a modern floor plan.
- The central foyer ushers guests past a study and on into the huge living room, which is highlighted by an 11-ft. ceiling, a corner fireplace and access to a big, covered backyard porch.
- An angled snack bar joins the living room to the bayed nook and the efficient kitchen. The formal dining room is easily reached from the kitchen and the foyer. A utility room and a half-bath are just off the garage entrance.
- The master suite, isolated for privacy, boasts a magnificent bath with a garden tub, a separate shower, double vanities and two walk-in closets.
- Two more bedrooms are located on the opposite side of the home and are separated by a hall bath.
- Ceilings in all rooms are at least 9 ft. high for added spaciousness.

Plan VL-2069

Bedrooms: 3	Baths: 2½
Living Area:	
Main floor	2,069 sq. ft.
Total Living Area:	**2,069 sq. ft.**
Garage	460 sq. ft.
Exterior Wall Framing:	2x4

Foundation Options:

Crawlspace

Slab

(All plans can be built with your choice of foundation and framing. A generic conversion diagram is available. See order form.)

BLUEPRINT PRICE CODE: **C**

REAR VIEW

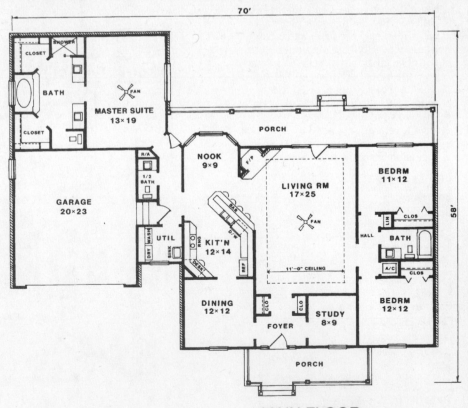

MAIN FLOOR

Plan VL-2069

PRICES AND DETAILS ON PAGES 12-15

Designed for Livability

- With the removal of the master suite from the rest of the home, this design is ideal for the maturing family.
- Off the columned porch, the sidelighted front entry offers views through the bright living room to the backyard.
- An elegant column visually sets off the formal dining room from the adjacent living room.
- The kitchen offers a sunny morning room, a pantry and handy access to the laundry facilities and the garage.
- The sunny bay created by the morning room and the sitting area of the master suite adds interior and exterior excitement to this plan.
- The master bath boasts an exciting oval garden tub and a separate shower, as well as a spacious walk-in closet and a dressing area with a dual-sink vanity.
- All of the rooms mentioned above feature soaring 10-ft. ceilings.
- Across the home, three additional bedrooms share another full bath.

Plan DD-1696

Bedrooms: 4	Baths: 2
Living Area:	
Main floor	1,748 sq. ft.
Total Living Area:	**1,748 sq. ft.**
Standard basement	1,748 sq. ft.
Garage	393 sq. ft.
Exterior Wall Framing:	2x4

Foundation Options:

Standard basement

Crawlspace

Slab

(All plans can be built with your choice of foundation and framing. A generic conversion diagram is available. See order form.)

BLUEPRINT PRICE CODE: B

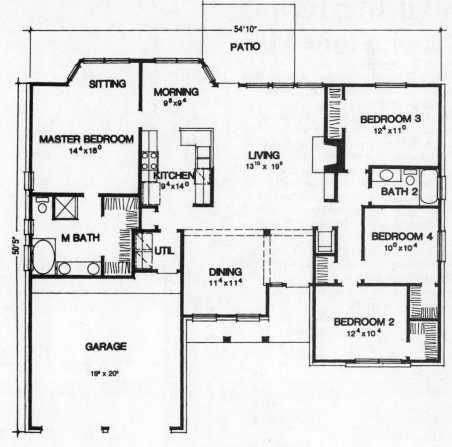

MAIN FLOOR

Stylish Exterior, Open Floor Plan

- With its simple yet stylish exterior, this modest-sized design is suitable for country or urban settings.
- A covered front porch and a gabled roof extension accent the facade while providing plenty of sheltered space for outdoor relaxation.
- Inside, the open floor plan puts available space to efficient use.
- The living room, which offers a warm fireplace, is expanded by a 10½-ft. cathedral ceiling. The addition of the kitchen and the bayed dining room creates an expansive gathering space.
- The master suite features a private bath and a large walk-in closet.
- Two more good-sized bedrooms share a second full bath.
- A utility area leads to the carport, which incorporates extra storage space.

Plan J-86155

Bedrooms: 3	Baths: 2
Living Area:	
Main floor	1,385 sq. ft.
Total Living Area:	**1,385 sq. ft.**
Standard basement	1,385 sq. ft.
Carport	380 sq. ft.
Storage	40 sq. ft.
Exterior Wall Framing:	2x4

Foundation Options:

Standard basement

Crawlspace

Slab

(All plans can be built with your choice of foundation and framing. A generic conversion diagram is available. See order form.)

BLUEPRINT PRICE CODE:	A

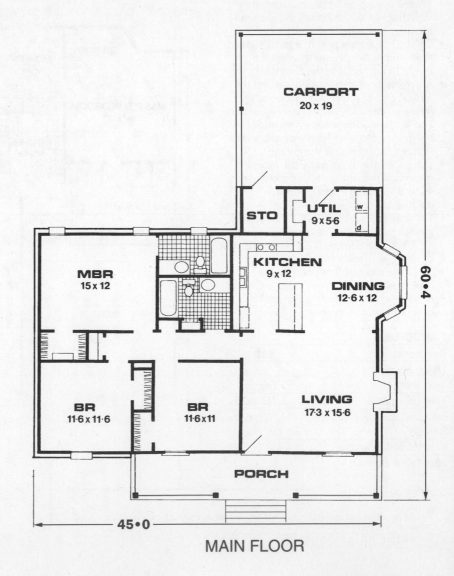

MAIN FLOOR

TO ORDER THIS BLUEPRINT, CALL TOLL-FREE 1-800-820-1283

Plan J-86155

PRICES AND DETAILS ON PAGES 12-15

Rural Roots

- This nostalgic farmhouse reminds you of country life, bringing back memories or maybe just fond daydreams.
- Authentic Victorian details contribute to the comforting facade. Lovely fishscale shingles above the bay window and oval glass in the front door will command attention from visitors.
- Receive the long-awaited kinfolk on the delightful wraparound porch; you may want to sit a spell and catch up on family news!
- Then usher everyone into the family room, for memorable moments in front of the corner fireplace.

- When the feast is ready, eyes will sparkle as the turkey is presented in the bay-windowed dining room. A French door leads to the back porch for after-dinner chatting in the cool evening.
- The efficient kitchen handles meal preparation with ease. The "east" wall features a pantry and double ovens.
- The secluded master suite lets you unwind before a good night's rest. A fabulous bath and direct porch access make this suite really sweet!
- Two secondary bedrooms share a split bath. The bayed front bedroom boasts a 10-ft. ceiling and a walk-in closet.
- The blueprints include plans for a detached, two-car garage (not shown).

Plan L-1772	
Bedrooms: 3	**Baths:** 2
Living Area:	
Main floor	1,772 sq. ft.
Total Living Area:	**1,772 sq. ft.**
Detached garage	576 sq. ft.
Exterior Wall Framing:	2x4

Foundation Options:

Slab
(All plans can be built with your choice of foundation and framing. A generic conversion diagram is available. See order form.)

BLUEPRINT PRICE CODE: B

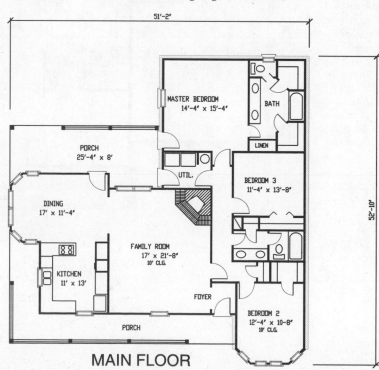

MAIN FLOOR

Masterful Master Suite

- This gorgeous home features front and rear covered porches and a master suite so luxurious it deserves its own wing.
- The expansive entry welcomes visitors into a spacious, skylighted living room, which boasts a handsome fireplace. The adjacent formal dining room overlooks the front porch.
- Designed for efficiency, the kitchen features an angled snack bar, a bayed eating area and views of the porch. An all-purpose utility room is conveniently located off the kitchen.
- The kitchen, eating area, living room and dining room are all heightened by 12-ft. ceilings.
- The sumptuous and secluded master suite features a tub and a separate shower, a double-sink vanity, a walk-in closet with built-in shelves and a compartmentalized toilet.
- The two secondary bedrooms share a hall bath at the other end of the home. The rear bedroom offers porch access.
- The garage features built-in storage and access to unfinished attic space.

Plan E-1811

Bedrooms: 3	Baths: 2
Living Area:	
Main floor	1,800 sq. ft.
Total Living Area:	**1,800 sq. ft.**
Garage and storage	634 sq. ft.
Exterior Wall Framing:	2x6

Foundation Options:

Crawlspace

Slab

(All plans can be built with your choice of foundation and framing. A generic conversion diagram is available. See order form.)

BLUEPRINT PRICE CODE: B

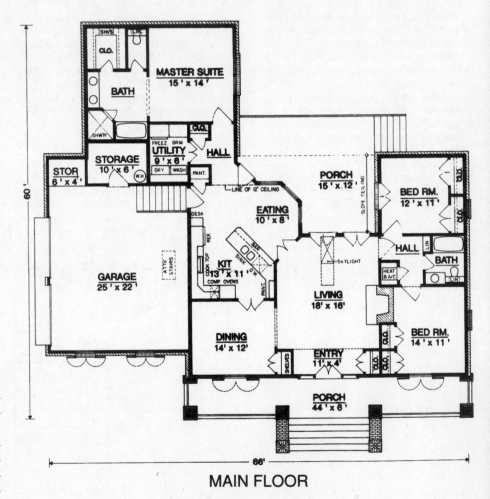

MAIN FLOOR

Plan E-1811

TO ORDER THIS BLUEPRINT,
CALL TOLL-FREE 1-800-820-1283

PRICES AND DETAILS
ON PAGES 12-15

Fresh Air

- With its nostalgic look and country style, this lovely home brings a breath of fresh air into any neighborhood.
- Past the inviting wraparound porch, the foyer is brightened by an arched transom window above the front door.
- The adjoining formal dining room is defined by decorative columns and features a 9-ft., 4-in. stepped ceiling.
- The bright and airy kitchen includes a pantry, a windowed sink and a sunny breakfast area with porch access.
- Enhanced by an 11-ft stepped ceiling, the spacious Great Room is warmed by a fireplace flanked by sliding glass doors to a covered back porch.
- The lush master bedroom boasts an 11-ft. tray ceiling and a bayed sitting area. The master bath showcases a circular spa tub with a glass-block wall.
- The two remaining bedrooms are serviced by a second bath and a nearby laundry room. The protruding bedroom has a 12-ft. vaulted ceiling.
- Additional living space can be made available by finishing the upper floor.

Plan AX-93308

Bedrooms: 3+	Baths: 2
Living Area:	
Main floor	1,793 sq. ft.
Total Living Area:	**1,793 sq. ft.**
Standard basement	1,793 sq. ft.
Unfinished upper floor	779 sq. ft.
Garage and utility	471 sq. ft.
Exterior Wall Framing:	2x4
Foundation Options:	
Standard basement	
Crawlspace	
Slab	

(All plans can be built with your choice of foundation and framing. A generic conversion diagram is available. See order form.)

BLUEPRINT PRICE CODE:	B

VIEW INTO GREAT ROOM

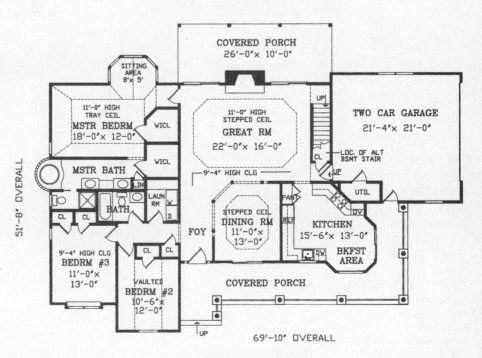

MAIN FLOOR

Versatile
Sun Room

- This cozy country-style home offers an inviting front porch and an interior just as welcoming.
- The spacious living room features a warming fireplace and windows that overlook the porch.
- The living room opens to a dining area, where French doors access a covered porch and a sunny patio.
- The island kitchen has a sink view, plenty of counter space, and a handy pass-through to the adjoining sun room. The bright sun room is large enough to serve as a formal dining room, a family room or a hobby room.
- The private master suite is secluded to the rear. A garden spa tub, dual walk-in closets and separate dressing areas are nice features found in the master bath.

Plan J-90014

Bedrooms: 3	Baths: 2½
Living Area:	
Main floor	2,190 sq. ft.
Total Living Area:	**2,190 sq. ft.**
Standard basement	2,190 sq. ft.
Garage	465 sq. ft.
Storage	34 sq. ft.
Exterior Wall Framing:	2x6

Foundation Options:

Standard basement

Crawlspace

Slab

(All plans can be built with your choice of foundation and framing. A generic conversion diagram is available. See order form.)

BLUEPRINT PRICE CODE: C

MAIN FLOOR

Plan J-90014

PRICES AND DETAILS ON PAGES 12-15

Classic Country-Style

- At the center of this rustic country-style home is an enormous living room with a flat beamed ceiling and a massive stone fireplace. A sunny patio and a covered rear porch are just steps away.
- The adjoining eating area and kitchen provide plenty of room for casual dining and meal preparation. The eating area is visually enhanced by a 14-ft. sloped ceiling with false beams. The kitchen includes a snack bar, a pantry closet and a built-in spice cabinet.
- The formal dining room gets plenty of pizzazz from a stone-faced wall and an arched planter facing the living room.
- The secluded master suite has it all, including a private bath, a separate dressing area and a large walk-in closet with built-in shelves.
- The two remaining bedrooms have big closets and easy access to a full bath.

Plan E-1808	
Bedrooms: 3	**Baths:** 2
Living Area:	
Main floor	1,800 sq. ft.
Total Living Area:	**1,800 sq. ft.**
Garage	605 sq. ft.
Exterior Wall Framing:	2x4

Foundation Options:

Crawlspace

Slab

(All plans can be built with your choice of foundation and framing. A generic conversion diagram is available. See order form.)

BLUEPRINT PRICE CODE:	B

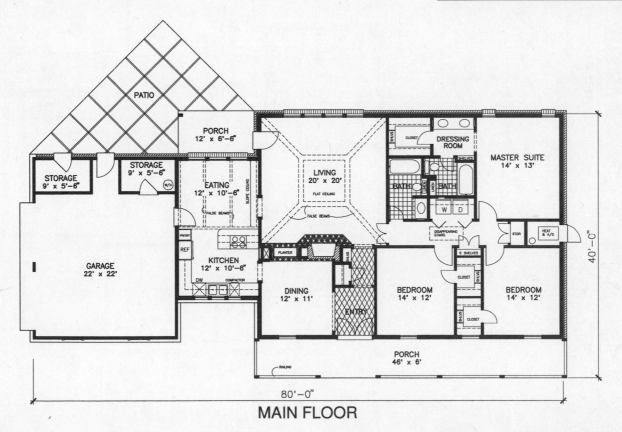

MAIN FLOOR

Wonderful Detailing

- The wonderfully detailed front porch, with its graceful arches, columns and railings, gives this home a character all its own. Dormer windows and arched transoms further accentuate the porch.
- The floor plan features a central living room with a 10-ft.-high ceiling and a fireplace framed by French doors. These doors open to a covered porch or a sun room, and a sheltered deck beyond.
- Just off the living room, the island kitchen and breakfast area provide a spacious place for family or guests. The nearby formal dining room has arched transom windows and a 10-ft. ceiling, as does the bedroom off the foyer. All of the remaining rooms have 9-ft. ceilings.
- The unusual master suite includes a window alcove, access to the porch and a fantastic bath with a garden tub.
- A huge utility room, a storage area off the garage and a 1,000-sq.-ft. attic space are other bonuses of this design.

Plan J-90019

Bedrooms: 3	Baths: 2½
Living Area:	
Main floor	2,410 sq. ft.
Total Living Area:	**2,410 sq. ft.**
Standard basement	2,410 sq. ft.
Garage	512 sq. ft.
Storage	86 sq. ft.
Exterior Wall Framing:	2x6

Foundation Options:

Standard basement
Crawlspace
Slab

(All plans can be built with your choice of foundation and framing. A generic conversion diagram is available. See order form.)

BLUEPRINT PRICE CODE: C

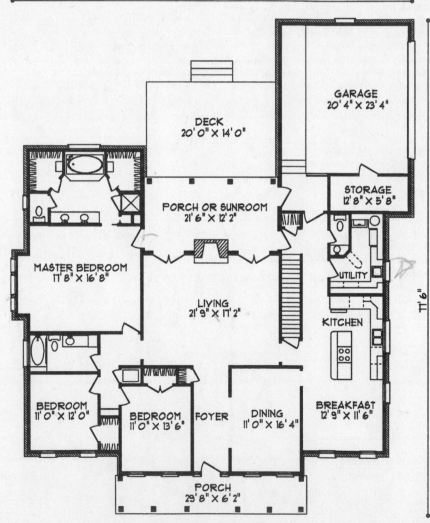

MAIN FLOOR

TO ORDER THIS BLUEPRINT, CALL TOLL-FREE 1-800-820-1283

Plan J-90019

PRICES AND DETAILS ON PAGES 12-15

Photo by Mark Englund/HomeStyles

Country Masterpiece!

- A handsome railed veranda punctuated by colonial columns bids a warm welcome to this French Country home.
- Historic hardwood floors in the foyer and dining room coupled with an abundance of windows, glass doors and 9-ft. ceilings give the interior the style and character of a masterpiece!
- Pocket doors isolate the study or guest room from the noise of incoming traffic.
- At the core of the informal spaces is an airy kitchen that interacts with the family room and the breakfast area over a 42-in.-high snack counter.
- The sprawling master suite basks in the comfort of a garden bath and a sunny sitting area that opens to the backyard.
- A window seat is centered between built-in bookshelves in the second main-floor bedroom.
- The upper-floor bedrooms share the use of a full bath and a huge game room.
- A detached three-car garage is included with the blueprints.

Plan L-308-FC

Bedrooms: 4+	Baths: 3
Living Area:	
Upper floor	787 sq. ft.
Main floor	2,519 sq. ft.
Total Living Area:	**3,306 sq. ft.**
Detached three-car garage	942 sq. ft.
Exterior Wall Framing:	2x4

Foundation Options:

Slab

(All plans can be built with your choice of foundation and framing. A generic conversion diagram is available. See order form.)

BLUEPRINT PRICE CODE: E

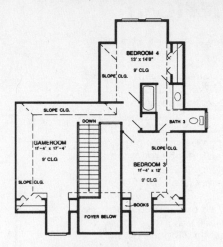

NOTE: The above photographed home may have been modified by the homeowner. Please refer to floor plan and/or drawn elevation shown for actual blueprint details.

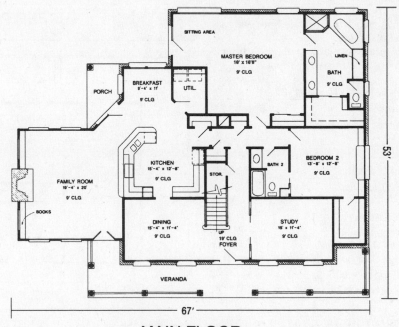

UPPER FLOOR

MAIN FLOOR

All-American Country Home

- The covered wraparound porch of this popular all-American home creates an old-fashioned country appeal.
- Off the entryway is the generous-sized living room, which offers a fireplace and French doors that open to the porch.
- The large adjoining dining room further expands the entertaining area.
- The country kitchen has a handy island and flows into the cozy family room, which is enhanced by exposed beams. A handsome fireplace warms the entire informal area, while windows overlook the porch.
- The quiet upper floor hosts four good-sized bedrooms and two baths. The master suite includes a walk-in closet, a dressing area and a private bath with a sit-down shower.
- This home is available with or without a basement and with or without a garage.

Plans H-3711-1, -1A, -2 & -2A

Bedrooms: 4	Baths: 2½
Living Area:	
Upper floor	1,176 sq. ft.
Main floor	1,288 sq. ft.
Total Living Area:	**2,464 sq. ft.**
Standard basement	1,176 sq. ft.
Garage	505 sq. ft.
Exterior Wall Framing:	2x6
Foundation Options:	**Plan #**
Basement with garage	H-3711-1
Basement without garage	H-3711-2
Crawlspace with garage	H-3711-1A
Crawlspace without garage	H-3711-2A

(All plans can be built with your choice of foundation and framing. A generic conversion diagram is available. See order form.)

BLUEPRINT PRICE CODE:	C

PLANS H-3711-1 & -1A WITH GARAGE

NOTE:
The above photographed home may have been modified by the homeowner. Please refer to floor plan and/or drawn elevation shown for actual blueprint details.

PLANS H-3711-2 & -2A WITHOUT GARAGE

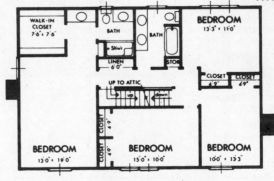

UPPER FLOOR

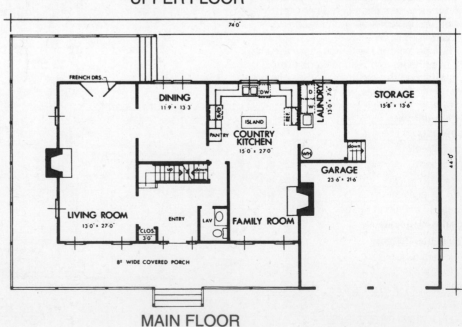

MAIN FLOOR

TO ORDER THIS BLUEPRINT, CALL TOLL-FREE 1-800-820-1283

Plans H-3711-1, -1A, -2 & -2A

PRICES AND DETAILS ON PAGES 12-15

Open, Flowing Floor Plan

- Open, flowing rooms punctuated with wonderful windows enhance this spacious four-bedroom home.
- The two-story-high foyer is brightened by an arched window above. To the left lies the living room, which flows into the family room. An inviting fireplace and windows overlooking a rear terrace highlight the family room.
- The centrally located kitchen serves both the formal dining room and the dinette, with a view of the family room beyond. Sliding glass doors in the dinette open to a lovely terrace.
- Upstairs, the master suite features an arched window and a walk-in closet with a dressing area. The private master bath includes a dual-sink vanity, a skylighted whirlpool tub and a separate shower.
- The three remaining bedrooms share another skylighted bath.

Plan AHP-9020

Bedrooms: 4	Baths: 2½
Living Area:	
Upper floor	1,021 sq. ft.
Main floor	1,125 sq. ft.
Total Living Area:	**2,146 sq. ft.**
Standard basement	1,032 sq. ft.
Garage	480 sq. ft.
Exterior Wall Framing:	2x6

Foundation Options:

Standard basement

Crawlspace

Slab

(All plans can be built with your choice of foundation and framing. A generic conversion diagram is available. See order form.)

BLUEPRINT PRICE CODE: C

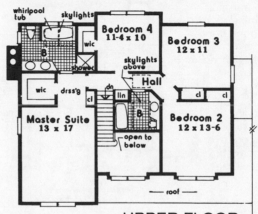

NOTE: The above photographed home may have been modified by the homeowner. Please refer to floor plan and/or drawn elevation shown for actual blueprint details.

UPPER FLOOR

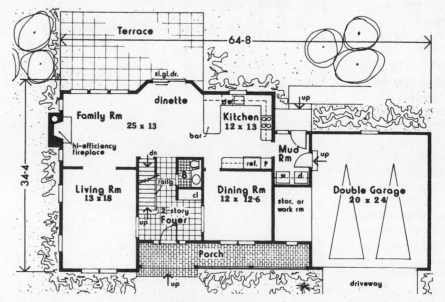

MAIN FLOOR

Classic Beauty

- The classic style of this beautiful home has retained its popularity for generations.
- The main floor includes abundant space for entertaining as well as for private family life. This spaciousness is enhanced by 10-foot ceilings throughout most of the first floor, with 9-foot ceilings in the master bedroom, master bath, and the utility areas.
- An impressive foyer leads guests to the formal dining room on the left and the large living room straight ahead. The living room features a fireplace framed by built-in shelves and patio doors that open to the backyard.
- A delightful breakfast nook adjoins the open kitchen that includes an island counter. The connecting dining room has French doors leading to the front porch.
- The secluded master suite has access to the backyard and enjoys a luxurious private bath with spa tub, separate shower and two vanities.
- The upstairs includes two more bedrooms with ceilings that slope up to 9 feet. An optional bonus room over the garage and a storage room above the master bedroom maximize the home's potential space.

Plan J-8601

Bedrooms: 3-4	Baths: 2½
Space:	
Upper floor	641 sq. ft.
Main floor	1,922 sq. ft.
Bonus area	516 sq. ft.
Total Living Area	**3,079 sq. ft.**
Basement	1,922 sq. ft.
Garage	474 sq. ft.
Storage	364 sq. ft.
Shop	121 sq. ft.
Exterior Wall Framing	2x4
Ceiling Heights:	
Upper floor	8' & 9'
Main floor	9' & 10'

Foundation options:
Standard Basement
Crawlspace
Slab
(Foundation & framing conversion diagram available—see order form.)

Blueprint Price Code	E

Photo by Mark Englund/HomeStyles

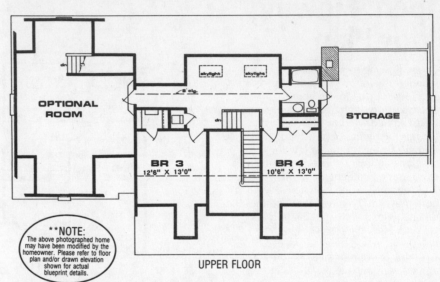

NOTE:
The above photographed home may have been modified by the homeowner. Please refer to floor plan and/or drawn elevation shown for actual blueprint details.

UPPER FLOOR

OPTIONAL ROOM

STORAGE

BR 3
12'6" X 13'0"

BR 4
10'6" X 13'0"

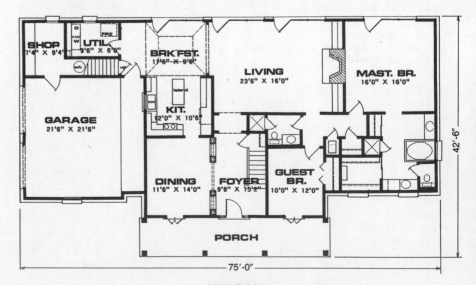

MAIN FLOOR

SHOP
7'4" X 9'4"

UTIL
9'6" X 6'8"

BRK'FST.
11'6" X 9'6"

LIVING
23'6" X 16'0"

MAST. BR.
16'0" X 16'0"

GARAGE
21'6" X 21'6"

KIT.
12'0" X 10'6"

DINING
11'6" X 14'0"

FOYER
9'8" X 15'2"

GUEST BR.
10'0" X 12'0"

PORCH

75'-0"

42'-6"

Photo courtesy of Breland & Farmer Designers, Inc.

Stylish and Compact

- This country-style home has a classic exterior and a space-saving and compact interior.
- A quaint covered porch extends along the front of the home. The oval-glassed front door opens to the entry, which leads to the spacious living room with a handsome fireplace, windows at either end and access to a big screened porch.
- The formal dining room flows from the living room and is easily served by the convenient U-shaped kitchen.
- A nice-sized laundry room and a full bath are nearby. The two-car garage offers a super storage area.
- The deluxe master suite features a huge walk-in closet. A separate dressing area leads to an adjoining, dual-access bath.
- The upper floor offers two more bedrooms and another full bath. Each bedroom has generous closet space and independent access to attic space.

Plan E-1626

Bedrooms: 3	Baths: 2
Living Area:	
Upper floor	464 sq. ft.
Main floor	1,136 sq. ft.
Total Living Area:	**1,600 sq. ft.**
Garage	462 sq. ft.
Exterior Wall Framing:	2x6

Foundation Options:

Crawlspace

Slab

(All plans can be built with your choice of foundation and framing. A generic conversion diagram is available. See order form.)

BLUEPRINT PRICE CODE: B

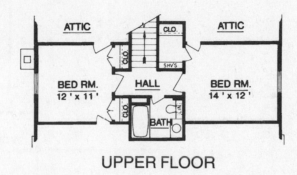

UPPER FLOOR

NOTE: The above photographed home may have been modified by the homeowner. Please refer to floor plan and/or drawn elevation shown for actual blueprint details.

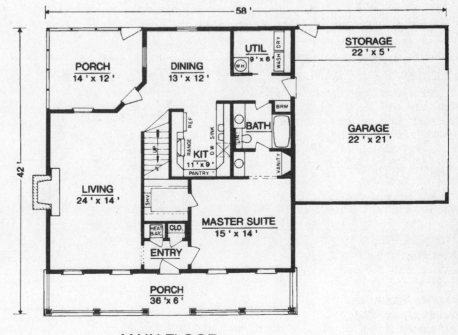

MAIN FLOOR

Elegant Interior

- An inviting covered porch welcomes guests into the elegant interior of this spectacular country home.
- Just past the entrance, the formal dining room boasts a stepped ceiling and a nearby server with a sink.
- The adjoining island kitchen has an eating bar that serves the breakfast room, which is enhanced by a 12-ft. cathedral ceiling and a bayed area of 8- and 9-ft.-high windows. Sliding glass doors lead to a covered side porch.
- Brightened by a row of 8-ft.-high windows and a glass door to the backyard, the spacious Great Room features a stepped ceiling, a built-in media center and a corner fireplace.
- The master bedroom has a tray ceiling and a cozy sitting area. The skylighted master bath boasts a whirlpool tub, a separate shower and a walk-in closet.
- A second main-floor bedroom, or optional study, offers private access to a compartmentalized bath. Two more bedrooms share a third bath on the upper floor. Generous storage space is also included.

Plan AX-3305-B

Bedrooms: 3+	Baths: 3
Living Area:	
Upper floor	550 sq. ft.
Main floor	2,017 sq. ft.
Total Living Area:	**2,567 sq. ft.**
Upper-floor storage	377 sq. ft.
Standard basement	2,017 sq. ft.
Garage	415 sq. ft.
Exterior Wall Framing:	2x4
Foundation Options:	
Standard basement	
Crawlspace	
Slab	

(All plans can be built with your choice of foundation and framing. A generic conversion diagram is available. See order form.)

BLUEPRINT PRICE CODE: D

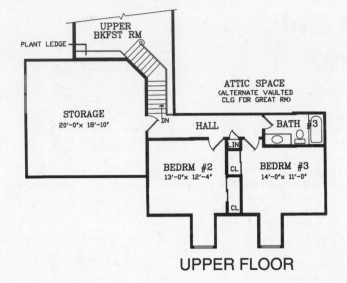

UPPER FLOOR

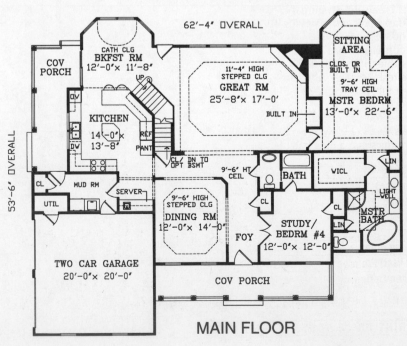

MAIN FLOOR

TO ORDER THIS BLUEPRINT, CALL TOLL-FREE 1-800-820-1283   Plan AX-3305-B   *PRICES AND DETAILS ON PAGES 12-15*

Rapt in Country Memories

- This beautiful home's wraparound porch will carry you away to a time when all was right with the world.
- Triple dormers and nostalgic shuttered windows combine with gorgeous oval glass in the front door to make the facade charming indeed!
- Looks can be deceiving, however. The interior of the home is thoroughly up-to-date, with every conceivable feature.
- Straight back from the foyer, a fireplace and tall windows under a 19-ft.-high cathedral ceiling make the living room a thing to behold.
- The roomy kitchen serves formal or casual meals with minimal effort. A breakfast nook and a serving counter host quick snacks.
- Two corner porches are easily accessible for thoughtful moments.
- Or, refresh yourself in the master suite's garden tub. A good book will keep you there for hours.
- Upstairs, the game room's balcony offers sweeping views; two big bedrooms share a nice bath.

Plan L-2449-VC

Bedrooms: 3	Baths: 2½
Living Area:	
Upper floor	780 sq. ft.
Main floor	1,669 sq. ft.
Total Living Area:	**2,449 sq. ft.**
Exterior Wall Framing:	2x4

Foundation Options:

Slab

(All plans can be built with your choice of foundation and framing. A generic conversion diagram is available. See order form.)

BLUEPRINT PRICE CODE:	C

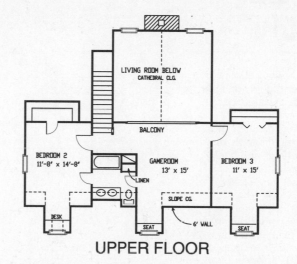

UPPER FLOOR

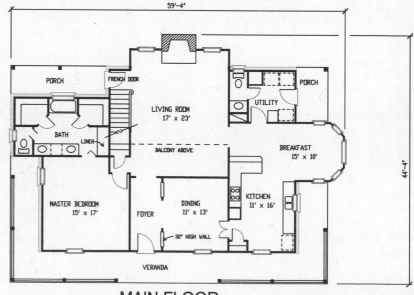

MAIN FLOOR

Window on the World

- Imagine the warmth you'll feel in this two-story charmer, as you relax in the living room and gaze out through the front windows to the nostalgic porch and beyond.
- Wrapping around the side of the home, the porch brings to mind simple days of endless summer evenings and backyard games of croquet and horseshoes.
- Sliding glass doors set into a bayed window arrangement grace the dining area, which opens to the kitchen for effortless serving. Past the sliding glass doors waits a huge deck presiding over the backyard. Here, a picnic table and planter boxes bursting with geraniums would add just the right touch.
- The upper-floor bedrooms gather about a full bath, with a linen closet easily accessible to all.
- Anyone like to tinker? The roomy storage space in the garage should satisfy the budding mechanic or carpenter in the family!

Plan GL-1243

Bedrooms: 3	Baths: 1½
Living Area:	
Upper floor	633 sq. ft.
Main floor	610 sq. ft.
Total Living Area:	**1,243 sq. ft.**
Standard basement	519 sq. ft.
Garage and storage	500 sq. ft.
Exterior Wall Framing:	2x4
Foundation Options:	

Standard basement
(All plans can be built with your choice of foundation and framing. A generic conversion diagram is available. See order form.)

BLUEPRINT PRICE CODE:	A

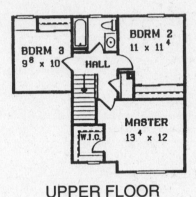

UPPER FLOOR

MAIN FLOOR

TO ORDER THIS BLUEPRINT, CALL TOLL-FREE 1-800-820-1283

Plan GL-1243

PRICES AND DETAILS ON PAGES 12-15

Gracious Days

- As it brings a touch of Victorian flair to this country-style home, a charming gazebo provides a gracious spot for afternoon visits and lemonade.
- Inside, the living and dining rooms flank the foyer, creating an elegant setting for parties. With a closet and private access to a bath, the living room could also be used as a bedroom or a home office.
- Straight ahead, handsome columns frame the Great Room, where puddles of sunshine will form under the two skylights. Sliding glass doors let in the fresh scent of spring blooms. A corner fireplace warms chilled fingers after an afternoon of raking leaves.
- In the kitchen, a sizable island doubles as a workstation and a snack bar. The sunny bay in the breakfast nook will rouse the sleepiest child.
- Across the home, the owners receive some extra special treatment in the master suite. Features here include a pair of walk-in closets, a linen closet and a bath with a dual-sink vanity.

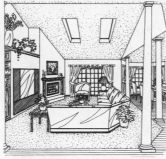

VIEW INTO GREAT ROOM

Plan AX-95349

Bedrooms: 3+	Baths: 3
Living Area:	
Upper floor	728 sq. ft.
Main floor	2,146 sq. ft.
Total Living Area:	**2,874 sq. ft.**
Unfinished loft	300 sq. ft.
Standard basement	2,146 sq. ft.
Garage	624 sq. ft.
Exterior Wall Framing:	2x6

Foundation Options:

Standard basement
Crawlspace
Slab

(All plans can be built with your choice of foundation and framing. A generic conversion diagram is available. See order form.)

BLUEPRINT PRICE CODE:	D

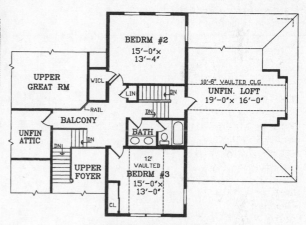

UPPER FLOOR

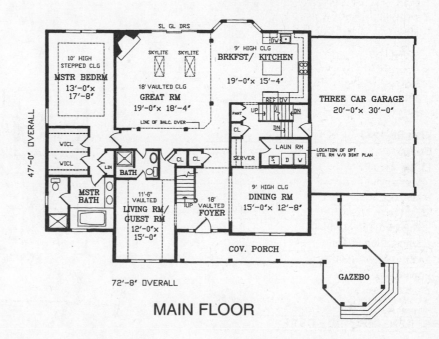

MAIN FLOOR

Country Charm

- While the facade of this home features country details, the interior includes many up-to-date amenities.
- Inside, a stepped ceiling crowns the dining room, where French doors allow guests to enjoy the sounds of raindrops. A wet bar makes serving easy.
- With a closet and private access to a split bath, the office near the entry would also serve well as a bedroom. A 9-ft. ceiling here adds a spacious feel.
- An 18-ft., 5-in. vaulted ceiling soars over the Great Room, which will be the setting for many family meetings.
- In the kitchen, an island counter makes room for baking sprees. A 12-ft. vaulted ceiling tops the breakfast nook, where sliding French doors lead to a porch.
- Across the home, a window seat in the master suite is perfect for relaxing.
- Upstairs, a raised loft would be a neat place to set up the kids' computer nook.
- The foyer, the master suite, the dining room and the two bedrooms upstairs include 9½-ft. ceilings.

Plan AX-94314

Bedrooms: 3+	Baths: 3
Living Area:	
Upper floor	646 sq. ft.
Main floor	2,118 sq. ft.
Total Living Area:	**2,764 sq. ft.**
Storage/future space	400 sq. ft.
Standard basement	2,118 sq. ft.
Garage and storage	497 sq. ft.
Exterior Wall Framing:	2x4

Foundation Options:

Standard basement
Crawlspace
Slab
(All plans can be built with your choice of foundation and framing. A generic conversion diagram is available. See order form.)

BLUEPRINT PRICE CODE: D

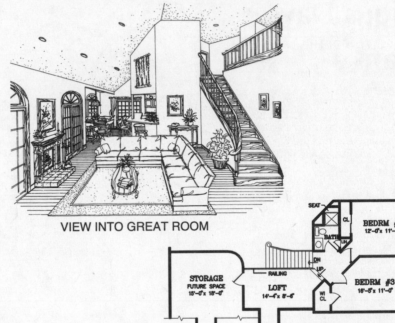

VIEW INTO GREAT ROOM

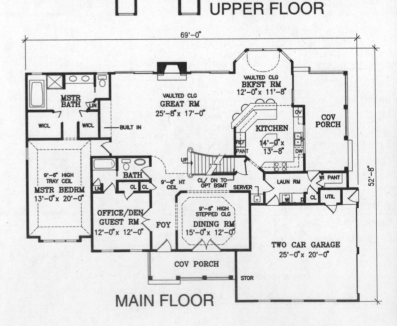

UPPER FLOOR

MAIN FLOOR

Plan AX-94314

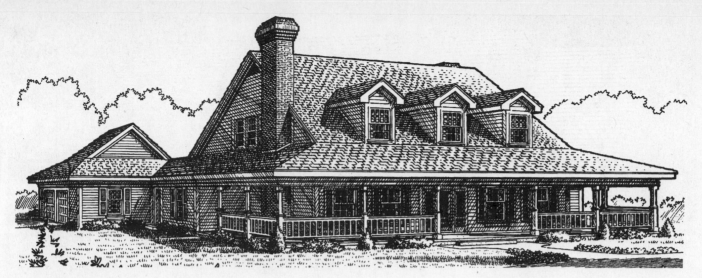

Rambling Romance

- The wonderful wraparound veranda of this rambling farmhouse provides hours of outdoor leisure and romance.
- Inside, there's plenty of space for the whole family to enjoy privacy, as well as conversation and togetherness.
- The airy foyer spills directly into the living room, which presents the first of the home's three handsome fireplaces.

In the adjoining dining room, built-in glass cabinets attractively store china.
- The central kitchen includes a pantry and a snack bar; its location is ideal for hosting formal or casual occasions. Sunny views of the backyard are possible through the window wall of the attached breakfast room.
- A dramatic brick fireplace wall in the family room backs up to a much more private flame in the lavish master suite.
- Recreation and exercise are combined on the upper floor, which also offers three more bedrooms and two baths.

Plan L-337-VC	
Bedrooms: 4+	**Baths:** 3½
Living Area:	
Upper floor	1,169 sq. ft.
Main floor	2,166 sq. ft.
Total Living Area:	**3,335 sq. ft.**
Garage	588 sq. ft.
Exterior Wall Framing:	2x4

Foundation Options:

Slab

(All plans can be built with your choice of foundation and framing. A generic conversion diagram is available. See order form.)

BLUEPRINT PRICE CODE:	E

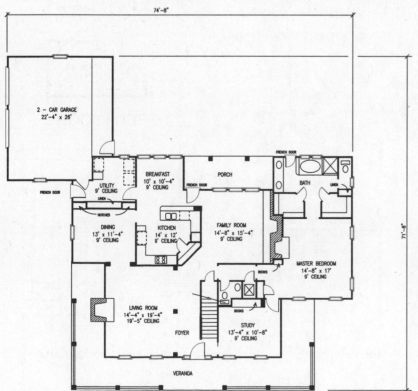

MAIN FLOOR

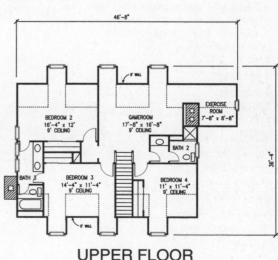

UPPER FLOOR

TO ORDER THIS BLUEPRINT,
CALL TOLL-FREE 1-800-820-1283

Plan L-337-VC

PRICES AND DETAILS
ON PAGES 12-15

101

New-Fashioned Farmhouse

- Traditional styling and a highly contemporary floor plan distinguish this new-fashioned farmhouse.
- The home is embraced by a covered porch, which is accessible from the foyer and the family room.
- The floor plan is zoned for formal and casual living. The casual living spaces are oriented to the rear and integrated for family interaction. The family room's inviting fireplace can be seen from the adjoining kitchen, which features a handy snack bar and a bayed breakfast nook.
- Upstairs are three bedrooms. The larger master bedroom has a vaulted ceiling that soars to approximately 12 feet. Two walk-in closets and a private, vaulted bath with an oval tub, a separate shower and dual sinks are also included. The secondary bedrooms share another full bath.

Plan S-62893

Bedrooms: 3	Baths: 2½
Living Area:	
Upper floor	774 sq. ft.
Main floor	963 sq. ft.
Total Living Area:	**1,737 sq. ft.**
Standard basement	930 sq. ft.
Garage	520 sq. ft.
Exterior Wall Framing:	2x6

Foundation Options:

Standard basement

Crawlspace

Slab

(All plans can be built with your choice of foundation and framing. A generic conversion diagram is available. See order form.)

BLUEPRINT PRICE CODE: B

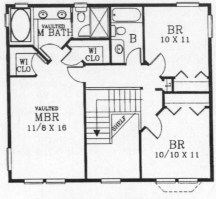

UPPER FLOOR

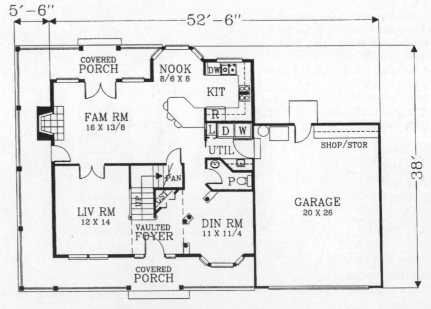

MAIN FLOOR

TO ORDER THIS BLUEPRINT, CALL TOLL-FREE 1-800-820-1283 Plan S-62893 **PRICES AND DETAILS ON PAGES 12-15**

Compact, Cozy, Inviting

- Full-width porches at the front and the rear of this home add plenty of space for outdoor living and entertaining.
- The huge, centrally located living room is the core of this three-bedroom home. The room features a corner fireplace, a 16-ft. sloped, open-beam ceiling and access to the back porch.
- The dining room combines with the kitchen to create an open, more spacious atmosphere. A long, central work island and a compact laundry closet are other space-saving features.
- The main-floor master suite offers a private bath with dual vanities and a large walk-in closet. Two additional bedrooms, a full bath and an intimate sitting area that overlooks the living room and entry are upstairs.
- A separate two-car garage is included with the blueprints.

Plan E-1421

Bedrooms: 3	Baths: 2
Living Area:	
Upper floor	561 sq. ft.
Main floor	924 sq. ft.
Total Living Area:	**1,485 sq. ft.**
Standard basement	924 sq. ft.
Exterior Wall Framing:	2x6

Foundation Options:

Standard basement

Crawlspace

Slab

(All plans can be built with your choice of foundation and framing. A generic conversion diagram is available. See order form.)

BLUEPRINT PRICE CODE: A

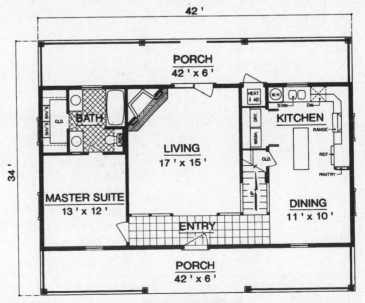

UPPER FLOOR

- ATTIC
- HALL
- BED RM. 16' x 12'
- BATH
- SITTING AREA
- BED RM. 13' x 11'
- OPEN TO LIVING AND ENTRY BELOW
- BEAMS

MAIN FLOOR

42'

34'

- PORCH 42' x 6'
- BATH
- KITCHEN
- HEAT & A/C
- W.H.
- SINK
- DW
- DRY.
- WASH
- RANGE
- REF.
- PANTRY
- LIVING 17' x 15'
- MASTER SUITE 13' x 12'
- ENTRY
- DINING 11' x 10'
- PORCH 42' x 6'

Warm Country

- Three beautiful fireplaces exude wonderful warmth and ambience throughout this stately country home.
- A wide wraparound porch encloses the facade and frames the sidelighted entry. The 23-ft.-high foyer shows off a sweeping stairway as it flows into the formal dining room.
- On the opposite side of the foyer, a roomy study is accessed by French doors and features a handsome fireplace accented by built-in bookshelves.
- A gallery unfolds to the family room, where a French door opens to a porch.
- This porch can also be accessed from the master bedroom. The master bath boasts a large walk-in closet, a Jacuzzi tub and a separate shower.
- The kitchen has a long snack/serving bar that is also great for meal preparation. The adjacent nook sports a built-in breakfast booth and a French door to another porch.
- Along the 14-ft.-high balcony hall are three more bedrooms. One bedroom flaunts its own private bath; another has a built-in desk.
- Unless otherwise specified, all rooms are topped by 9-ft. ceilings.

Plan L-934-VSB

Bedrooms: 4+	Baths: 3½
Living Area:	
Upper floor	933 sq. ft.
Main floor	1,999 sq. ft.
Total Living Area:	**2,932 sq. ft.**
Garage	530 sq. ft.
Exterior Wall Framing:	2x4

Foundation Options:

Slab

(All plans can be built with your choice of foundation and framing. A generic conversion diagram is available. See order form.)

BLUEPRINT PRICE CODE: **D**

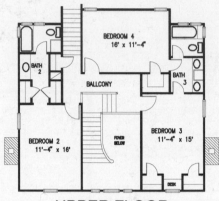

UPPER FLOOR

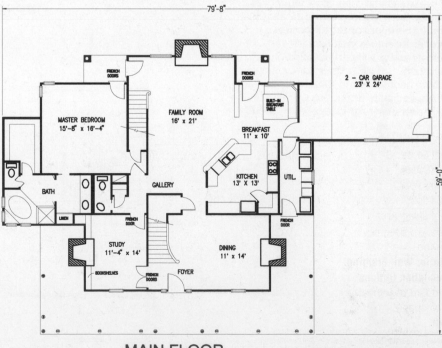

MAIN FLOOR

TO ORDER THIS BLUEPRINT, CALL TOLL-FREE 1-800-820-1283

Plan L-934-VSB

PRICES AND DETAILS ON PAGES 12-15

Country Living

- A covered porch, half-round transom windows and three dormers give this home its warm, nostalgic appeal. Shuttered windows and a louvered vent beautify the side-entry, two-car garage.

- Designed for the ultimate in country living, the floor plan starts off with a dynamic Great Room that flows to a bayed dining area. A nice fireplace adds warmth, while a French door provides access to a backyard covered porch. A powder room is just steps away.

- A 12-ft., 4-in. vaulted ceiling presides over the large country kitchen, which offers a bayed nook, an oversized breakfast bar and a convenient pass-through to the rear porch.

- The exquisite master suite boasts a tray ceiling, a bay window and an alcove for built-in shelves or extra closet space. Other amenities include a large walk-in closet and a compartmentalized bath.

- Upstairs, 9-ft. ceilings enhance two more bedrooms and a second full bath. Each bedroom boasts a cozy dormer window and two closets.

Plan AX-93311

Bedrooms: 3	Baths: 2½
Living Area:	
Upper floor	570 sq. ft.
Main floor	1,375 sq. ft.
Total Living Area:	**1,945 sq. ft.**
Standard basement	1,280 sq. ft.
Garage	450 sq. ft.
Exterior Wall Framing:	2x4

Foundation Options:

Standard basement
Crawlspace
Slab
(All plans can be built with your choice of foundation and framing. A generic conversion diagram is available. See order form.)

BLUEPRINT PRICE CODE: **B**

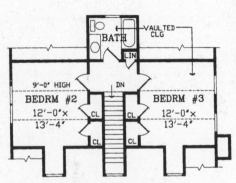

UPPER FLOOR

VIEW INTO GREAT ROOM

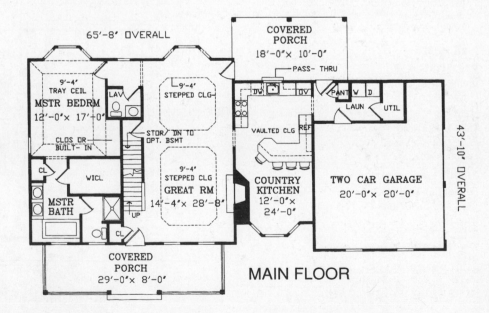

MAIN FLOOR

TO ORDER THIS BLUEPRINT,
CALL TOLL-FREE 1-800-820-1283

Plan AX-93311

PRICES AND DETAILS
ON PAGES 12-15

105

Casual Country Living

- With its covered wraparound porch, this gracious design is ideal for warm summer days or starry evenings.
- The spacious living room boasts a handsome brick-hearth fireplace and built-in book and gun storage. A French door accesses the backyard.
- The open kitchen design provides plenty of space for food storage and preparation with its pantry and oversized central island.
- Two mirror-imaged baths service the three bedrooms on the upper floor. Each secondary bedroom features a window seat and two closets. The master bedroom has a large walk-in closet and a private bath.
- A versatile hobby or sewing room is also included.
- An optional carport off the dining room is available upon request. Please specify when ordering.

Plan J-8895

Bedrooms: 3	Baths: 2½
Living Area:	
Upper floor	860 sq. ft.
Main floor	919 sq. ft.
Total Living Area:	**1,779 sq. ft.**
Standard basement	919 sq. ft.
Optional carport	462 sq. ft.
Exterior Wall Framing:	2x4

Foundation Options:
Standard basement
Crawlspace
Slab
(All plans can be built with your choice of foundation and framing. A generic conversion diagram is available. See order form.)

BLUEPRINT PRICE CODE: B

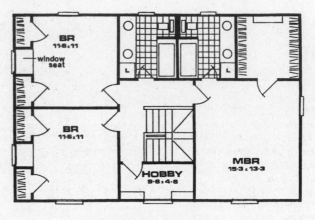

UPPER FLOOR

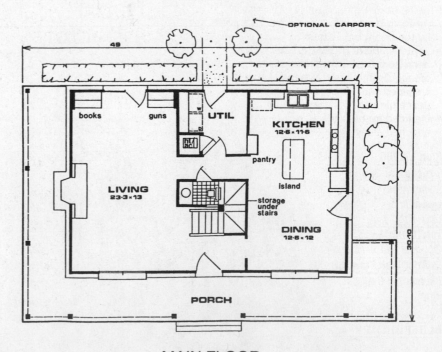

MAIN FLOOR

TO ORDER THIS BLUEPRINT, CALL TOLL-FREE 1-800-820-1283

Plan J-8895

PRICES AND DETAILS ON PAGES 12-15

Some Romantic Feeling

- Seemingly saved from some romantic era, this picturesque Victorian-style home will capture your heart.
- You can spend almost the entire day outside if you want; a great wraparound veranda in front and a covered porch in back are nice spots to while away a sunny day.
- Indoors, the family room offers an incredible amount of space, highlighted by a huge bay window and a heartwarming fireplace.
- Gourmets will appreciate the ambience of the formal dining room, while casual meals in the breakfast room are sparked by the bright bay window.
- Upstairs, the deluxe master suite handles you with care. A bayed sitting area, a skylighted private bath and an L-shaped walk-in closet ensure the peacefulness of this gorgeous retreat.
- Included in the blueprints is an optional attached garage off the utility room.

Plan L-2066

Bedrooms: 3	Baths: 2½
Living Area:	
Upper floor	1,069 sq. ft.
Main floor	997 sq. ft.
Total Living Area:	**2,066 sq. ft.**
Optional attached garage	506 sq. ft.
Exterior Wall Framing:	2x4
Foundation Options:	

Slab
(All plans can be built with your choice of foundation and framing. A generic conversion diagram is available. See order form.)

BLUEPRINT PRICE CODE:	C

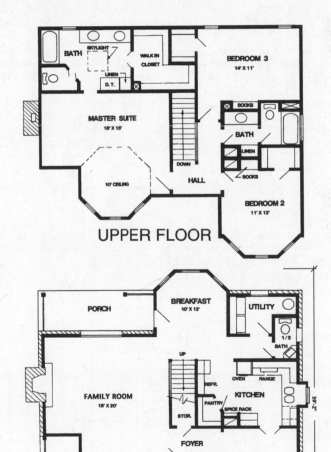

UPPER FLOOR

MAIN FLOOR

Modern Country Life

- Classic country features like a wrap-around porch, round louvered vents and a covered entry accent the exterior of this modern home.
- Just past the inviting entry, the spacious 17-ft.-high living room is separated from the dining room by a see-through fireplace.

- The dining room features a bright bay window. The adjacent kitchen, which serves the family room over a stylish counter, has a pantry and corner windows over the sink.
- The family room is brightened by sliding glass doors to a backyard patio. A convenient half-bath and a laundry room are nearby.
- Upstairs, the master bedroom boasts a 10½-ft.-high vaulted ceiling. The master bath has a double-sink vanity, a walk-in closet and a linen closet.

Plan AG-1603

Bedrooms: 4	Baths: 2½
Living Area:	
Upper floor	853 sq. ft.
Main floor	789 sq. ft.
Total Living Area:	**1,642 sq. ft.**
Standard basement	760 sq. ft.
Garage	440 sq. ft.
Exterior Wall Framing:	2x4

Foundation Options:

Standard basement
(All plans can be built with your choice of foundation and framing. A generic conversion diagram is available. See order form.)

BLUEPRINT PRICE CODE: B

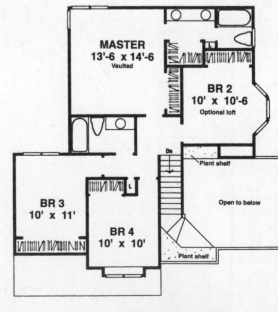

MAIN FLOOR

UPPER FLOOR

TO ORDER THIS BLUEPRINT, CALL TOLL-FREE 1-800-820-1283

Plan AG-1603

PRICES AND DETAILS ON PAGES 12-15

Soul Delight

- Ensconced in its quaint, country-flavored facade, this efficient home will delight your soul.
- Consider the comfortable living room, with its cute windows and generous space for the sofa, loveseat and big-screen TV.
- Formal or casual meals may be taken in the dining room, which flows into the kitchen. On summery Saturdays, herd the kids through the sliding glass doors and seat them at a picnic table for

lemonade, burgers and your famous potato salad!
- The main-floor master suite, which is tucked away for extra privacy, pampers you with loads of closet space and private access to a full bath.
- In the hall, laundry facilities are tucked neatly away; a closet gives you a spot to shuck off that winter jacket.
- Two upper-floor bedrooms give the kids their privacy. The larger of the two bedrooms has a nook, where your budding philatelist may set up her growing stamp collection.

Plan GL-1201

Bedrooms: 3	Baths: 2
Living Area:	
Upper floor	437 sq. ft.
Main floor	764 sq. ft.
Total Living Area:	**1,201 sq. ft.**
Standard basement	679 sq. ft.
Garage	400 sq. ft.
Exterior Wall Framing:	2x4

Foundation Options:

Standard basement
(All plans can be built with your choice of foundation and framing. A generic conversion diagram is available. See order form.)

BLUEPRINT PRICE CODE:	**A**

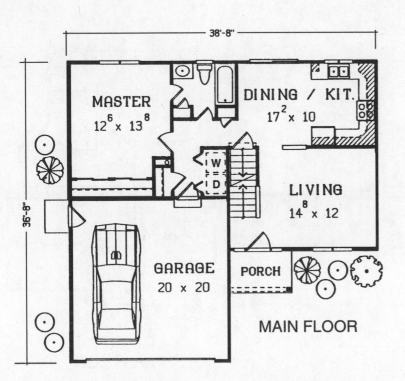

MAIN FLOOR

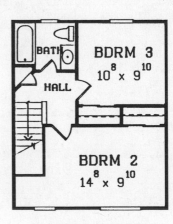

UPPER FLOOR

TO ORDER THIS BLUEPRINT,
CALL TOLL-FREE 1-800-820-1283

Plan GL-1201

PRICES AND DETAILS
ON PAGES 12-15

109

Elegant, with a Country Heart

- A columned porch and a dramatic arched window help to create a country-style home with a twist of urbane elegance.
- The dramatic two-story foyer greets visitors with its sunlit brilliance.
- Entertaining big crowds can easily be done in the large family room or the even larger living room/dining room area. Take the party outdoors via sliding glass doors to a handy terrace.
- The master suite features its own secluded terrace, and is also highlighted by a 12-ft. cathedral ceiling, a walk-in closet and a skylighted private bath with a sensuous whirlpool tub under a dazzling glass-block wall.
- A majestic curved stairway leads gracefully to the upper floor, where four more bedrooms and a second full bath are featured.

Plan K-804-R

Bedrooms: 5	Baths: 2½
Living Area:	
Upper floor	937 sq. ft.
Main floor	1,808 sq. ft.
Total Living Area:	**2,745 sq. ft.**
Standard basement	1,795 sq. ft.
Garage	483 sq. ft.
Exterior Wall Framing:	2x4 or 2x6

Foundation Options:

Standard basement

Slab

(All plans can be built with your choice of foundation and framing. A generic conversion diagram is available. See order form.)

BLUEPRINT PRICE CODE:	D

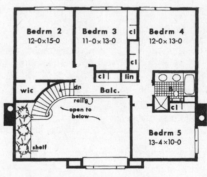

UPPER FLOOR

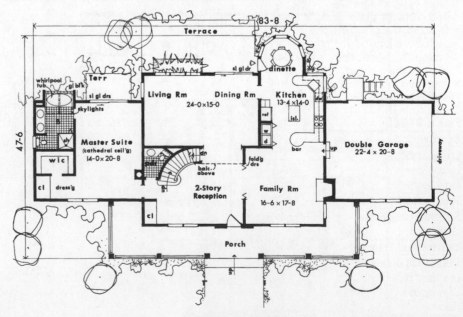

MAIN FLOOR

TO ORDER THIS BLUEPRINT, CALL TOLL-FREE 1-800-820-1283   Plan K-804-R   *PRICES AND DETAILS ON PAGES 12-15*

Farmhouse for Today

- An inviting covered porch and decorative dormer windows lend traditional warmth and charm to this attractive design.
- The up-to-date interior includes ample space for entertaining as well as for daily family activities.
- The elegant foyer is flanked on one side by the formal, sunken living room and on the other by a sunken family room with a fireplace and an entertainment center. Each room features an 8½-ft. tray ceiling and views of the porch.
- The dining room flows from the living room to increase the entertaining space.
- The kitchen/nook/laundry area forms a large expanse for casual family living and domestic chores.
- Upstairs, the grand master suite includes a large closet and a private bath with a garden tub, a designer shower and a private deck.
- A second full bath serves the two secondary bedrooms.

Plan U-87-203

Bedrooms: 3	Baths: 2½
Living Area:	
Upper floor	857 sq. ft.
Main floor	1,064 sq. ft.
Total Living Area:	**1,921 sq. ft.**
Standard basement	1,064 sq. ft.
Garage	552 sq. ft.
Exterior Wall Framing:	2x4 or 2x6

Foundation Options:

Standard basement

Crawlspace

Slab

(All plans can be built with your choice of foundation and framing. A generic conversion diagram is available. See order form.)

BLUEPRINT PRICE CODE: B

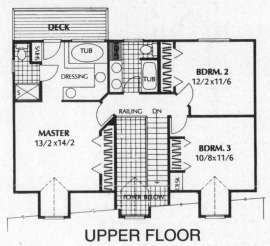

UPPER FLOOR

MAIN FLOOR

Easy to Build

- The basic rectangular shape of this two-story home makes it economical to build. The well-zoned interior isolates all four bedrooms on the upper floor.
- Off the covered porch, the airy foyer reveals the open stairway and unfolds to each of the living areas.
- The formal rooms are positioned at the front of the home and overlook the porch. The large living room boasts a handsome fireplace and extends to a rear porch through sliding glass doors.
- The central family room hosts casual family activities and shows off a rustic wood-beam ceiling. This room also opens to the porch and integrates with the kitchen and the bright dinette for a big, open atmosphere.
- A half-bath, a laundry area and a handy service porch are located near the entrance from the garage.
- Two dual-sink bathrooms serve the bedrooms upstairs. The spacious master bedroom has a private bath and a big walk-in closet.

Plan HFL-1070-RQ

Bedrooms: 4	Baths: 2½
Living Area:	
Upper floor	1,013 sq. ft.
Main floor	1,082 sq. ft.
Total Living Area:	**2,095 sq. ft.**
Standard basement	889 sq. ft.
Garage and storage	481 sq. ft.
Exterior Wall Framing:	2x6

Foundation Options:

Standard basement
Slab

(All plans can be built with your choice of foundation and framing. A generic conversion diagram is available. See order form.)

BLUEPRINT PRICE CODE:	C

VIEW INTO FAMILY ROOM, KITCHEN AND DINETTE

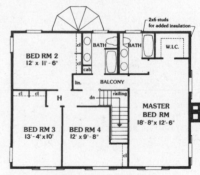

UPPER FLOOR

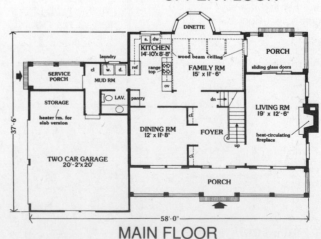

MAIN FLOOR

TO ORDER THIS BLUEPRINT, CALL TOLL-FREE 1-800-820-1283

Plan HFL-1070-RQ

PRICES AND DETAILS ON PAGES 12-15

Formal, Casual Entertainment

- This charming home has plenty of space for both formal and casual entertaining.
- On the main floor, the huge central living room will pamper your guests with an impressive fireplace, a wet bar and two sets of French doors that expand the room to a backyard porch.
- The large formal dining room hosts those special, sit-down dinners.
- There's still more space in the roomy island kitchen and breakfast nook to gather for snacks and conversation.
- For quiet evenings alone, the plush master suite offers pure relaxation! A romantic two-way fireplace between the bedroom and the bath serves as the focal point, yet the whirlpool garden tub is just as inviting.
- The main-floor rooms are enhanced by 10-ft. ceilings; the upper-floor rooms have 9-ft. ceilings.
- The kids' recreation time can be spent in the enormous game room on the upper floor. Private baths service each of the vaulted upper-floor bedrooms.

Plan L-105-VC

Bedrooms: 4+	Baths: 4
Living Area:	
Upper floor	1,077 sq. ft.
Main floor	1,995 sq. ft.
Total Living Area:	**3,072 sq. ft.**
Garage	529 sq. ft.
Storage	184 sq. ft.
Exterior Wall Framing:	2x4

Foundation Options:

Slab

(All plans can be built with your choice of foundation and framing. A generic conversion diagram is available. See order form.)

BLUEPRINT PRICE CODE:	E

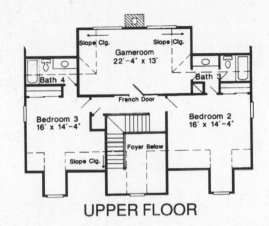

UPPER FLOOR

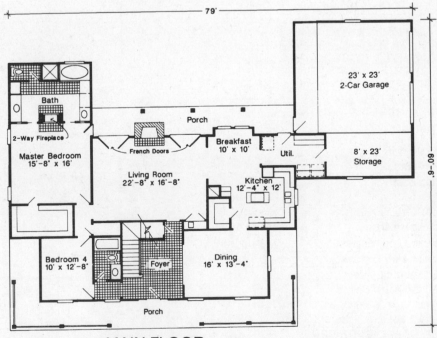

MAIN FLOOR

Cottage with Open Interior

- The exterior of this contemporary cottage features a delightful covered porch and a pair of matching dormers.
- The entry has a dramatic 13-ft. ceiling and flows into an expansive Great Room. The Great Room is also highlighted by a vaulted ceiling that rises to a height of 17 feet. Tall windows brighten both corners, while a fireplace serves as a handsome centerpiece. Sliding doors between the Great Room and the breakfast nook open to an angled backyard deck.
- The sunny vaulted nook provides a cozy setting for family dining with a view of the backyard.
- Ample cabinets and counter space are offered in the efficient galley kitchen, which also features a handy snack counter that extends into the nook.
- The main-floor master bedroom has a walk-in closet and easy access to the full bath beyond.
- The upper floor offers another bedroom, plus a full bath with space for a laundry closet. The loft could serve as an extra bedroom.

Plan JWB-9307

Bedrooms: 2+	Baths: 2
Living Area:	
Upper floor	349 sq. ft.
Main floor	795 sq. ft.
Total Living Area:	**1,144 sq. ft.**
Standard basement	712 sq. ft.
Exterior Wall Framing:	2x4 or 2x6

Foundation Options:

Standard basement
(Typical foundation & framing conversion diagram available—see order form.)

BLUEPRINT PRICE CODE: A

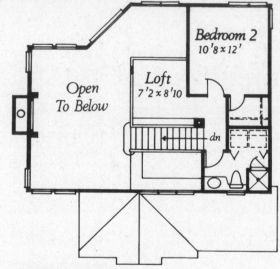

UPPER FLOOR

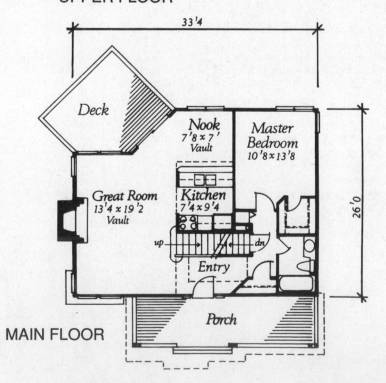

MAIN FLOOR

Plan JWB-9307

Octagonal Dining Bay

- Classic traditional styling is recreated with a covered front porch and triple dormers with half-round windows.
- Off the entry porch, double doors reveal the reception area, with a walk-in closet and a half-bath.

- The living room features a striking fireplace and leads to the dining room, with its octagonal bay.
- The island kitchen overlooks the dinette and the family room, which features a second fireplace and sliding glass doors to a rear deck.
- Upstairs, the master suite boasts a walk-in closet and a whirlpool bath. A skylighted hallway connects three more bedrooms and another full bath.

Plan K-680-R

Bedrooms: 4	**Baths:** 2½
Living Area:	
Upper floor	853 sq. ft.
Main floor	1,047 sq. ft.
Total Living Area:	**1,900 sq. ft.**
Standard basement	1,015 sq. ft.
Garage and storage	472 sq. ft.
Exterior Wall Framing:	2x4 or 2x6
Foundation Options:	
Standard basement	
Slab	

(All plans can be built with your choice of foundation and framing. A generic conversion diagram is available. See order form.)

BLUEPRINT PRICE CODE:	**B**

MAIN FLOOR

UPPER FLOOR

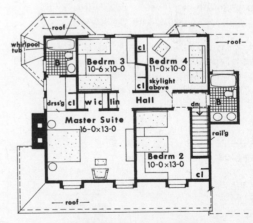

VIEW INTO LIVING ROOM AND DINING ROOM

Comfortable Country Home

- A central gable and a wide, welcoming front porch with columns give this design comfortable country charm.
- The large living room is open to the dining room, which features a tray ceiling and views to the backyard.
- The kitchen offers an oversized island counter with a snack bar. The adjoining breakfast area has a sliding glass door to the backyard and a half-wall that separates it from the family room. This inviting room includes a fireplace and a bay window with a cozy seat.
- Upstairs, the master suite boasts three windows, including a lovely arched window, that overlook the front yard. The private bath offers a whirlpool tub and a separate shower.
- Three more bedrooms, a second full bath and a multipurpose den make this a great family-sized home.

Plan OH-165

Bedrooms: 4+	Baths: 2½
Living Area:	
Upper floor	1,121 sq. ft.
Main floor	1,000 sq. ft.
Total Living Area:	**2,121 sq. ft.**
Standard basement	1,000 sq. ft.
Garage	400 sq. ft.
Exterior Wall Framing:	2x4

Foundation Options:

Standard basement

(All plans can be built with your choice of foundation and framing. A generic conversion diagram is available. See order form.)

BLUEPRINT PRICE CODE: C

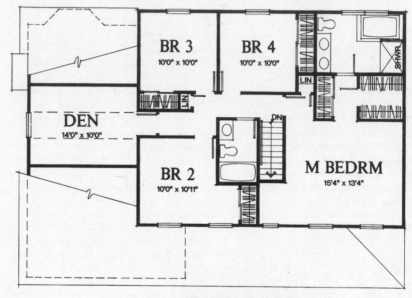

UPPER FLOOR

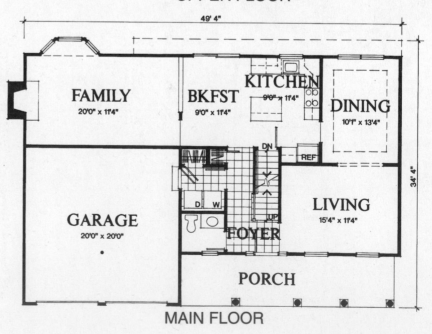

MAIN FLOOR

TO ORDER THIS BLUEPRINT, CALL TOLL-FREE 1-800-820-1283   Plan OH-165   **PRICES AND DETAILS ON PAGES 12-15**

City House, Country Home

- Gingerbread detailing and a covered front porch give this charming home a country-style feel, while its modest width makes it suitable for a city lot.
- The inviting entry leads directly into the spacious Great Room, which boasts a 14-ft. vaulted ceiling. An impressive brick fireplace adds warmth and atmosphere.

- A French door in the adjoining dining area opens to a covered back porch.
- The efficient L-shaped kitchen is open to the dining area and brightened by a window above the sink. The nearby laundry room also accesses the porch.
- The quiet master bedroom is furnished with a roomy walk-in closet. The central full bath is just steps away.
- An elegant open-railed stairway overlooks the entry and leads to the upper floor, where two additional bedrooms share a hallway linen closet and a second full bath.

Plan V-1098

Bedrooms: 3	Baths: 2
Living Area:	
Upper floor	396 sq. ft.
Main floor	702 sq. ft.
Total Living Area:	**1,098 sq. ft.**
Exterior Wall Framing:	2x6

Foundation Options:

Crawlspace
(All plans can be built with your choice of foundation and framing. A generic conversion diagram is available. See order form.)

BLUEPRINT PRICE CODE: A

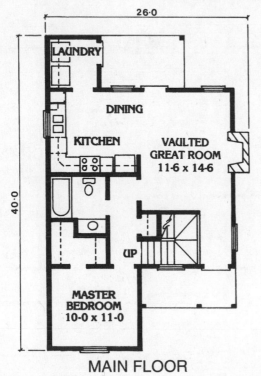

MAIN FLOOR

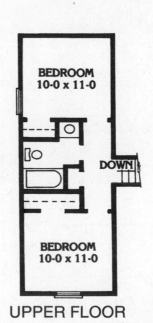

UPPER FLOOR

Picture-Perfect

- Those tall, cold glasses of summertime lemonade will taste even better when enjoyed on the shady front porch of this picture-perfect home.
- Inside, the two-story, sidelighted foyer unfolds to the formal living areas and the Great Room beyond.
- Fireplaces grace the living room and the Great Room, which are separated by French pocket doors. A TV nook borders the fireplace in the Great Room, letting the kids catch their favorite show while Mom and Dad fix dinner in the kitchen. Two sets of French doors swing wide to reveal a backyard deck.
- A glassy dinette with an 8-ft. ceiling makes breakfasts cozy and comfortable.
- Restful nights will be the norm in the master suite, which boasts a 14-ft. cathedral ceiling. Next to the walk-in closet, the private bath has a whirlpool tub in a fabulous boxed-out window.
- Unless otherwise noted, all main-floor rooms are topped by 9-ft. ceilings.
- At day's end, guests and children may retire to the upper floor, where four big bedrooms and a full bath await them.

Plan AHP-9512

Bedrooms: 5	Baths: 2½
Living Area:	
Upper floor	928 sq. ft.
Main floor	1,571 sq. ft.
Total Living Area:	**2,499 sq. ft.**
Standard basement	1,571 sq. ft.
Garage and storage	420 sq. ft.
Exterior Wall Framing:	**2x4 or 2x6**

Foundation Options:

Standard basement

Crawlspace

Slab

(All plans can be built with your choice of foundation and framing. A generic conversion diagram is available. See order form.)

BLUEPRINT PRICE CODE: C

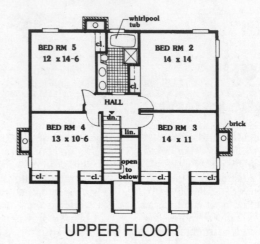

UPPER FLOOR

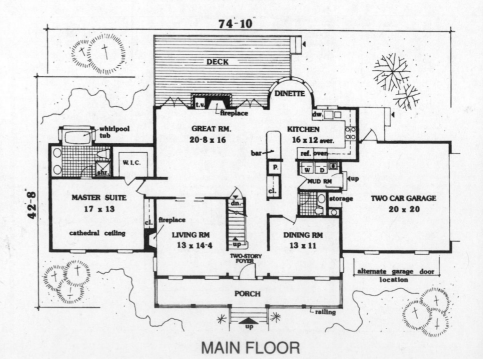

MAIN FLOOR

Wonderful Expectations

- This home's huge wraparound porch creates wonderful expectations about what awaits inside; and its remarkable design doesn't disappoint!
- Large, open areas work great for gathering family and friends. The family room and the living room each offer lots of space, and both are cheered by a friendly fireplace.

- A third fireplace is found in the heartwarming master suite, which also boasts dual walk-in closets, a secluded bath and access to the backyard via a lovely French door.
- The outstanding kitchen has lots of nooks and crannies for storage—including a corner pantry. Located between the dining and morning rooms, it's convenient for any meal.
- Upstairs, you'll find three nice-sized bedrooms and an entertainment/study area that can convert to a fifth bedroom if necessary.

Plan L-182-FCC	
Bedrooms: 4+	**Baths:** 3½
Living Area:	
Upper floor	943 sq. ft.
Main floor	2,237 sq. ft.
Total Living Area:	**3,180 sq. ft.**
Garage and work area	603 sq. ft.
Exterior Wall Framing:	2x4
Foundation Options:	
Slab	

(All plans can be built with your choice of foundation and framing. A generic conversion diagram is available. See order form.)

| **BLUEPRINT PRICE CODE:** | E |

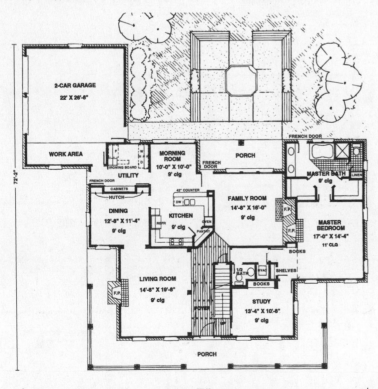

MAIN FLOOR

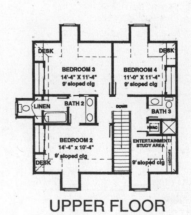

UPPER FLOOR

Traditional Retreat

- This traditional vacation retreat maximizes space by offering an open, flowing floor plan.
- The spacious living room's luxurious features include a cathedral ceiling, fireplace and wet bar; its openness is extended by an exciting adjoining covered deck.
- Sweeping diagonally from the living room is the formal dining room with both front-facing and roof windows.
- The merging kitchen is separated from the living areas by a counter bar.
- The first floor bedroom features a unique triangular window seat, a dressing area and a full bath.
- The second floor is devoted entirely to a private master suite, complete with a lovely window seat, walk-in closet and attached bath.

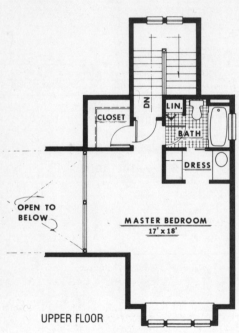

UPPER FLOOR

OPEN TO BELOW

CLOSET / DN / LIN. / BATH / DRESS

MASTER BEDROOM
17' x 18'

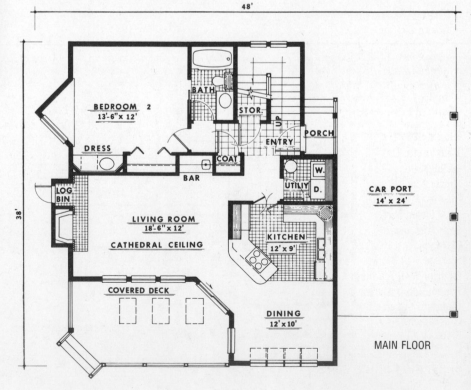

MAIN FLOOR

48'

38'

BEDROOM 2
13'-6" x 12'

DRESS

BATH / STOR. / UP / PORCH

ENTRY

COAT

BAR

LOG BIN

W. / UTILIY / D. / CAR PORT 14' x 24'

LIVING ROOM
18'-6" x 12'
CATHEDRAL CEILING

KITCHEN
12' x 9'

COVERED DECK

DINING
12' x 10'

Plan NW-334

Bedrooms: 2	Baths: 2

Space:

Upper floor:	438 sq. ft.
Main floor:	1,015 sq. ft.
Total living area:	**1,453 sq. ft.**
Carport:	336 sq. ft.

Exterior Wall Framing: 2x6

Foundation options:
Crawlspace.
(Foundation & framing conversion diagram available — see order form.)

Blueprint Price Code: A

Down-Home Country Flavor!

- Open living areas, decorative dormers and a spacious wraparound porch give this charming home its country feel.
- The main entrance opens into an enormous living room, which boasts a handsome fireplace flanked by bright windows and built-in cabinets.
- The adjoining dining room is brightened by windows on three sides. A rear French door opens to the porch.
- The modern kitchen serves the dining room over an eating bar. A half-bath and a laundry/utility area with access to the garage and porch are nearby.
- The removed master bedroom includes a roomy walk-in closet and a private bath with a corner shower and a dual-sink vanity with knee space.
- All main-floor rooms have 9-ft. ceilings.
- Two upper-floor bedrooms share a hallway bath, which is enhanced by one of three dormer windows.

Plan J-90013

Bedrooms: 3	Baths: 2½
Living Area:	
Upper floor	823 sq. ft.
Main floor	1,339 sq. ft.
Total Living Area:	**2,162 sq. ft.**
Standard basement	1,339 sq. ft.
Garage	413 sq. ft.
Storage	106 sq. ft.
Exterior Wall Framing:	2x4

Foundation Options:

Standard basement

Crawlspace

Slab

(All plans can be built with your choice of foundation and framing. A generic conversion diagram is available. See order form.)

BLUEPRINT PRICE CODE: C

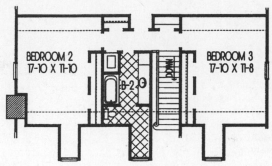

UPPER FLOOR

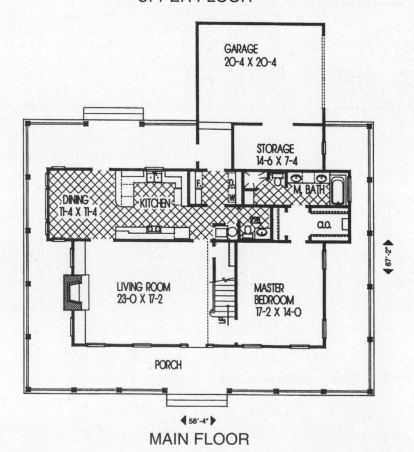

MAIN FLOOR

Cottage Suits Small Lot

- Designed to fit on a sloping or small lot, this compact country-style cottage has the amenities of a much larger home.
- The large front porch opens to the home's surprising two-story-high foyer, which views into the living room.
- The spacious living room is warmed by a handsome fireplace that is centered between built-in bookshelves.
- Enhanced by a sunny bay that opens to a backyard deck, the dining room offers a comfortable eating area that is easily served by the island kitchen.
- The secluded main-floor master bedroom includes a roomy walk-in closet. The spectacular master bath showcases a corner garden tub, a designer shower, a built-in bench and a dual-sink vanity.
- Upstairs, a railed balcony overlooks the foyer. Two secondary bedrooms with walk-in closets share a central bath.

Plan C-8870

Bedrooms: 3	Baths: 2
Living Area:	
Upper floor	664 sq. ft.
Main floor	1,100 sq. ft.
Total Living Area:	**1,764 sq. ft.**
Daylight basement/garage	1,100 sq. ft.
Exterior Wall Framing:	2x4

Foundation Options:

Daylight basement
(All plans can be built with your choice of foundation and framing. A generic conversion diagram is available. See order form.)

BLUEPRINT PRICE CODE:	**B**

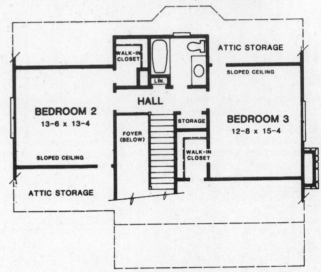

UPPER FLOOR

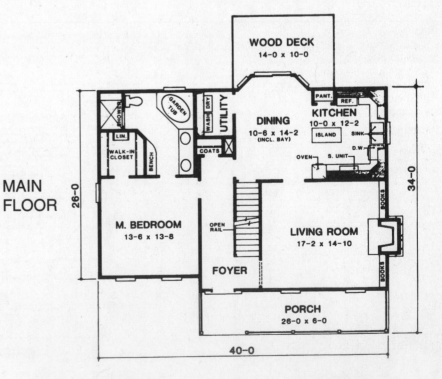

MAIN FLOOR

Plan C-8870

PRICES AND DETAILS ON PAGES 12-15

Relax in the Country

- This country home provides plenty of room to relax, with its covered porches and wide-open living spaces.
- Just off the front porch, the living room boasts a soothing fireplace with a raised brick hearth. The 18-ft. cathedral ceiling is shared with the adjoining dining room, which offers French-door access to the backyard porch.
- The walk-through kitchen features a handy pantry, plus a laundry closet that houses a stackable washer and dryer.
- A convenient pocket door leads to the secluded full bath.
- The master bedroom boasts two closets and private access to the bath.
- An open stairway with an oak handrail leads up to another bedroom, with a cozy seat under an arched window arrangement. Other features include a 9-ft. ceiling, a pair of closets and access to extra storage space.

Plan J-90016

Bedrooms: 2	Baths: 1
Living Area:	
Upper floor	203 sq. ft.
Main floor	720 sq. ft.
Total Living Area:	**923 sq. ft.**
Standard basement	720 sq. ft.
Exterior Wall Framing:	2x6

Foundation Options:

Standard basement

Crawlspace

Slab

(All plans can be built with your choice of foundation and framing. A generic conversion diagram is available. See order form.)

BLUEPRINT PRICE CODE:	**AA**

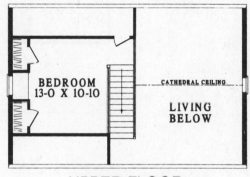

UPPER FLOOR

BEDROOM 13-0 X 10-10

CATHEDRAL CEILING

LIVING BELOW

32-0

38-6

PORCH 32-0 X 8-0

KITCHEN 11-6 X 7-4

DINING 14-2 X 8-0

MASTER BEDROOM 13-2 X 11-6

LIVING 14-2 X 13-6

PORCH 32-0 X 8-0

MAIN FLOOR

Five-Bedroom Traditional

- This sophisticated traditional home makes a striking statement both inside and out.
- The dramatic two-story foyer is flanked by the formal living spaces. The private dining room overlooks the front porch, while the spacious living room has outdoor views on two sides.
- A U-shaped kitchen with a snack bar, a sunny dinette area and a large family room flow together at the back of the home. The family room's fireplace warms the open, informal expanse, while sliding glass doors in the dinette access the backyard terrace.
- The second floor has five roomy bedrooms and two skylighted bathrooms. The luxurious master suite has a high ceiling with a beautiful arched window, a dressing area and a huge walk-in closet. The private bath offers dual sinks, a whirlpool tub and a separate shower.
- Attic space is located above the garage.

Plan AHP-9392

Bedrooms: 5	Baths: 2½
Living Area:	
Upper floor	1,223 sq. ft.
Main floor	1,193 sq. ft.
Total Living Area:	**2,416 sq. ft.**
Standard basement	1,130 sq. ft.
Garage	509 sq. ft.
Storage	65 sq. ft.
Exterior Wall Framing:	2x4 or 2x6

Foundation Options:

Standard basement

Crawlspace

Slab

(Typical foundation & framing conversion diagram available—see order form.)

BLUEPRINT PRICE CODE: C

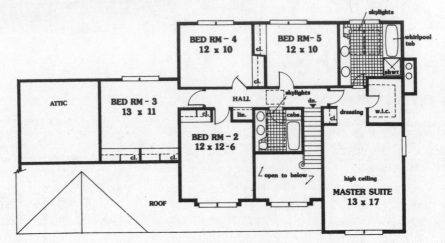

UPPER FLOOR

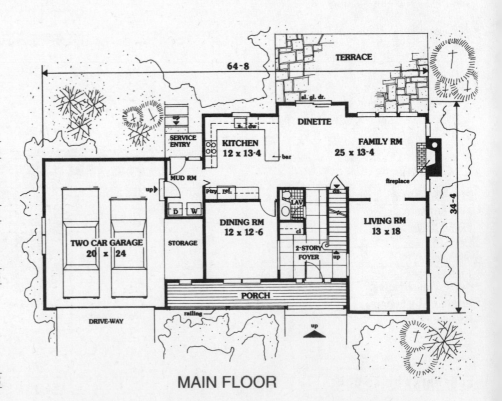

MAIN FLOOR

TO ORDER THIS BLUEPRINT, CALL TOLL-FREE 1-800-820-1283   Plan AHP-9392   *PRICES AND DETAILS ON PAGES 12-15*

A Hint of Romance

- An ornate front porch and a decorative gable with fishscale shingles give this lovely home a romantic Victorian look.
- The central foyer flows to all areas of the home, including the convenient powder room to the left.
- Directly ahead, the airy kitchen features a functional eating bar and a sunny breakfast area with sliding glass doors to a backyard deck. Access to both the garage and a fully appointed laundry room is also a cinch.
- The formal dining room expands into the spacious bayed family room, where a handsome fireplace adds warmth and character to the room.
- Upstairs, the incredible master bedroom boasts a stunning bay window and an optional 15-ft. vaulted ceiling. His-and-hers closets and a private bath with a spa tub, a separate shower and twin vanities are also included.
- A second full bath and two more bedrooms complete the upper floor.

Plan APS-1514

Bedrooms: 3	Baths: 2½
Living Area:	
Upper floor	786 sq. ft.
Main floor	812 sq. ft.
Total Living Area:	**1,598 sq. ft.**
Garage and storage	560 sq. ft.
Exterior Wall Framing:	2x4

Foundation Options:

Crawlspace

Slab

(All plans can be built with your choice of foundation and framing. A generic conversion diagram is available. See order form.)

BLUEPRINT PRICE CODE: B

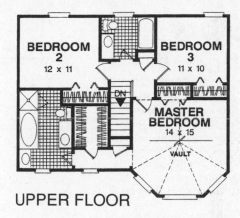

UPPER FLOOR

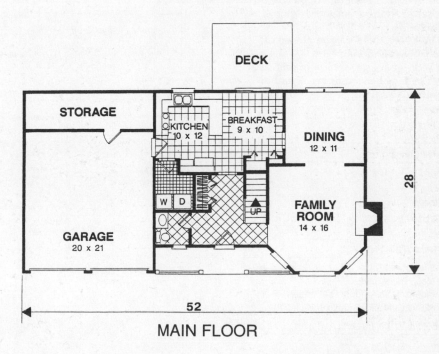

MAIN FLOOR

Two-Story Traditional

- A lovely front porch adorns the facade of this traditional beauty.
- Virtually barrier-free, this open design offers plenty of room to roam; the family room, kitchen and eating area form a continuous dining or entertaining expanse with fireplace, bay window and worktop island.
- Formal dining is done opposite the kitchen in the front-facing dining room.
- The living room can be closed off with pocket doors.
- The large master bedroom and two secondary bedrooms are found on the second floor, which also reveals an open balcony.

Plan GL-1950

Bedrooms: 3	Baths: 2½
Space:	
Upper floor:	912 sq. ft.
Main floor:	1,038 sq. ft.
Total living area:	1,950 sq. ft.
Garage:	484 sq. ft.
Exterior Wall Framing:	2x6

Foundation options:
Standard basement.
(Foundation & framing conversion diagram available — see order form.)

Blueprint Price Code: B

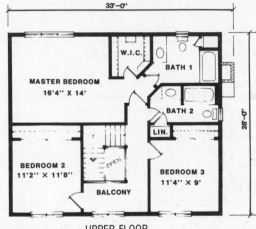

UPPER FLOOR

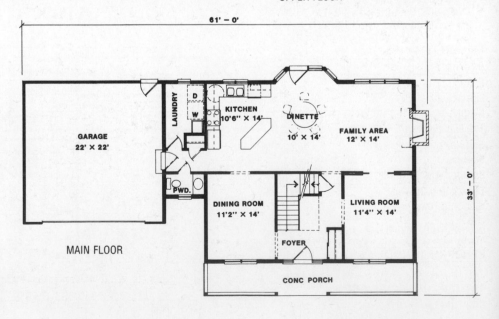

MAIN FLOOR

TO ORDER THIS BLUEPRINT, CALL TOLL-FREE 1-800-820-1283

Plan GL-1950

PRICES AND DETAILS ON PAGES 12-15

Country Appeal

- A spacious covered front porch adds to the country appeal of this classic farmhouse-style home.
- The inviting central foyer showcases a curved open-railed stairway. The adjacent living room boasts a handsome fireplace and a 9½-ft.-high vaulted sitting area brightened by a large Palladian-style window.
- Formal entertaining can be expanded to the dining room, which offers sliding glass doors to a backyard terrace.
- Updated and efficient, the good-sized kitchen includes an eating bar and a windowed sink. The adjoining dinette also expands to the terrace through sliding glass doors. Nearby is a laundry/mudroom with a service entry and garage access.
- Upstairs, an open-railed balcony overlooks the foyer. The deluxe master bedroom features a private bath and a separate dressing area.
- Three additional upper-floor bedrooms are serviced by a second full bath.

Plan HFL-1040-MB

Bedrooms: 4	Baths: 2½
Living Area:	
Upper floor	936 sq. ft.
Main floor	1,094 sq. ft.
Total Living Area:	**2,030 sq. ft.**
Standard basement	1,022 sq. ft.
Garage	420 sq. ft.
Exterior Wall Framing:	2x6

Foundation Options:

Standard basement

Slab

(All plans can be built with your choice of foundation and framing. A generic conversion diagram is available. See order form.)

BLUEPRINT PRICE CODE: C

VIEW INTO LIVING ROOM

UPPER FLOOR

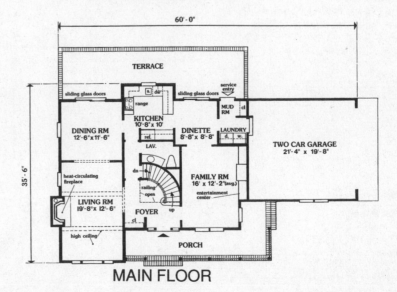

MAIN FLOOR

Classy Design

- Brick and wood construction, combined with traditional design overtones, gives this two-story home character and class.
- A covered entry porch opens to the 18-ft.-high foyer and the adjoining formal dining room.
- Past a handy powder room, the galley-style kitchen has much to offer. An angled serving bar, lots of counter space and a neat pantry are nice attractions. The laundry room and the two-car garage are within easy reach.
- The breakfast area includes a built-in desk and a French door to the backyard.
- The heart of the home is the spacious Great Room, which features an inviting fireplace framed by windows.
- The upper floor is highlighted by a spectacular overlook and an equally stunning master bedroom topped by a 10-ft., 8-in. tray ceiling. The master bath includes a 13-ft. vaulted ceiling and a corner spa tub under glass!

Plan FB-1563

Bedrooms: 3	Baths: 2½
Living Area:	
Upper floor	766 sq. ft.
Main floor	797 sq. ft.
Total Living Area:	**1,563 sq. ft.**
Daylight basement	797 sq. ft.
Garage	440 sq. ft.
Exterior Wall Framing:	2x4

Foundation Options:
Daylight basement
Slab
(All plans can be built with your choice of foundation and framing. A generic conversion diagram is available. See order form.)

BLUEPRINT PRICE CODE: B

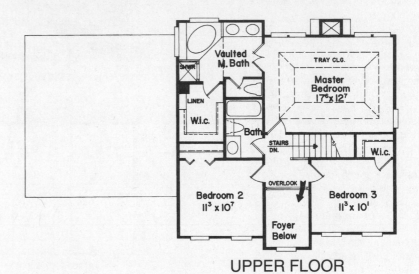

UPPER FLOOR

MAIN FLOOR

TO ORDER THIS BLUEPRINT, CALL TOLL-FREE 1-800-820-1283

Plan FB-1563

PRICES AND DETAILS ON PAGES 12-15

Pure Country

- This home's wraparound veranda, wood shutters and trio of dormers conjure up a nostalgic image of pure country.
- Behind the ornate entry door, the foyer unfolds to the formal dining room and the spacious central living room.
- Set off by columned half-walls, the dining room has a nice quiet location; cafe doors separate it from the kitchen.
- The living room enjoys the warmth of a majestic fireplace and the drama of a window wall that peaks at the room's 17-ft.-high cathedral ceiling and soaring trapezoid transoms.
- With a functional work island and a neat pantry, the kitchen is suited for efficiency and mobility.
- Its bay window and openness to the living spaces visually expand the breakfast room, which is accessible to the veranda through a French door.
- The master bedroom offers the owners of the home a huge walk-in closet, a step-up garden tub, a private toilet and a dual-sink vanity.
- A large split bath accommodates the upper-floor bedrooms, each with its own roomy closet and built-in desk.

Plan L-2194

Bedrooms: 3	Baths: 2½
Living Area:	
Upper floor	690 sq. ft.
Main floor	1,504 sq. ft.
Total Living Area:	**2,194 sq. ft.**
Exterior Wall Framing:	2x4

Foundation Options:

Slab

(All plans can be built with your choice of foundation and framing. A generic conversion diagram is available. See order form.)

BLUEPRINT PRICE CODE: C

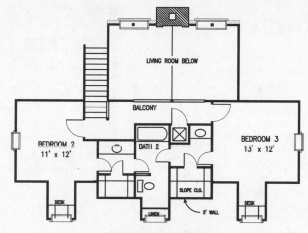

UPPER FLOOR

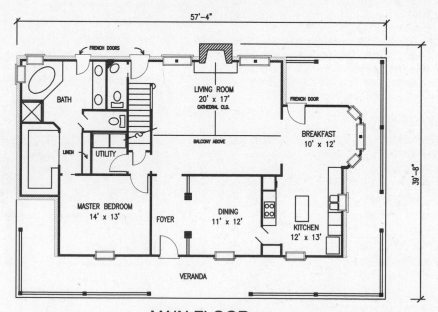

MAIN FLOOR

Relax on the Front Porch

- With its wraparound covered porch, this quaint two-story home makes summer evenings a breeze.
- Inside, a beautiful open stairway welcomes guests into the vaulted foyer, which connects the formal areas. The front-facing living and dining rooms have views of the covered front porch.
- French doors open from the living room to the family room, where a fireplace and corner windows warm and brighten this spacious activity area.
- The breakfast nook, set off by a half-wall, hosts a handy work desk and opens to the back porch.
- The country kitchen offers an oversized island, a pantry closet and illuminating windows flanking the corner sink.
- The upper-floor master suite boasts two walk-in closets and a private bath with a tub and a separate shower. Two more bedrooms, another full bath and a laundry room are also included.

Plan AGH-1997

Bedrooms: 3	Baths: 2½
Living Area:	
Upper floor	933 sq. ft.
Main floor	1,064 sq. ft.
Total Living Area:	**1,997 sq. ft.**
Standard basement	1,064 sq. ft.
Garage	662 sq. ft.
Exterior Wall Framing:	2x6

Foundation Options:

Standard basement

(All plans can be built with your choice of foundation and framing. A generic conversion diagram is available. See order form.)

BLUEPRINT PRICE CODE: B

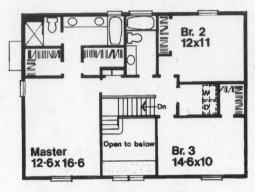

UPPER FLOOR

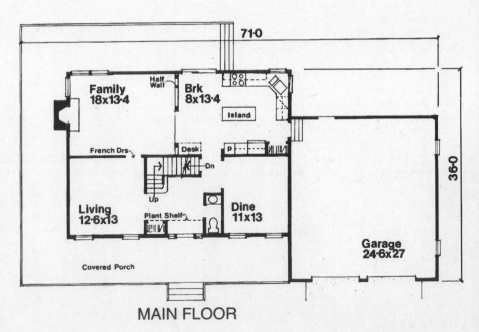

MAIN FLOOR

Sunny Charmer

- A huge wraparound porch highlights this bright and airy country charmer.
- Inside, the two-story vaulted foyer is bathed in sunlight from the expansive arched window above. The formal dining room and a cozy parlor complete the front area.
- Straight ahead is the spectacular family room, featuring a 17-ft. vaulted ceiling, a unique three-sided fireplace and double French doors leading to a large back porch and deck.
- A breakfast bar divides the U-shaped kitchen from the sunny breakfast nook, which overlooks the backyard.
- The expansive master bedroom features a large walk-in closet and private access to the front porch. The master bath includes dual vanities, a garden tub, a private toilet and a tray ceiling.
- Ceilings in all main-floor rooms are at least 9 ft. high for added spaciousness.
- Upstairs, the two remaining bedrooms share a second full bath.
- A two-car detached garage with an optional studio and bath above is included in the blueprints.

Plan APS-2218

Bedrooms: 3	Baths: 2½
Living Area:	
Upper floor	607 sq. ft.
Main floor	1,632 sq. ft.
Total Living Area:	**2,239 sq. ft.**
Detached garage	624 sq. ft.
Exterior Wall	2x4

Foundation Options:

Crawlspace
(All plans can be built with your choice of foundation and framing. A generic conversion diagram is available. See order form.)

BLUEPRINT PRICE CODE: **C**

UPPER FLOOR

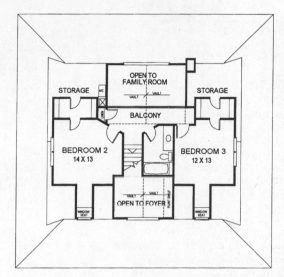

MAIN FLOOR

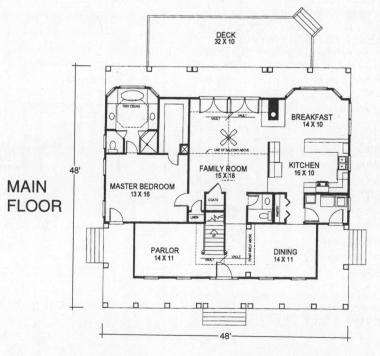

Essential Peace

- This home's nostalgic porch and charming interior wrap you up in peace and comfort.

- On a warm summer night, you can rig up a hammock on the porch and enjoy a cold drink while watching fireflies, the air around you so quiet you can hear the ice in your drink settling.

- Inside, a wide passageway joins the formal living room to the strikingly angled kitchen and dining room. An island greatly simplifies your food preparation efforts. Sliding glass doors let you deliver that potato salad to hungry picnickers in the backyard!

- A design option included with the blueprints for this home substitutes one main-floor bedroom for a greatly expanded master bedroom with an amenity-laden bath.

- Upstairs, two secondary bedrooms are placed at each end of a balcony hall for privacy. Dormer windows grace each room, and a third dormer between them houses an optional third bath.

- All rooms have 9-ft. ceilings.

VIEW INTO KITCHEN AND DINING ROOM

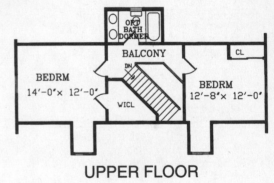

UPPER FLOOR

Plan AX-94341

Bedrooms: 4+	Baths: 1½-3
Living Area:	
Upper floor	597 sq. ft.
Main floor	1,040 sq. ft.
Total Living Area:	**1,637 sq. ft.**
Standard basement	1,040 sq. ft.
Exterior Wall Framing:	2x4

Foundation Options:

Standard basement

Crawlspace

Slab

(All plans can be built with your choice of foundation and framing. A generic conversion diagram is available. See order form.)

BLUEPRINT PRICE CODE: **B**

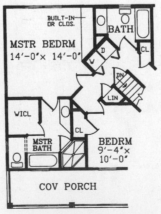

ALTERNATE MAIN FLOOR

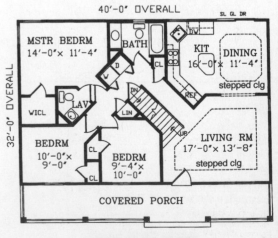

MAIN FLOOR

TO ORDER THIS BLUEPRINT, CALL TOLL-FREE 1-800-820-1283

Plan AX-94341

PRICES AND DETAILS ON PAGES 12-15

Gracious Country

- A peaceful and inviting covered porch introduces this gracious country home.
- Inside the sidelighted entry, the two-story foyer leads into the home's elegant formal area. The combined living and dining rooms allow a distinction between formal entertaining and everyday family life.
- Located just off the dining room, the well-planned island kitchen extends to a sunny dinette. Sliding glass doors open the dinette to a fun and relaxing backyard patio.
- An 11-ft. cathedral ceiling tops the family room nearby, where your family will enjoy years of casual gatherings in front of the warm fireplace.
- Upstairs, a railed balcony leads to the master bedroom, which features a striking 11-ft., 4-in. cathedral ceiling. The master bath includes a soothing whirlpool tub and a separate shower.
- A hall bath services two good-sized bedrooms down the hall.

Plan GL-2229

Bedrooms: 3	Baths: 2½
Living Area:	
Upper floor	983 sq. ft.
Main floor	1,246 sq. ft.
Total Living Area:	**2,229 sq. ft.**
Standard basement	1,241 sq. ft.
Garage and storage	532 sq. ft.
Exterior Wall Framing:	2x4

Foundation Options:

Standard basement

(All plans can be built with your choice of foundation and framing. A generic conversion diagram is available. See order form.)

BLUEPRINT PRICE CODE:	C

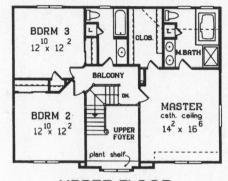

UPPER FLOOR

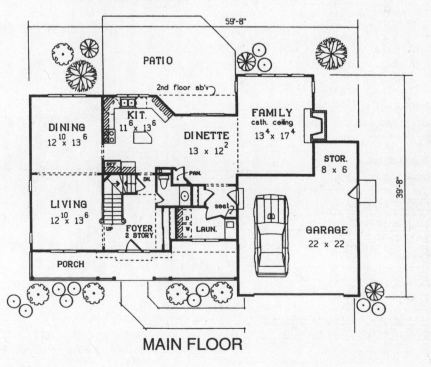

MAIN FLOOR

TO ORDER THIS BLUEPRINT,
CALL TOLL-FREE 1-800-820-1283

Plan GL-2229

PRICES AND DETAILS
ON PAGES 12-15

133

Three-Sided Porch Adds Country Charm

- This inviting wrap-around porch invites visitors to come up and say "Howdy."
- The interior is just as welcoming, with its large family room with a fireplace, and the adjoining dining/living rooms.
- The open-design kitchen includes a convenient work island and adjoins a bright breakfast nook.
- A den off the foyer would make a nice home office, if needed, or a fourth bedroom as well.
- Upstairs, note the majestic master suite with a big walk-in closet and luxury bath.
- Bedrooms 2 and 3 are served by a second full bath and include large closets.

Plan I-2531-A

Bedrooms: 3-4	Baths: 2½
Space:	
Upper floor:	1,064 sq. ft.
Main floor:	1,467 sq. ft.
Total living area:	2,531 sq. ft.
Garage:	608 sq. ft.
Exterior Wall Framing:	2x6

Foundation options:
Crawlspace.
(Foundation & framing conversion diagram available — see order form.)

Blueprint Price Code:	D

UPPER FLOOR

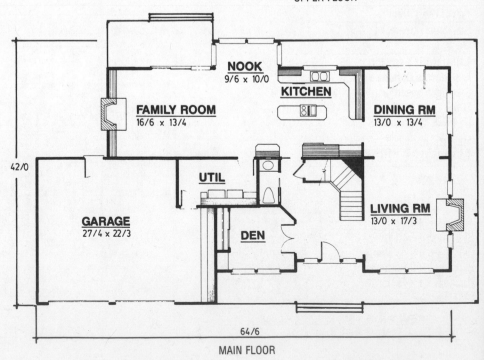

MAIN FLOOR

Plan I-2531-A

Traditional Treasure

- Arched windows lend elegance to the trio of dormers that accentuate this traditional treasure.
- Double doors off the covered front porch open to a dramatic two-story lobby with a curved stairway. The adjacent living room is set in a stunning glass alcove, lending sunlight and spaciousness to the design. A spectacular fireplace is angled to parallel the living room.
- The adjoining dining room offers sliding glass doors to a back terrace, which is perfect for outdoor dining or entertaining.
- The L-shaped island kitchen, the sunny dinette and the family room merge for a cozy ambience. A second fireplace enhances the comfortable feel. Sliding glass doors provide outdoor access.
- Off the upper-floor balcony are four bedrooms and two baths. The master bedroom offers a cathedral ceiling and a private balcony. The skylighted master bath has twin sinks and a bidet.

Plan K-690-D

Bedrooms: 4	Baths: 2½
Living Area:	
Upper floor	1,086 sq. ft.
Main floor	1,171 sq. ft.
Total Living Area:	**2,257 sq. ft.**
Standard basement	1,098 sq. ft.
Garage	420 sq. ft.
Exterior Wall Framing:	2x4 or 2x6

Foundation Options:
Standard basement
Slab
(Typical foundation & framing conversion diagram available—see order form.)

BLUEPRINT PRICE CODE: C

VIEW INTO THE LIVING ROOM
AND DINING ROOM

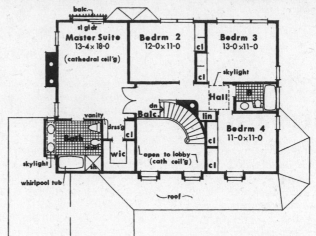

UPPER FLOOR

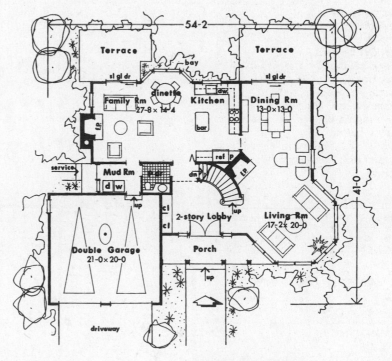

MAIN FLOOR

Modern Country Charm

- Charming window treatments, a covered porch and detailed railings give this modern home a country feeling.
- The inviting entry flows into the elegant living room, which features a 10-ft. ceiling and a striking corner fireplace.
- The sunny kitchen is built into a beautiful bay and easily serves the formal dining room.

- The spacious sunken family room enjoys bright windows and offers sliding glass doors to a backyard patio.
- A half-bath, a laundry/utility room and a storage area are conveniently located off the garage entrance.
- Upstairs, the master bedroom includes a private garden bath, a walk-in closet and a separate dressing area with a dual-sink vanity.
- Two additional upper-floor bedrooms share a full bath and a linen closet. Both rooms are enhanced by sizable closets and cozy window seats.

Plan NW-836	
Bedrooms: 3	**Baths:** 2½
Living Area:	
Upper floor	684 sq. ft.
Main floor	934 sq. ft.
Total Living Area:	**1,618 sq. ft.**
Garage	419 sq. ft.
Exterior Wall Framing:	2x6

Foundation Options:

Crawlspace
(All plans can be built with your choice of foundation and framing. A generic conversion diagram is available. See order form.)

BLUEPRINT PRICE CODE:	**B**

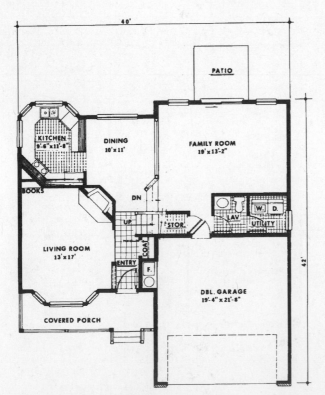

MAIN FLOOR

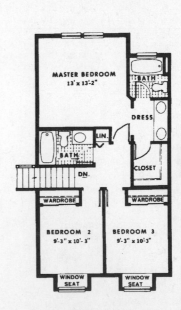

UPPER FLOOR

Plan NW-836

PRICES AND DETAILS ON PAGES 12-15

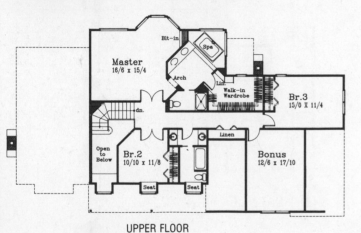

UPPER FLOOR

MAIN FLOOR

72'-0"

43'-11"

Nostalgic but New

- Triple dormers, a covered front porch and half-round windows lend a nostalgic country feel to this exciting two-story home.
- A dramatic two-story foyer makes an elegant introduction, leading into the vaulted living room with a fireplace, a window seat and round-top windows.
- The formal dining room, which features a tray ceiling, opens to the living room through an arch supported by stylish columns.
- The island kitchen has an open view into the breakfast nook and the family room with rear patio beyond.
- Upstairs, there are three bedrooms, plus a large bonus room that could be used as a fourth bedroom or as a playroom.
- The master suite dazzles with double doors, a sitting bay, a huge walk-in closet and an angled bath with a corner spa tub beneath windows.

Plan CDG-2031

Bedrooms: 3-5	Baths: 2½
Living Area:	
Upper floor	1,203 sq. ft.
Main floor	1,495 sq. ft.
Bonus room	238 sq. ft.
Total Living Area:	**2,936 sq. ft.**
Garage	811 sq. ft.
Exterior Wall Framing:	2x6

Foundation Options:

Crawlspace
(Typical foundation & framing conversion diagram available—see order form.)

BLUEPRINT PRICE CODE:	**D**

TO ORDER THIS BLUEPRINT,
CALL TOLL-FREE 1-800-820-1283

Plan CDG-2031

PRICES AND DETAILS
ON PAGES 12-15

137

Family Farmhouse

- There's more to this house than its charming front porch, steeply pitched roof and dormer windows.
- A feeling of spaciousness is emphasized by the open floor plan, with the living room adjoining the kitchen and bayed breakfast area. A snack bar allows easy service to the living room.
- The back door leads from the carport to the utility room, which is convenient to the kitchen and half-bath.
- The secluded main-floor master bedroom offers a large walk-in closet and a private bathroom.
- Upstairs, two bedrooms share another full bath. One includes dormer windows and the other a window seat. A door at the top of the stairs provides access to attic space that could be turned into an extra bedroom.

Plan J-86133

Bedrooms: 3	Baths: 2½
Living Area:	
Upper floor	559 sq. ft.
Main floor	1,152 sq. ft.
Total Living Area:	**1,711 sq. ft.**
Standard basement	1,152 sq. ft.
Carport	387 sq. ft.
Storage	85 sq. ft.
Exterior Wall Framing:	2x4

Foundation Options:

Standard basement

Crawlspace

Slab

(All plans can be built with your choice of foundation and framing. A generic conversion diagram is available. See order form.)

BLUEPRINT PRICE CODE: **B**

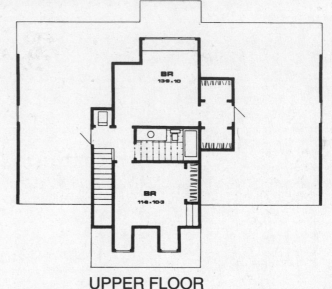

UPPER FLOOR

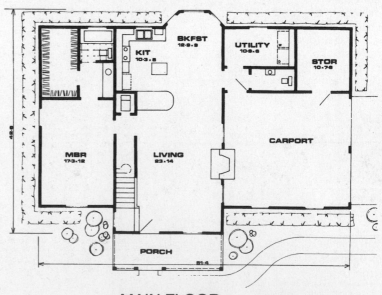

MAIN FLOOR

TO ORDER THIS BLUEPRINT, CALL TOLL-FREE 1-800-820-1283

Plan J-86133

PRICES AND DETAILS ON PAGES 12-15

Luxurious Country Home

- This country cottage hosts many luxuries, such as an expansive Great Room, good-sized sleeping areas and a large, screened back porch.
- The rustic front porch opens to the inviting Great Room, which is warmed by a handsome fireplace. Entertaining may be expanded to the rear porch when the weather is suitable.
- The bright kitchen features a huge work island and a windowed sink, and flows into both the formal dining room and the cozy breakfast bay.
- The two-car, side-entry garage is located nearby to facilitate the unloading of groceries. A handy storage room is perfect for the lawn mower and sports equipment.
- The removed master suite boasts a private bath with a spa tub, a separate shower, a dual-sink vanity and two walk-in closets.
- Upstairs are two oversized bedrooms, each with a dressing room that adjoins a shared bathing area.

Plan C-8535

Bedrooms: 3	Baths: 2½
Living Area:	
Upper floor	765 sq. ft.
Main floor	1,535 sq. ft.
Total Living Area:	**2,300 sq. ft.**
Partial daylight basement	1,091 sq. ft.
Garage	424 sq. ft.
Exterior Wall Framing:	2x4

Foundation Options:

Partial daylight basement
(All plans can be built with your choice of foundation and framing. A generic conversion diagram is available. See order form.)

BLUEPRINT PRICE CODE:	C

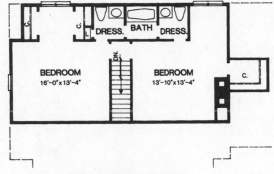

UPPER FLOOR

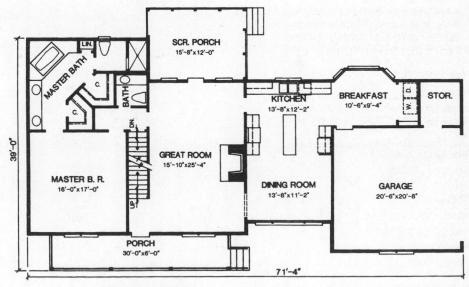

MAIN FLOOR

TO ORDER THIS BLUEPRINT,
CALL TOLL-FREE 1-800-820-1283

Plan C-8535

PRICES AND DETAILS
ON PAGES 12-15

139

Charm, Grace, Space

A charming front porch, brick masonry accents and a bayed front window at the living room all combine to enhance this comfortable family home. At only 1,661 square feet, this three-bedroom, two-bath dwelling combines many possibilities seldom found in such a compact living arrangement.

A multi-purpose loft overlooking the family room and nook area below graces a substantial portion of the second floor. A private master suite "get-away" rounds out the living area of the upper level. Not to be overlooked is the huge upstairs storage area.

The main floor offers separate living room and family areas for more or less formal gatherings. A kitchen with an angled eating bar and corner pantry make food preparation a joy. Two bedrooms complete the main floor.

Main floor:	1,065 sq. ft.
Upper floor:	596 sq. ft.
Total living area: (Not counting garage)	1,661 sq. ft.

PLAN R-2004
WITHOUT BASEMENT
(CRAWLSPACE FOUNDATION)

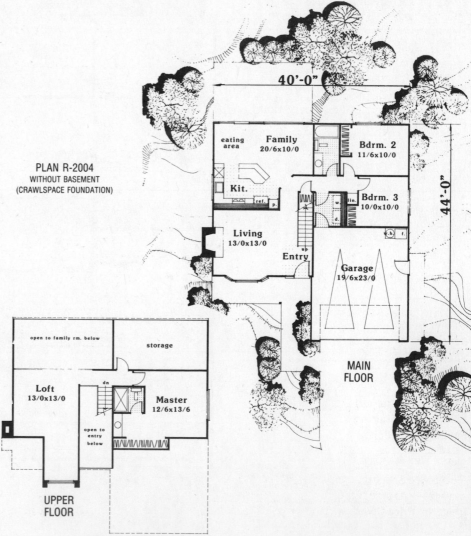

Blueprint Price Code B
Plan R-2004

PRICES AND DETAILS
ON PAGES 12-15

Open Floor Plan Enjoys Outdoors

- Luxurious family living begins with a spectacular central Great Room; a fireplace is flanked by double doors that access the large wrapping rear porch.
- Casual dining can take place in the adjoining breakfast nook or island kitchen, with snack bar; access to a convenient laundry room, plus the front porch and rear veranda is also offered in the kitchen.
- Formal dining and living rooms flank the foyer.
- For privacy, you'll find the master suite on the main floor; it features a spacious walk-in closet and large bath with dual vanities, whirlpool tub and separate shower.
- Two extra bedrooms, each with personal dressing areas, share the upper level.

Plan VL-3038

Bedrooms: 3	Baths: 2 ½
Space:	
Upper floor	836 sq. ft.
Main floor	2,202 sq. ft.
Total Living Area	**3,038 sq. ft.**
Exterior Wall Framing	2x4

Foundation options:

Crawlspace

Slab

(Foundation & framing conversion diagram available—see order form.)

Blueprint Price Code	E

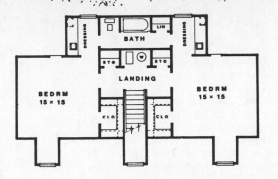

UPPER FLOOR

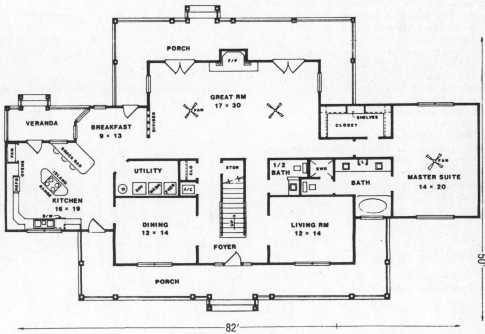

MAIN FLOOR

Big, Bright Country Kitchen

- Decorative dormers, shuttered windows and a large covered front porch give this charming two-story home a pleasant country flavor.
- Inside, the central Great Room is warmed by a handsome fireplace. The adjoining dining room offers sliding glass doors to a backyard deck.
- The enormous country kitchen features a sunny bay-windowed eating area and a convenient island counter. The nearby laundry/utility area accesses the garage and the backyard.
- The main-floor master bedroom boasts a roomy walk-in closet and private access to a compartmentalized bath with an oversized linen closet.
- Upstairs, two bedrooms with window seats share a full bath. An easy-to-access storage area is above the garage. Another convenient storage area can be reached from the garage.

Plan C-8040

Bedrooms: 3	Baths: 2
Living Area:	
Upper floor	718 sq. ft.
Main floor	1,318 sq. ft.
Total Living Area:	**2,036 sq. ft.**
Daylight basement	1,221 sq. ft.
Garage	436 sq. ft.
Exterior Wall Framing:	2x4

Foundation Options:

Daylight basement
Crawlspace
Slab

(All plans can be built with your choice of foundation and framing. A generic conversion diagram is available. See order form.)

BLUEPRINT PRICE CODE: C

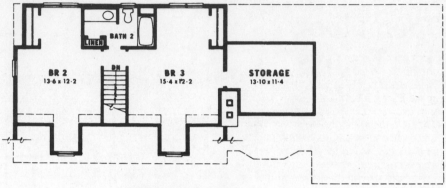

UPPER FLOOR

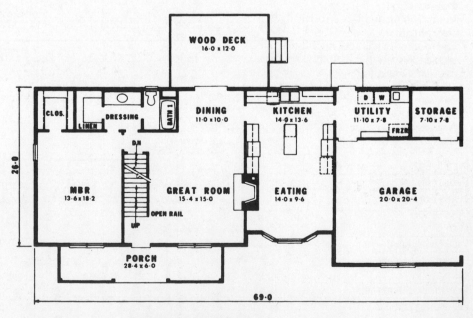

MAIN FLOOR

TO ORDER THIS BLUEPRINT, CALL TOLL-FREE 1-800-820-1283

Plan C-8040

PRICES AND DETAILS ON PAGES 12-15

Timeless Styling

- This home's timeless gables and classic front porch conceal an expansive interior with modern styling.
- Sidelighted double doors open from the porch to the elegant two-story gallery and its curved, open-railed staircase.
- The living room boasts stylish windows, a fireplace with built-in wood storage and a 14-ft., 6-in. cathedral ceiling.
- The semi-circular dining room basks in light from a radiant arrangement of windows, offering a panoramic view.
- The kitchen features a bright sink, a nifty snack bar and a sunny half-circle dinette with views to the backyard.
- Another fireplace warms the family room, which also features sliding glass doors to a backyard terrace.
- The mudroom has laundry facilities, plus access to a half-bath and to the two-car garage.
- The upper-floor master suite offers a balcony and a private bath with a whirlpool tub and a separate shower. A skylighted bath serves the three secondary bedrooms.

Plan K-692-T

Bedrooms: 4	Baths: 2½
Living Area:	
Upper floor	950 sq. ft.
Main floor	1,498 sq. ft.
Total Living Area:	**2,448 sq. ft.**
Daylight basement	1,430 sq. ft.
Garage	440 sq. ft.
Exterior Wall Framing:	2x4 or 2x6

Foundation Options:
Daylight basement
Slab
(All plans can be built with your choice of foundation and framing. A generic conversion diagram is available. See order form.)

BLUEPRINT PRICE CODE: C

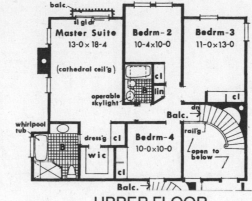

UPPER FLOOR

VIEW INTO FAMILY ROOM

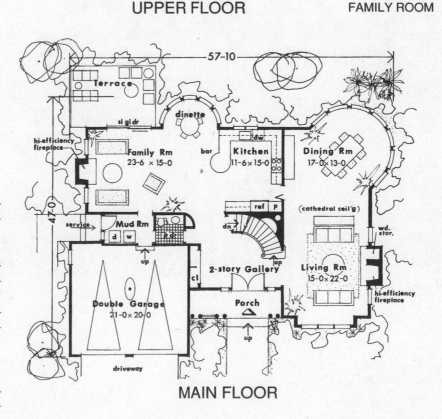

MAIN FLOOR

TO ORDER THIS BLUEPRINT, CALL TOLL-FREE 1-800-820-1283

PRICES AND DETAILS ON PAGES 12-15

Plan K-692-T

Tradition Recreated

- Classic traditional styling is recreated in this home with its covered porch, triple dormers and half-round windows.
- A central hall stems from the two-story-high foyer and accesses each of the main living areas.
- A large formal space is created with the merging of the living room and the dining room. The living room boasts a fireplace and a view of the front porch.
- The informal spaces merge at the rear of the home. The kitchen features an oversized cooktop island. The sunny dinette is enclosed with a circular glass wall. The family room boasts a media center and access to the rear terrace.
- A convenient main-floor laundry room sits near the garage entrance.
- The upper floor includes three secondary bedrooms that share a full bath, and a spacious master bedroom that offers dual walk-in closets and a large private bath.

Plan AHP-9393

Bedrooms: 4+	**Baths:** 3
Living Area:	
Upper floor	989 sq. ft.
Main floor	1,223 sq. ft.
Total Living Area:	**2,212 sq. ft.**
Standard basement	1,223 sq. ft.
Garage and storage	488 sq. ft.
Exterior Wall Framing:	2x4 or 2x6

Foundation Options:

Standard basement
Crawlspace
Slab
(Typical foundation & framing conversion diagram available—see order form.)

BLUEPRINT PRICE CODE: C

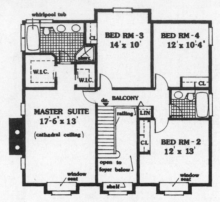

UPPER FLOOR

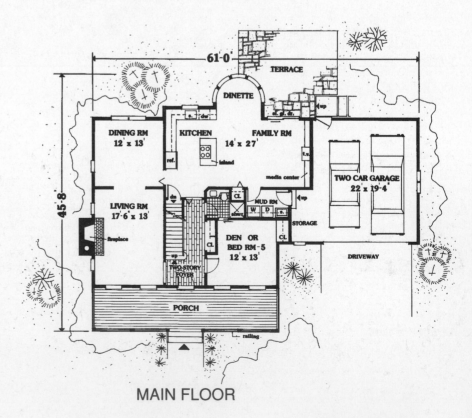

MAIN FLOOR

144

TO ORDER THIS BLUEPRINT,
CALL TOLL-FREE 1-800-820-1283

Plan AHP-9393

PRICES AND DETAILS
ON PAGES 12-15

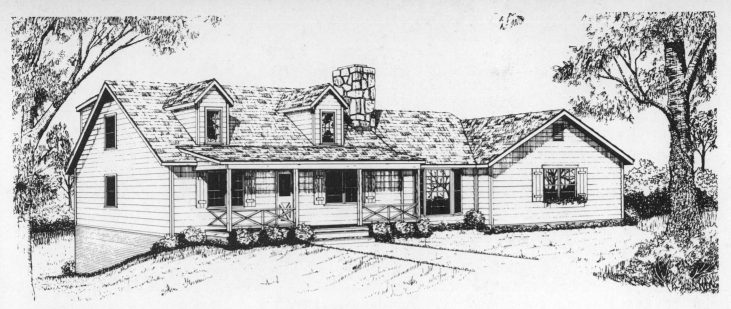

Rustic Country Design

- A welcoming front porch, window shutters and a bay window on the exterior of this rustic design are complemented by a comfortable, informal interior.
- A spacious country kitchen includes a bay-windowed breakfast area, center work island and abundant counter and cabinet space.
- Note the large utility room in the garage entry area.
- The large Great Room includes an impressive fireplace and another informal eating area with double doors opening to a deck, patio or screened porch. Also note the half-bath.

- The main floor master suite features a walk-in closet and compartmentalized private bath.
- Upstairs, you will find two more bedrooms, another full bath and a large storage area.

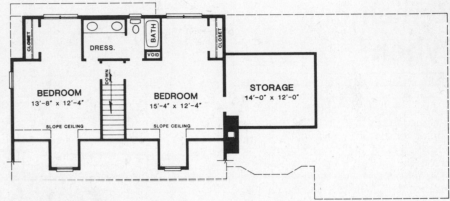

UPPER FLOOR

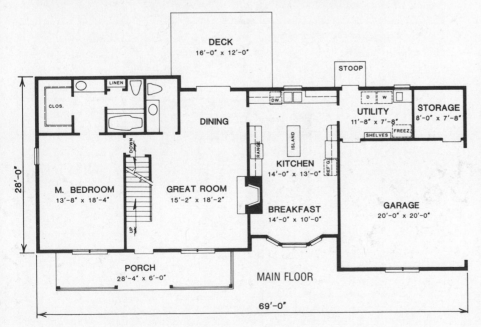

MAIN FLOOR

Plan C-8476

Bedrooms: 3	Baths: 2½

Space:

Upper floor:	720 sq. ft.
Main floor:	1,277 sq. ft.

Total living area:	1,997 sq. ft.
Basement:	approx. 1,200 sq. ft.
Garage:	400 sq. ft.
Storage:	(in garage) 61 sq. ft.

Exterior Wall Framing:	2x4

Foundation options:
Daylight basement.
Standard basement.
Crawlspace.
Slab.
(Foundation & framing conversion diagram available — see order form.)

Blueprint Price Code:	B

TO ORDER THIS BLUEPRINT,
CALL TOLL-FREE 1-800-820-1283

Plan C-8476

PRICES AND DETAILS
ON PAGES 12-15

145

Remember When?

- Remember when porch swings creaked in the summer air, a glass of iced tea sweated beside you and the nights seemed to last forever? This country home recalls those days with a nostalgic covered porch and a peaceful interior.
- From the sidelighted foyer, the massive Great Room unfolds, offering a rustic stone fireplace that rises to the ceiling. French doors lead to a backyard patio.
- Wide-open spaces enhance the kitchen and the adjoining dining area. The big island snack bar will be a favorite spot when the kids come home from school.
- The upper-floor master bedroom provides plenty of room to relax, and includes a private bath.
- Business matters may be attended to in the home office space just down the hall, while two bedrooms with desks allow private space for children or overnight guests.

Plan J-9507

Bedrooms: 3	Baths: 2½
Living Area:	
Upper floor	947 sq. ft.
Main floor	931 sq. ft.
Total Living Area:	**1,878 sq. ft.**
Standard basement	931 sq. ft.
Carport	455 sq. ft.
Exterior Wall Framing:	2x4

Foundation Options:

Standard basement
Crawlspace
Slab

(All plans can be built with your choice of foundation and framing. A generic conversion diagram is available. See order form.)

BLUEPRINT PRICE CODE:	B

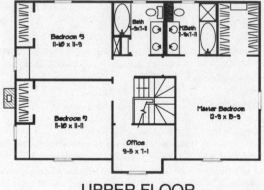

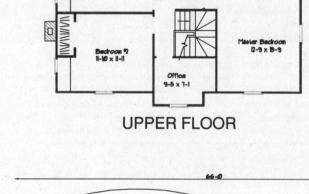

UPPER FLOOR

BASEMENT STAIRWAY LOCATION

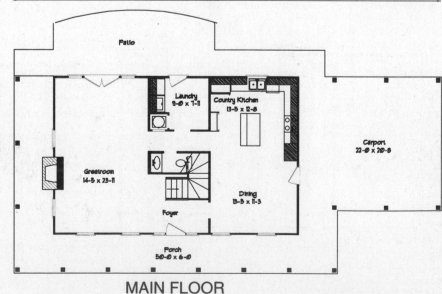

MAIN FLOOR

TO ORDER THIS BLUEPRINT, CALL TOLL-FREE 1-800-820-1283

Plan J-9507

PRICES AND DETAILS ON PAGES 12-15

Formal Meets Informal

- The charming, columned front porch of this appealing home leads visitors into a two-story-high foyer with a beautiful turned staircase.
- The gracious formal living room shares a 15-ft. cathedral ceiling and a dramatic see-through fireplace with the adjoining family room.
- A railing separates the family room from the spacious breakfast area and the island kitchen. A unique butler's pantry joins the kitchen to the dining room, which is enhanced by a tray ceiling.
- A convenient laundry room is located between the kitchen and the entrance to the garage .
- All four bedrooms are located on the upper level. The master suite boasts an 11-ft. cathedral ceiling, a walk-in closet and a large, luxurious bath.

Plan OH-132

Bedrooms: 4	Baths: 2½
Living Area:	
Upper floor	1,118 sq. ft.
Main floor	1,396 sq. ft.
Total Living Area:	**2,514 sq. ft.**
Standard basement	1,396 sq. ft.
Garage	413 sq. ft.
Storage/workshop	107 sq. ft.
Exterior Wall Framing:	2x4

Foundation Options:

Standard basement
(All plans can be built with your choice of foundation and framing. A generic conversion diagram is available. See order form.)

BLUEPRINT PRICE CODE: D

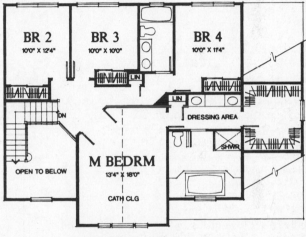

UPPER FLOOR

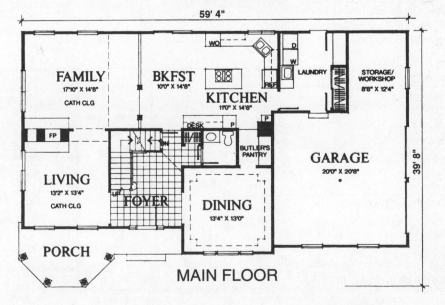

MAIN FLOOR

TO ORDER THIS BLUEPRINT,
CALL TOLL-FREE 1-800-820-1283

Plan OH-132

PRICES AND DETAILS
ON PAGES 12-15

147

Country Classic

- A wrap-around front porch, narrow lap siding and a brick chimney all add classic country styling to this updated two-story design.
- The Great Room has windows on three sides and offers a handsome fireplace and access to a screened porch for bug-free outdoor living.
- The informal family room can house the TV and video games, as well as the other toys of the active family.
- The island kitchen overlooks the dining bay and the rear yard.
- There are four bedrooms and two full baths upstairs.

Plan CPS-1117-E

Bedrooms: 4	Baths: 2½
Space:	
Upper floor:	1,008 sq. ft.
Main floor:	1,139 sq. ft.
Total living area:	2,147 sq. ft.
Basement:	1,139 sq. ft.
Garage:	647 sq. ft.
Exterior Wall Framing:	2x6

Foundation options:
Standard basement.
(Foundation & framing conversion diagram available — see order form.)

Blueprint Price Code: C

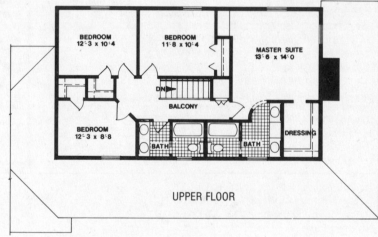

UPPER FLOOR

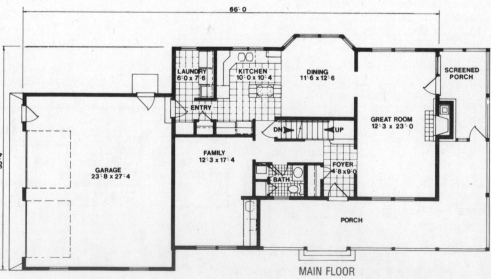

MAIN FLOOR

Plan CPS-1117-E

PRICES AND DETAILS ON PAGES 12-15

Fill Your Life with Sunshine

- This home is as warm and inviting on the inside as it is on the outside. Two fireplaces, lots of sunny living spaces and a superb master suite are among its many attributes.
- The master suite claims one of the fireplaces, plus offers a luxurious bath and twin walk-in closets. French doors lead both to the rear garden and to the relaxing front porch.
- The living room hosts the remaining fireplace and also has French doors opening to the front porch. The adjoining dining room includes an elegant bow window.
- The kitchen and the breakfast room overlook an inviting sun room. A half-bath and a utility room are close by.
- The main floor has 9-ft. ceilings throughout, while the upper floor has 8-ft. ceilings. The blueprints include a choice of three bedrooms on the second floor or two bedrooms separated by a game room.

Plan J-91068

Bedrooms: 3-4	Baths: 2½
Space:	
Upper floor	893 sq. ft.
Main floor	1,947 sq. ft.
Total Living Area	**2,840 sq. ft.**
Basement	1,947 sq. ft.
Garage	441 sq. ft.
Exterior Wall Framing	**2x4**

Foundation options:

Standard Basement
Crawlspace
Slab
(Foundation & framing conversion diagram available—see order form.)

Blueprint Price Code   **D**

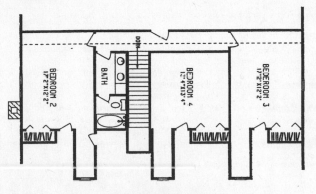

UPPER FLOOR
WITH THREE BEDROOMS

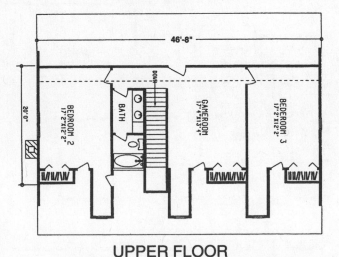

UPPER FLOOR
WITH TWO BEDROOMS AND GAME ROOM

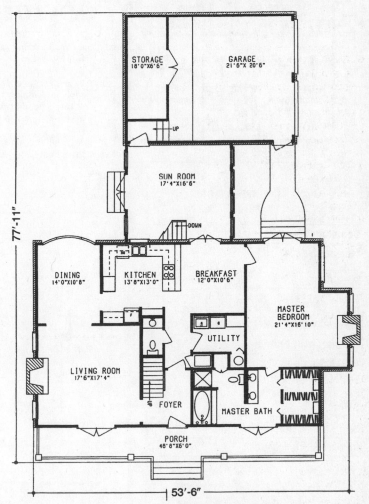

MAIN FLOOR

Farm House with Victorian Flair

- Wrap-around porch, fancy trim, and fish-scale shingles lend a Victorian flair to this farmhouse.
- Central foyer leads to formal living room and dining room.
- Large family room with fireplace has access to a half-bath and a deck in the rear.
- Large kitchen has all the necessary ingredients and ample cabinet space.
- Breakfast nook with bay provides a place for warm sunny mornings.
- Master suite has large closets. Master bath offers a garden tub, shower, twin vanities and a planter.
- Two large bedrooms and full bath complete the second floor. Open stair and hall give spacious feeling.
- Utility room provides a buffer between house and garage.

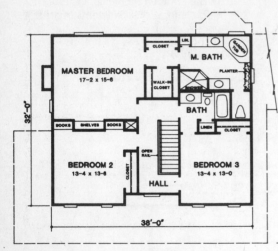

UPPER FLOOR

Plan C-8865-S

Bedrooms: 3	Baths: 3
Finished space:	
Upper floor:	1,196 sq. ft.
Main floor:	1,366 sq. ft.
Total living area:	2,562 sq. ft.
Basement:	1,250 sq. ft.
Garage:	455 sq. ft.
Exterior Wall Framing:	2x4

Foundation options: (Specify)
Daylight basement.
Standard basement.
Crawlspace.
(Foundation & framing conversion diagram available — see order form.)

Blueprint Price Code: D

MAIN FLOOR

Plan C-8865-S

Simple Elegance

- This simple, yet elegant exterior houses an interior that is efficient and functional.
- Four bedrooms, lots of closet space, two full baths upstairs and a powder room on the main level leave little to complain about in the efficiency department.
- Flowing together at the rear of the home are the family activity areas; only a half-wall separates the large family room from the adjoining dinette and kitchen. The formal dining room joins the kitchen on the opposite side.
- An optional fireplace can add drama to the formal living room at the front of the home.
- Two mid-sized bedrooms, a spacious master bedroom and a large, fourth bedroom share the upper level with two full baths.

Plan GL-1926

Bedrooms: 4	Baths: 2 ½
Space:	
Upper floor	972 sq. ft.
Main floor	954 sq. ft.
Total Living Area	**1,926 sq. ft.**
Basement	954 sq. ft.
Garage	484 sq. ft.
Exterior Wall Framing	**2x6**

Foundation options:

Standard Basement

(Foundation & framing conversion diagram available—see order form.)

Blueprint Price Code	**B**

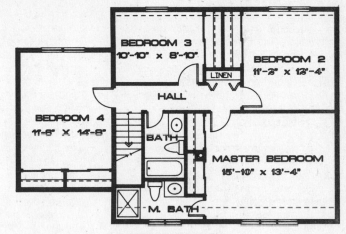

UPPER FLOOR

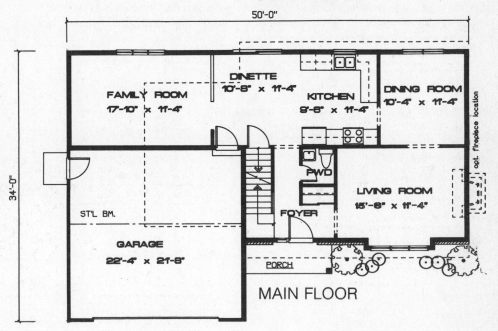

MAIN FLOOR

TO ORDER THIS BLUEPRINT,
CALL TOLL-FREE 1-800-820-1283

Plan GL-1926

PRICES AND DETAILS
ON PAGES 12-15

151

Gracious, Open Living

- A wonderfully open floor plan gives this gracious country-style home a feeling of freedom. A full wraparound porch extends the openness to the outdoors.
- The sidelighted foyer offers views into the formal dining room and the study, and displays a unique two-way staircase to the upper floor.
- The quiet study, which would make a great den or guest room, is the perfect spot for reading your favorite novel or catching up on correspondence.
- The serene dining room is large enough to host a turkey dinner for the relatives.
- At the rear of the home, the Great Room, breakfast nook and island kitchen combine for an informal setting.
- The Great Room's fireplace warms the entire area on cold winter evenings. On

either side of the bayed breakfast nook, French doors open to the porch.
- A laundry/utility room and a full bath flank the hallway to the two-car, side-entry garage, which includes a wide storage room.
- Three bedrooms, two baths and an exciting playroom are located on the upper floor.
- The railed playroom is brightened by a beautiful Palladian window. The kids will enjoy this room for hours on end, playing cards or video games. The playroom is large enough to be finished as a bedroom if needed.
- The master bedroom boasts a huge sleeping area and a walk-in closet. The luxurious private bath features a nice oval tub housed in a beautiful window bay. A separate shower, a dual-sink vanity and a private toilet are other notable amenities.
- Two secondary bedrooms share a roomy hall bath.

Plan J-9289	
Bedrooms: 3+	**Baths:** 3
Living Area:	
Upper floor	1,212 sq. ft.
Main floor	1,370 sq. ft.
Total Living Area:	**2,582 sq. ft.**
Standard basement	1,370 sq. ft.
Garage and storage	720 sq. ft.
Exterior Wall Framing:	2x4

Foundation Options:
Standard basement
Crawlspace
Slab
(All plans can be built with your choice of foundation and framing. A generic conversion diagram is available. See order form.)

BLUEPRINT PRICE CODE:	D

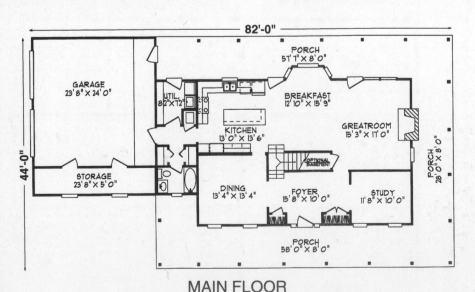

MAIN FLOOR

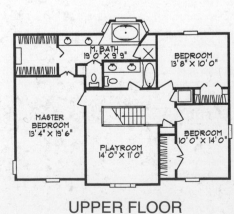

UPPER FLOOR

TO ORDER THIS BLUEPRINT, CALL TOLL-FREE 1-800-820-1283

Plan J-9289

PRICES AND DETAILS ON PAGES 12-15

Dramatic, Updated Farmhouse

- This unique farmhouse style home is updated by a dramatic, multiple circle-top window and an exciting floor plan with the master suite on the main level.
- The high vaulted ceiling over the entry merges into the second floor and living room ceilings, creating a marvelous sense of space.
- A beautiful vaulted ceiling and wood-burning fireplace highlight the front-facing living room, one step up from the center hall.
- The master suite features a dramatic, angled entry and an attached bath with a raised, corner whirlpool tub, vaulted ceiling and skylite.
- The second floor balcony accommodates two bedrooms and a bath. An optional alternate plan included provides for four bedrooms.

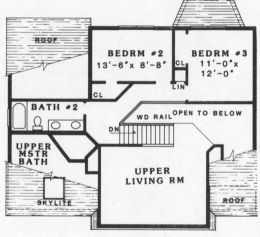

UPPER FLOOR

Plan AX-89320

Bedrooms: 3	Baths: 2½

Space:	
Upper floor:	486 sq. ft.
Main floor:	1,582 sq. ft.

Total living area:	2,068 sq. ft.
Optional 4th bedroom	164 sq. ft.
Basement:	1,582 sq. ft.
Garage:	436 sq. ft.

Exterior Wall Framing:	2x4

Foundation options:
Standard basement.
Slab.
(Foundation & framing conversion diagram available — see order form.)

Blueprint Price Code:	C

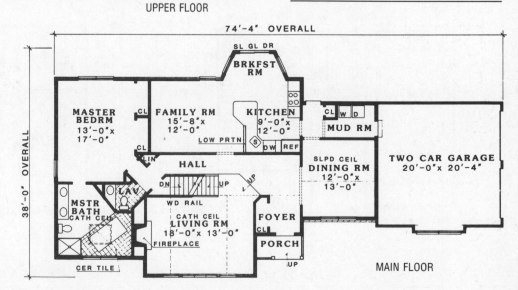

MAIN FLOOR

Economical Two-Story

- A choice of a traditional or a more contemporary-looking exterior is offered with this economical two-story home. Please specify Elevation A or Elevation B when ordering.
- Decorative and functional interior features make the most of the modest total living area.
- The living room offers a bayed window seat. The adjoining dining room boasts a tray ceiling.
- A modern walk-through kitchen is nestled between the dining room and the family room. A snack counter and a pantry are nice extras.
- An inviting fireplace and rear sliders to the outdoor patio add interest and volume to the family room.
- Three bedrooms and two baths share the upper level.

ELEVATION A

ELEVATION B

Plan AG-1601

Bedrooms: 3	Baths: 2½
Space:	
Upper floor	728 sq. ft.
Main floor	875 sq. ft.
Total Living Area	**1,603 sq. ft.**
Basement	875 sq. ft.
Garage	400 sq. ft.
Exterior Wall Framing	2x6
Foundation options:	
Standard Basement	
(Foundation & framing conversion diagram available—see order form.)	
Blueprint Price Code	B

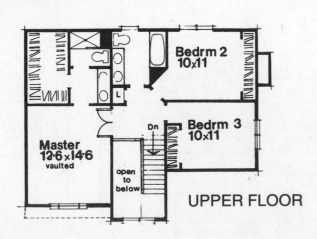

UPPER FLOOR

Bedrm 2
10x11

Bedrm 3
10x11

Master
12·6 x14·6
vaulted

Dn

open to below

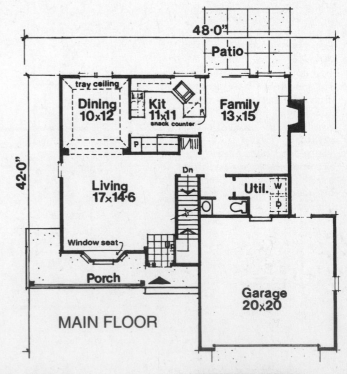

MAIN FLOOR

48·0"

42·0"

Patio

tray ceiling

Dining
10x12

Kit
11x11
snack counter

Family
13x15

P

Living
17x14·6

Dn

Util.
W

Window seat

Porch

Garage
20x20

TO ORDER THIS BLUEPRINT, CALL TOLL-FREE 1-800-820-1283

Plan AG-1601

PRICES AND DETAILS ON PAGES 12-15

Open Kitchen/Family Room Combination

- This compact plan is designed to provide maximum casual living space for a small but busy family.
- A large family room/kitchen combination opens onto a large deck.
- The great room features an impressive corner fireplace and a vaulted ceiling and adjoins the dining room to create a liberal space for entertaining.
- Upstairs, the master suite includes a private bath and large closet.
- Bedroom 2 boasts a large gable window, two closets and easy access to a second upstairs bath.
- The loft area is available for study, play, an exercise area or third bedroom.

Plan B-88006	
Bedrooms: 2-3	**Baths:** 2½
Space:	
Upper floor:	732 sq. ft.
Main floor:	818 sq. ft.
Total living area:	1,550 sq. ft.
Basement:	818 sq. ft.
Garage:	374 sq. ft.
Exterior Wall Framing:	2x4

Foundation options:
Standard basement only.
(Foundation & framing conversion diagram available — see order form.)

Blueprint Price Code:	B

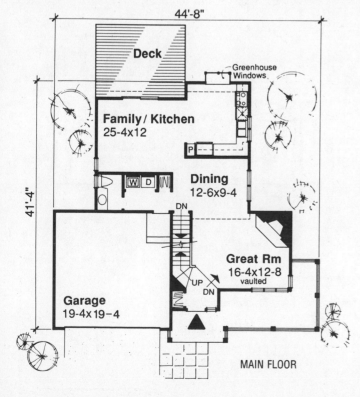

MAIN FLOOR

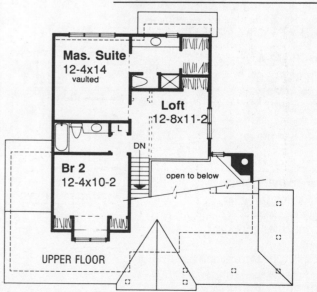

UPPER FLOOR

TO ORDER THIS BLUEPRINT,
CALL TOLL-FREE 1-800-820-1283

Plan B-88006

PRICES AND DETAILS
ON PAGES 12-15

155

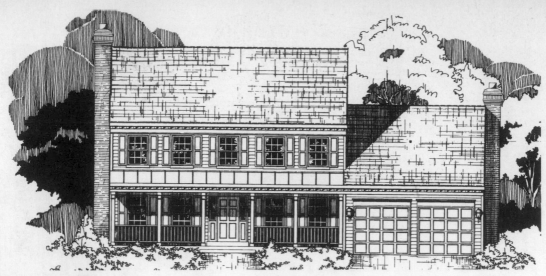

Great Family Living Areas

- The covered front porch and multi-windowed facade give this home its countrypolitan appeal and comfort.
- Inside, a wonderful kitchen, breakfast nook and family room combination steals the show. The step-saving kitchen includes a large pantry closet, an over-sized worktop island/snack bar and a built-in desk. The bay-windowed breakfast nook steps down to the vaulted family room with fireplace.
- The formal living room includes an optional fireplace, while the dining room has an optional bay window.
- A half-bath is just off the foyer, as is a study. The laundry room is convenient to both the kitchen and the garage.
- The upper floor features a spectacular master suite, offering a vaulted ceiling in the sleeping area, a dressing area with a walk-in closet and a skylighted bath with a corner platform tub.
- The blueprints for this plan include details for finishing the exterior with brick or with wood siding.

Plan CH-240-A

Bedrooms: 4-5	Baths: 2½
Living Area:	
Upper floor	1,019 sq. ft.
Main floor	1,300 sq. ft.
Total Living Area:	**2,319 sq. ft.**
Basement	1,300 sq. ft.
Garage	384 sq. ft.
Exterior Wall Framing:	2x4

Foundation Options:
Daylight basement
Standard basement
Crawlspace
(Typical foundation & framing conversion diagram available—see order form.)

BLUEPRINT PRICE CODE: C

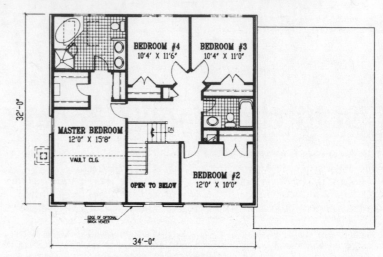

UPPER FLOOR

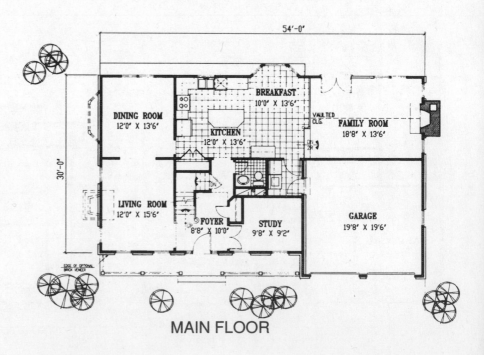

MAIN FLOOR

TO ORDER THIS BLUEPRINT, CALL TOLL-FREE 1-800-820-1283

Plan CH-240-A

PRICES AND DETAILS ON PAGES 12-15

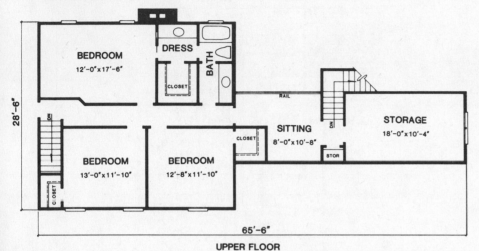

BEDROOM
12'-0"x17'-6"

DRESS

BATH

CLOSET

BEDROOM
13'-0"x11'-10"

BEDROOM
12'-8"x11'-10"

CLOSET

SITTING
8'-0"x10'-8"

RAIL

STORAGE
18'-0"x10'-4"

DN

STOR

28'-6"

65'-6"

UPPER FLOOR

Bay Windows Enhance a Country Home

A large master bedroom suite includes a deluxe bath with separate shower, garden tub, twin vanities and two large walk in closets. Kitchen has direct access to both the breakfast nook and the dining room, which features a large bay window. Three bedrooms, a sitting area and storage or bonus room combine to form the second level.

First floor:	2,005 sq. ft.
Second floor:	1,063 sq. ft.
Total living area:	3,068 sq. ft.
(Not counting basement or garage)	

SCREENED PORCH
23'-10"x16'-0"

WOOD DECK
18'-0"x8'-0"

MASTER BATH

LINEN

DESK

BAR

BREAKFAST AREA
13'-6x10'-6

PANTRY

WASH DRY

CLOSET

BATH

FAMILY ROOM
23'-2"x14'-10"

UTILITY
8'-4"x10'-0"

CLOSET

DN

COATS

KITCHEN
13'-0"x9'-6"

UP

33'-0"

MASTER BEDROOM
12'-10"x16'-10"

FOYER
10'-6"x12'-0"

UP

LIVING ROOM
18'-6"x12'-0"

DINING ROOM
13'-0"x11'-10"

2 CAR GARAGE
21'-6"x21'-0"

MAIN FLOOR

PORCH
29'-6"x4'-6"

78'-10"

Specify daylight basement, crawlspace or slab foundation.

TO ORDER THIS BLUEPRINT,
CALL TOLL-FREE 1-800-820-1283

Blueprint Price Code E
Plan C-8409

PRICES AND DETAILS
ON PAGES 12-15

157

Country Highlights

- A roomy front porch, narrow lap siding and paned windows give this two-story home a warm country feel.
- A sidelighted French door leads to the two-story foyer, brightened by a large half-round window above.
- Just off the foyer, the living room is warmed by a stone-hearthed fireplace and equipped with a wet bar. Sliding glass doors in the adjoining dining room and the nearby Great Room access the rear terrace.
- The large kitchen, just steps from the Great Room and the mudroom, includes a sunny breakfast nook with a broad bay window overlooking the front porch.
- The upper floor boasts a tray-ceilinged master suite with a luxurious bath, featuring a whirlpool tub, a dual-sink vanity and a separate shower.
- A balcony hall leads to two more bedrooms that share a full bath.

Plan AHP-9394

Bedrooms: 3+	Baths: 2½
Living Area:	
Upper floor	602 sq. ft.
Main floor	1,099 sq. ft.
Total Living Area:	**1,701 sq. ft.**
Standard basement	1,099 sq. ft.
Garage and storage	510 sq. ft.
Exterior Wall Framing:	2x4 or 2x6

Foundation Options:

Standard basement

Crawlspace

Slab

(All plans can be built with your choice of foundation and framing. A generic conversion diagram is available. See order form.)

BLUEPRINT PRICE CODE:	B

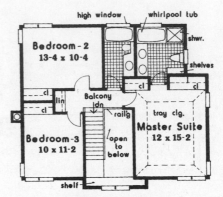

UPPER FLOOR

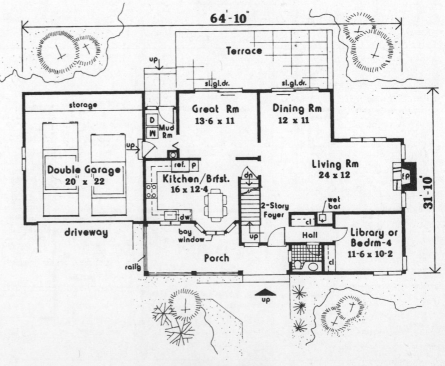

MAIN FLOOR

TO ORDER THIS BLUEPRINT, CALL TOLL-FREE 1-800-820-1283   Plan AHP-9394   *PRICES AND DETAILS ON PAGES 12-15*

Modern Features with Traditional Flair

- This affordable design offers a traditional flair to its modern floor plan.
- Formal living areas share the left side of the home; the living room offers an array of front windows that overlook the porch and optional fireplace. The adjoining dining room may be accented by a bay window.
- At the center of the floor plan is an open, updated kitchen with a handy work island, a laundry closet and an adjoining breakfast bay.
- The large vaulted family room features a fireplace and backyard access.
- The sleeping area on the upper level includes a vaulted master bedroom with private garden bath, generous closet space and an optional sitting room entered through double doors. The sitting room may also be used as a fourth bedroom.

Plan CH-230-A

Bedrooms: 3-4	Baths: 2½
Space:	
Upper floor	971 sq. ft.
Main floor	1,207 sq. ft.
Total Living Area	**2,178 sq. ft.**
Basement	1,207 sq. ft.
Garage	400 sq. ft.
Exterior Wall Framing	2x4

Foundation options:
Standard Basement
Daylight Basement
(Foundation & framing conversion diagram available—see order form.)

Blueprint Price Code	C

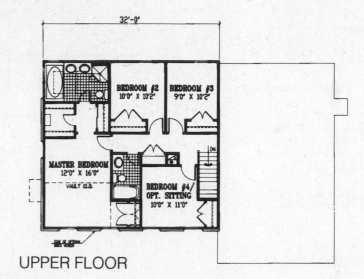

UPPER FLOOR

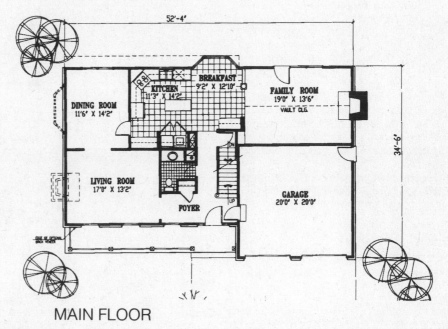

MAIN FLOOR

TO ORDER THIS BLUEPRINT,
CALL TOLL-FREE 1-800-820-1283

Plan CH-230-A

PRICES AND DETAILS
ON PAGES 12-15

159

Striking Traditional Farmhouse

- This eye-catching design will attract compliments wherever it is built, with its wide front porch, decorative columns and gables.
- The interior is equally fascinating, with an abundance of space for formal entertaining and casual family living.
- A large kitchen and eating area are at the heart of the home, and a spacious family room with a fireplace opens onto a secluded back porch.
- For formal occasions, the living and dining rooms adjoin each other to create a fine space for entertaining.
- The master suite is fit for royalty, with its bright sitting area, majestic bath and enormous walk-in closet.
- The upstairs bedrooms are also roomy, and one boasts a private bath. All three feature walk-in closets.

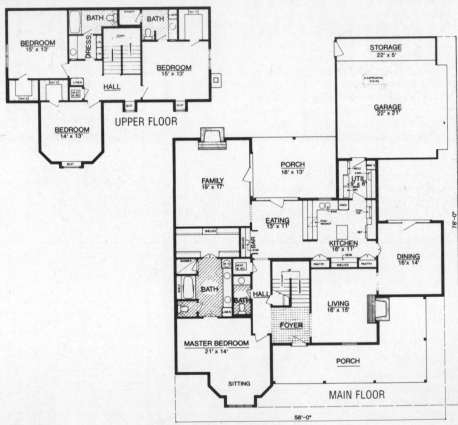

Plan E-3101

Bedrooms: 4		Baths: 2½
Space:		
Upper floor		1,074 sq. ft.
Main floor		2,088 sq. ft.
Total Living Area		**3,162 sq. ft.**
Basement	(approx.)	2,088 sq. ft.
Garage		462 sq. ft.
Storage		110 sq. ft.
Porches		598 sq. ft.

Exterior Wall Framing   2x6
Foundation options:
Standard basement
Crawlspace
Slab
(Foundation & framing conversion diagram available—see order form.)

Blueprint Price Code   E

Innovative Floor Plan

- The wide, covered front porch, arched windows and symmetrical lines of this traditional home conceal the modern, innovative floor plan found within.
- A two-story-high foyer guides guests to the front-oriented formal areas, which have views to the front porch.
- The hotspot of the home is the Great Room, with one of the home's three fireplaces and a media wall. Flanking doors open to a large backyard deck.
- The island kitchen and glassed-in eating nook overlook the deck and access a handy mudroom. High 9-ft. ceilings add to the aura of warmth and hospitality found on the main floor of this home.
- Another of the fireplaces is offered in the master suite. This private oasis also boasts a 13-ft.-high cathedral ceiling and a delicious bath with a garden tub.
- Upstairs, one bedroom has a sloped ceiling and a private bath. Three more bedrooms share another full bath.

Plan AHP-9360

Bedrooms: 5	Baths: 3½
Living Area:	
Upper floor	970 sq. ft.
Main floor	1,735 sq. ft.
Total Living Area:	**2,705 sq. ft.**
Standard basement	1,550 sq. ft.
Garage and utility area	443 sq. ft.
Exterior Wall Framing:	2x6

Foundation Options:

Standard basement
Crawlspace
Slab

(All plans can be built with your choice of foundation and framing. A generic conversion diagram is available. See order form.)

BLUEPRINT PRICE CODE: D

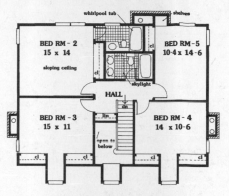

UPPER FLOOR

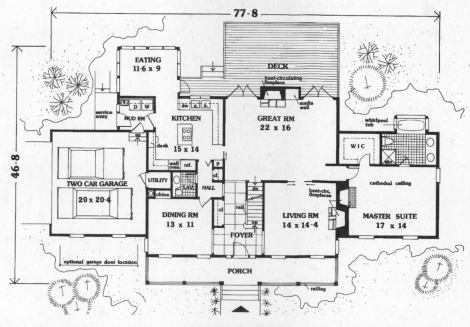

MAIN FLOOR

TO ORDER THIS BLUEPRINT,
CALL TOLL-FREE 1-800-820-1283

Plan AHP-9360

PRICES AND DETAILS
ON PAGES 12-15

161

Surrounded by Shade

- Comfort reigns in this delightful domicile, which boasts a shaded veranda that nearly surrounds the home. There's enough room for a porch hammock! When it rains during the family reunion, the festivities can be moved to this glorious covered area.
- Inside, a fireplace-blessed living room joins seamlessly with the welcoming foyer. Opposite, the big dining room will hold the largest dinner parties.

- Your whole family can participate in meal preparation, since the kitchen and connecting breakfast room flow into each other. A French door gives veranda access.
- In the master bedroom, an atrium door offers private passage to the veranda. The private bath includes a bubbly tub, a separate shower and a planter for your lush greenery.
- Upstairs, two more bedrooms flank a peaceful sitting area. A large split bath features a dual-sink vanity.
- All rooms in the home are topped by airy 9-ft. ceilings, for added spaciousness.

Plan L-88-VB

Bedrooms: 3	Baths: 2½
Living Area:	
Upper floor	751 sq. ft.
Main floor	1,308 sq. ft.
Total Living Area:	**2,059 sq. ft.**
Detached two-car garage	505 sq. ft.
Exterior Wall Framing:	2x4

Foundation Options:

Slab

(All plans can be built with your choice of foundation and framing. A generic conversion diagram is available. See order form.)

BLUEPRINT PRICE CODE:	**C**

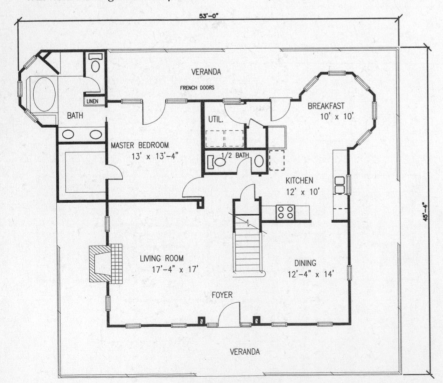

MAIN FLOOR

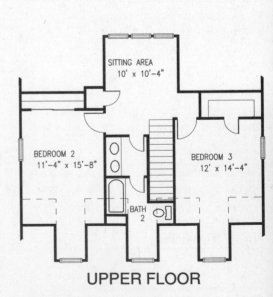

UPPER FLOOR

TO ORDER THIS BLUEPRINT, CALL TOLL-FREE 1-800-820-1283

Plan L-88-VB

PRICES AND DETAILS ON PAGES 12-15

Photo by Mark Englund/HomeStyles

Luxury and Livability

- Big on style, this modest-sized home features a quaint Colonial exterior and an open interior.
- The covered front porch leads to a two-story foyer that opens to the formal living and dining rooms. A coat closet, an attractive display niche and a powder room are centrally located, as is the stairway to the upper floor.
- The kitchen, breakfast nook and family room are designed so that each room has its own definition yet also functions as part of a whole. The angled sink separates the kitchen from the breakfast nook, which is outlined by a bay window. The large family room includes a fireplace.
- The upper floor has an exceptional master suite, featuring an 8½-ft. tray ceiling in the sleeping area and an 11-ft. vaulted ceiling in the spa bath.
- Two more bedrooms and a balcony hall add to this home's luxury and livability.

Plan FB-1600

Bedrooms: 3	Baths: 2½
Living Area:	
Upper floor	772 sq. ft.
Main floor	828 sq. ft.
Total Living Area:	**1,600 sq. ft.**
Daylight basement	828 sq. ft.
Garage	473 sq. ft.
Exterior Wall Framing:	2x4

Foundation Options:

Daylight basement
Crawlspace
Slab

(All plans can be built with your choice of foundation and framing. A generic conversion diagram is available. See order form.)

BLUEPRINT PRICE CODE: B

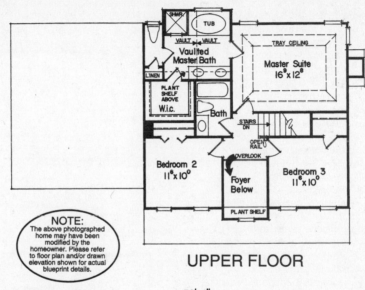

NOTE:
The above photographed home may have been modified by the homeowner. Please refer to floor plan and/or drawn elevation shown for actual blueprint details.

UPPER FLOOR

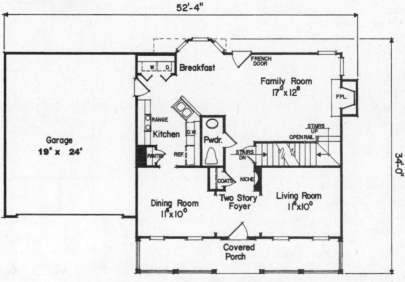

MAIN FLOOR

Classic Victorian

- This classic exterior is built around an interior that offers all the amenities desired by today's families.
- In from the covered front porch, the entry features a curved stairway and a glass-block wall to the dining room.
- A step down from the entry, the Great Room boasts a dramatic 24½-ft. cathedral ceiling and provides ample space for large family gatherings.
- The formal dining room is available for special occasions, while the 13-ft.-high breakfast nook serves everyday needs.
- The adjoining island kitchen offers plenty of counter space and opens to a handy utility room and a powder room.
- The deluxe main-floor master suite features a 14½-ft. cathedral ceiling and an opulent private bath with a garden spa tub and a separate shower.
- Upstairs, two secondary bedrooms share a full bath and a balcony overlooking the Great Room below.
- Plans for a two-car garage are available upon request.

Plan DW-2112

Bedrooms: 3	Baths: 2½
Living Area:	
Upper floor	514 sq. ft.
Main floor	1,598 sq. ft.
Total Living Area:	**2,112 sq. ft.**
Standard basement	1,598 sq. ft.
Exterior Wall Framing:	2x4

Foundation Options:

Standard basement
Crawlspace
Slab

(All plans can be built with your choice of foundation and framing. A generic conversion diagram is available. See order form.)

BLUEPRINT PRICE CODE: C

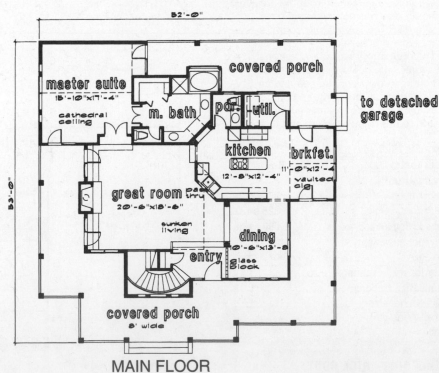

UPPER FLOOR

MAIN FLOOR

Plan DW-2112

PRICES AND DETAILS ON PAGES 12-15

Poised and Pure

- This pure country-style home stands poised with plenty of eye-catching features to grab your attention.
- Relaxation is the rule on the railed veranda in front; on starry summer nights it's the perfect place to cuddle up with your loved ones.
- From the raised foyer you can step down to the living room or dining room. The living room features a cozy boxed-out window and a pleasant fireplace to cheer up the large space.
- The dining room also contains a boxed-out window, and is just a step from the island kitchen, which helps to make serving and cleaning up meals fast and easy.
- Sunshine pours into the corner breakfast nook via two walls of windows. Sit down and enjoy the great views or step outside via a handy French door.
- French doors are also a key feature in the beautiful master suite—they invite you to a private patio. Other highlights include a huge bath and an equally spacious walk-in closet.
- Two more bedrooms complete the main floor. A large game room upstairs converts easily to a fourth bedroom.

Plan L-284-VB

Bedrooms: 3+	Baths: 3
Living Area:	
Upper floor	445 sq. ft.
Main floor	1,837 sq. ft.
Total Living Area:	**2,282 sq. ft.**
Exterior Wall Framing:	2x4

Foundation Options:

Slab

(All plans can be built with your choice of foundation and framing. A generic conversion diagram is available. See order form.)

BLUEPRINT PRICE CODE: C

UPPER FLOOR

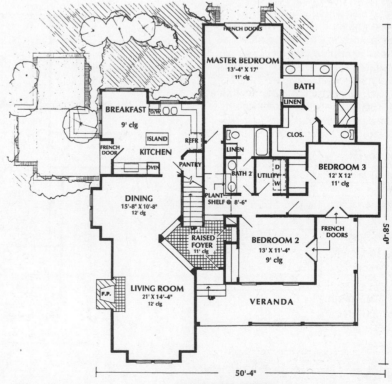

MAIN FLOOR

Sunny Comfort

- A covered wraparound porch and lovely arched windows give this home a comfortable country style.
- Inside, an elegant columned archway introduces the formal dining room.
- The huge Great Room features an 18-ft. vaulted ceiling, a dramatic wall of windows and two built-in wall units on either side of the fireplace.
- Ample counter space and a convenient work island allow maximum use of the roomy kitchen.
- The sunny breakfast nook opens to a porch through sliding glass doors.
- On the other side of the home, a dramatic bay window and a 10-ft. ceiling highlight the master bedroom. The enormous master bath features a luxurious whirlpool tub.
- Unless otherwise noted, all main-floor rooms have 9-ft. ceilings.
- Open stairs lead up to a balcony with a magnificent view of the Great Room. Two upstairs bedrooms, one with an 11-ft. vaulted ceiling, share a bath.

Plan AX-94317

Bedrooms: 3	Baths: 2½
Living Area:	
Upper floor	525 sq. ft.
Main floor	1,720 sq. ft.
Total Living Area:	**2,245 sq. ft.**
Standard basement	1,720 sq. ft.
Garage	502 sq. ft.
Storage/utility	51 sq. ft.
Exterior Wall Framing:	2x4

Foundation Options:

Standard basement
Crawlspace
Slab

(All plans can be built with your choice of foundation and framing. A generic conversion diagram is available. See order form.)

BLUEPRINT PRICE CODE: **C**

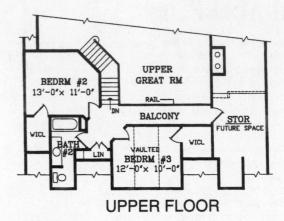

UPPER FLOOR

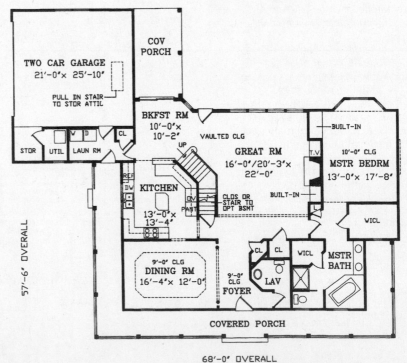

MAIN FLOOR

TO ORDER THIS BLUEPRINT, CALL TOLL-FREE 1-800-820-1283

Plan AX-94317

PRICES AND DETAILS ON PAGES 12-15

Country Kitchen

- A lovely front porch, dormers and shutters give this home a country-style exterior and complement its comfortable and informal interior.
- The roomy country kitchen connects with the sunny breakfast nook and the formal dining room.
- The central portion of the home consists of a large family room with a handsome fireplace and easy access to a backyard deck.
- The main-floor master suite, particularly impressive for a home of this size, features a majestic master bath with a corner garden tub, two walk-in closets and a dual-sink vanity with knee space.
- Upstairs, you will find two more good-sized bedrooms, a double bath and a large storage area.

Plan C-8645	
Bedrooms: 3	**Baths:** 2½
Living Area:	
Upper floor	704 sq. ft.
Main floor	1,477 sq. ft.
Total Living Area:	**2,181 sq. ft.**
Daylight basement	1,400 sq. ft.
Garage and storage	561 sq. ft.
Exterior Wall Framing:	2x4

Foundation Options:

Daylight basement
Crawlspace
Slab
(All plans can be built with your choice of foundation and framing. A generic conversion diagram is available. See order form.)

BLUEPRINT PRICE CODE: C

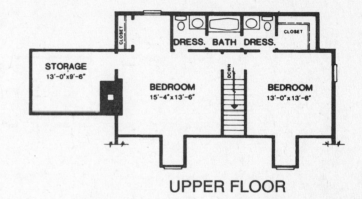

UPPER FLOOR

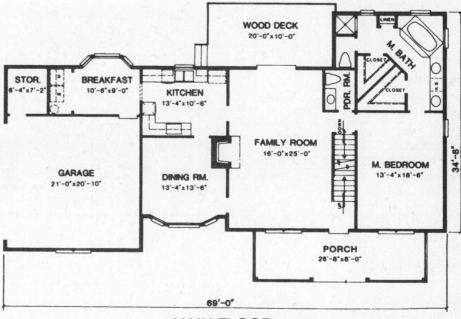

MAIN FLOOR

TO ORDER THIS BLUEPRINT,
CALL TOLL-FREE 1-800-820-1283

Plan C-8645

PRICES AND DETAILS
ON PAGES 12-15

167

Spacious Economy

- This economical country cottage features wide, angled spaces and 9-ft., 4-in. ceilings in both the Great Room and the master bedroom for roomy appeal and year-round comfort.
- The Great Room boasts a cozy fireplace with a raised hearth and a built-in niche for a TV, making this room perfect for winter gatherings. On warm nights, a homey covered porch at the rear can be accessed through sliding glass doors.
- Amenities in the luxurious master bedroom include a large walk-in closet, a private whirlpool bath and a dual-sink vanity.
- The nicely appointed kitchen offers nearby laundry facilities and porch access. A serving bar allows for casual dining and relaxed conversation.
- The optional daylight basement includes a tuck-under, two-car garage.

Plan AX-94322

Bedrooms: 3	Baths: 2½
Living Area:	
Upper floor	545 sq. ft.
Main floor	1,134 sq. ft.
Total Living Area:	**1,679 sq. ft.**
Daylight basement	618 sq. ft.
Standard basement	1,134 sq. ft.
Tuck-under garage	516 sq. ft.
Exterior Wall Framing:	2x4

Foundation Options:
Daylight basement
Standard basement
Crawlspace
Slab
(All plans can be built with your choice of foundation and framing. A generic conversion diagram is available. See order form.)

BLUEPRINT PRICE CODE: B

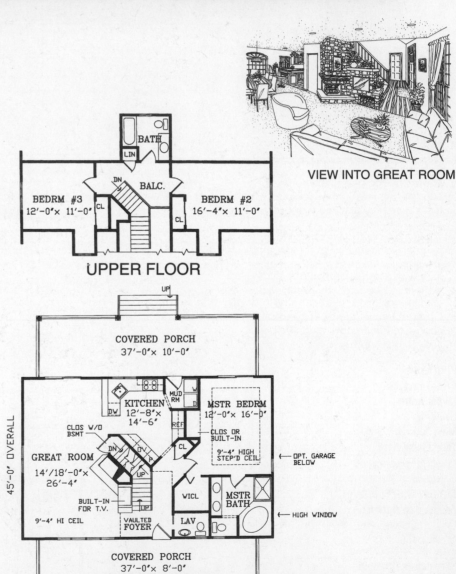

VIEW INTO GREAT ROOM

UPPER FLOOR

MAIN FLOOR

TO ORDER THIS BLUEPRINT, CALL TOLL-FREE 1-800-820-1283

Plan AX-94322

PRICES AND DETAILS ON PAGES 12-15

Compact Three-Bedroom

- Both openness and privacy are possible in this economical three-bedroom home design.
- The bright living room boasts a 17-ft. vaulted ceiling, a warming fireplace and a corner window. A high clerestory window lets in additional natural light.
- The modern, U-shaped kitchen features a handy corner pantry and a versatile snack bar.
- The adjacent open dining area provides access to a backyard deck through sliding glass doors.
- A lovely corner window brightens the secluded master bedroom, which also includes a roomy walk-in closet and private access to a compartmentalized hall bath.
- Upstairs, two good-sized bedrooms share a second split bath.

Plan B-101-8501

Bedrooms: 3	**Baths:** 2

Living Area:	
Upper floor	400 sq. ft.
Main floor	846 sq. ft.
Total Living Area:	**1,246 sq. ft.**
Garage	400 sq. ft.
Standard basement	846 sq. ft.
Exterior Wall Framing:	2x4

Foundation Options:

Standard basement

(All plans can be built with your choice of foundation and framing. A generic conversion diagram is available. See order form.)

BLUEPRINT PRICE CODE: A

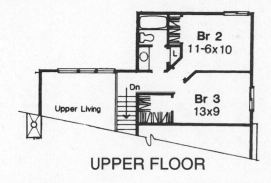

UPPER FLOOR

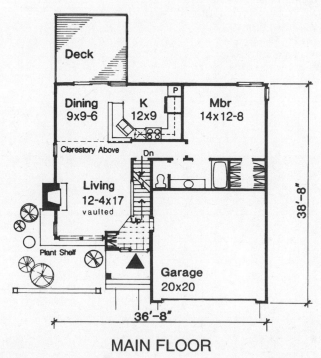

MAIN FLOOR

Large-Scale Living

- Eye-catching windows and an appealing wraparound porch highlight the exterior of this outstanding home.
- Inside, high ceilings and large-scale living spaces prevail, beginning with the foyer, which has an 18-ft. ceiling.
- The spacious living room flows into the formal dining room, which opens to the porch and to an optional rear deck.
- The island kitchen extends to a bright breakfast room with deck access. The family room offers an 18-ft. vaulted ceiling and a corner fireplace.
- Unless otherwise noted, every main-floor room boasts a 9-ft. ceiling.
- Upstairs, the lush master bedroom boasts an 11-ft. vaulted ceiling and two walk-in closets. The skylighted master bath features a spa tub, a separate shower and a dual-sink vanity.
- Three more bedrooms are reached by a balcony, which overlooks the family room. In one bedroom, the ceiling jumps to 10 ft. at the beautiful window.

Plan AX-93309

Bedrooms: 4	Baths: 2½
Living Area:	
Upper floor	1,180 sq. ft.
Main floor	1,290 sq. ft.
Total Living Area:	**2,470 sq. ft.**
Basement	1,290 sq. ft.
Garage and storage	421 sq. ft.
Exterior Wall Framing:	2x4

Foundation Options:

Daylight basement
Standard basement
Slab
(All plans can be built with your choice of foundation and framing. A generic conversion diagram is available. See order form.)

BLUEPRINT PRICE CODE: C

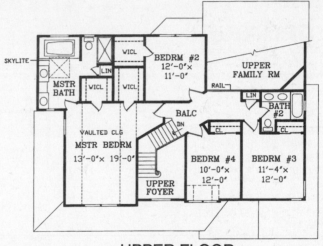

UPPER FLOOR

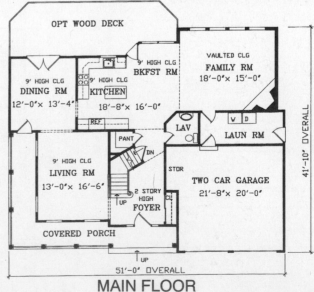

MAIN FLOOR

TO ORDER THIS BLUEPRINT, CALL TOLL-FREE 1-800-820-1283

Plan AX-93309

PRICES AND DETAILS ON PAGES 12-15

Blend of Old and New

- In this design, a traditional wraparound porch encompasses an interior filled with the best features in today's homes.
- Inside, columns and bookshelves introduce the living room, which hosts gatherings in style. A sunny garden room shares the living room's two-way fireplace, and would be a quiet, pleasant spot for reading.
- For most activities, the family room at the rear will suit you well, as it interacts nicely with the kitchen and the breakfast nook.
- In the master suite, a number of perks offer special treatment. The secluded patio provides a private spot for coffee, while twin vanities and bountiful closet space easily accommodate two.
- The bedrooms upstairs also include neat features like built-in shelves, private bath access and good-sized closets. In the two front-facing bedrooms, pretty dormers would serve well as cozy places to sit and reflect on the day.
- Every main-floor room boasts a 10-ft. ceiling, while each of the upper-floor rooms features a 9-ft. ceiling.

Plan L-3050-C

Bedrooms: 4	Baths: 3½
Living Area:	
Upper floor	787 sq. ft.
Main floor	2,263 sq. ft.
Total Living Area:	**3,050 sq. ft.**
Exterior Wall Framing:	2x4

Foundation Options:

Slab

(All plans can be built with your choice of foundation and framing. A generic conversion diagram is available. See order form.)

BLUEPRINT PRICE CODE:	E

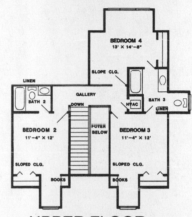

UPPER FLOOR

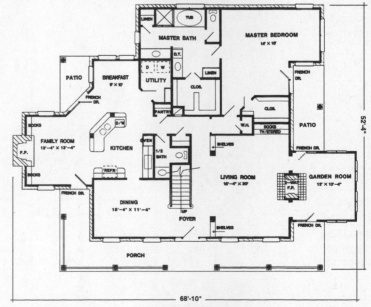

MAIN FLOOR

REAR VIEW

Fantastic Facade, Stunning Spaces

- Matching dormers and a generous covered front porch give this home its fantastic facade. Inside, the open living spaces are just as stunning.
- A two-story foyer bisects the formal living areas. The living room offers three bright windows, an inviting fireplace and sliding French doors to the Great Room. The formal dining room overlooks the front porch and has easy access to the kitchen.
- The Great Room is truly grand, featuring a fireplace and a TV center flanked by French doors that lead to a large deck.
- A circular dinette connects the Great Room to the kitchen, which is handy to a mudroom and a powder room.
- The main-floor master suite boasts a 14-ft. cathedral ceiling, a walk-in closet and a private bath with a whirlpool tub.
- Upstairs, four large bedrooms share another whirlpool bath. One bedroom offers a 12-ft. sloped ceiling.

Plan AHP-9397

Bedrooms: 5	Baths: 2½
Living Area:	
Upper floor	928 sq. ft.
Main floor	1,545 sq. ft.
Total Living Area:	**2,473 sq. ft.**
Standard basement	1,545 sq. ft.
Garage and storage	432 sq. ft.
Exterior Wall Framing:	2x4 or 2x6

Foundation Options:

Standard basement
Crawlspace
Slab
(All plans can be built with your choice of foundation and framing. A generic conversion diagram is available. See order form.)

BLUEPRINT PRICE CODE: C

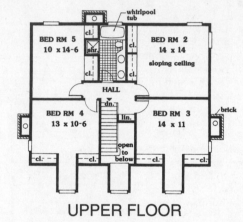

UPPER FLOOR

MAIN FLOOR

Plan AHP-9397

PRICES AND DETAILS ON PAGES 12-15

Front Porch Invites Visitors

- This neat and well-proportioned design exudes warmth and charm.
- The roomy foyer connects the formal dining room and living room for special occasions, and the living and family rooms join together to create abundant space for large gatherings.
- The large kitchen, dinette and family room flow from one to the other for great casual family living.
- Upstairs, the roomy master suite is complemented by a master bath available in two configurations. The unique library is brightened by a beautiful arched window.

Plan GL-2161

Bedrooms: 3	Baths: 2½
Living Area:	
Upper floor	991 sq. ft.
Main floor	1,170 sq. ft.
Total Living Area	**2,161 sq. ft.**
Standard basement	1,170 sq. ft.
Garage	462 sq. ft.
Exterior Wall Framing	2x6

Foundation Options:

Standard basement
(All plans can be built with your choice of foundation and framing. A generic conversion diagram is available. See order form.)

BLUEPRINT PRICE CODE	C

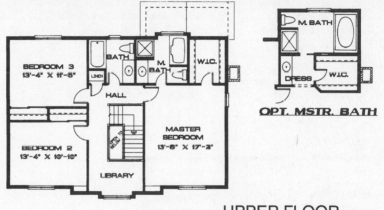

UPPER FLOOR

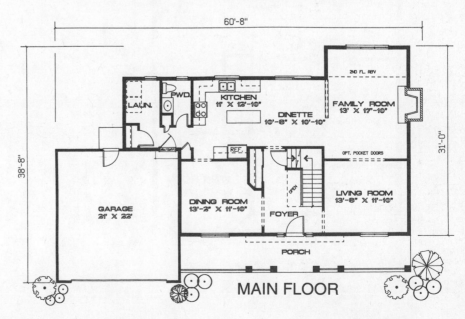

MAIN FLOOR

TO ORDER THIS BLUEPRINT,
CALL TOLL-FREE 1-800-820-1283

Plan GL-2161

PRICES AND DETAILS
ON PAGES 12-15

173

Affordable Victorian

- This compact Victorian design incorporates four bedrooms and three full baths into an attractive, affordable home that's only 30 ft. wide.
- Just in from the covered front porch, family members and guests will gather in the spacious parlor to relax in front of the soothing fireplace. A beautiful bay window adds cheer and elegance to the formal dining room nearby.

- The galley-style kitchen offers efficient service to the breakfast nook. A laundry closet and a pantry are nearby.
- The main-floor bedroom makes a great office or guest bedroom, with a convenient full bath nearby.
- Upstairs, the master suite features an adjoining sitting room with a 14-ft. cathedral ceiling. The luxurious master bath includes a dual-sink vanity and a whirlpool tub with a shower. Two more bedrooms share another bath.
- An attached two-car garage off the kitchen is available upon request.

Plan C-8347-A

Bedrooms: 3+	Baths: 3
Living Area:	
Upper floor	783 sq. ft.
Main floor	954 sq. ft.
Total Living Area:	**1,737 sq. ft.**
Exterior Wall Framing:	2x4

Foundation Options:
Crawlspace
Slab
(All plans can be built with your choice of foundation and framing. A generic conversion diagram is available. See order form.)

BLUEPRINT PRICE CODE:	B

MAIN FLOOR

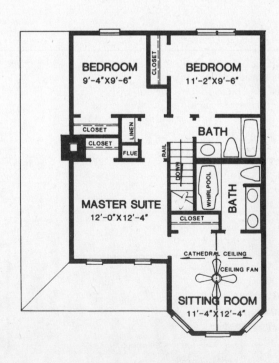

UPPER FLOOR

TO ORDER THIS BLUEPRINT, CALL TOLL-FREE 1-800-820-1283   Plan C-8347-A   *PRICES AND DETAILS ON PAGES 12-15*

Irresistible Master Suite

- This traditional three-bedroom home features a main-floor master suite that is hard to resist, with an inviting window seat and a delightful bath.
- The home is introduced by a covered front entry, topped by a dormer with a half-round window.
- Just off the front entry, the formal dining room is distinguished by a tray ceiling and a large picture window overlooking the front porch.
- Straight back, the Great Room features a 16-ft.-high vaulted ceiling with a window wall facing the backyard. The fireplace can be enjoyed from the adjoining kitchen and breakfast area.
- The gourmet kitchen includes a corner sink, an island cooktop and a walk-in pantry. A 12-ft. vaulted ceiling expands the breakfast nook, which features a built-in desk and backyard deck access.
- The spacious master suite offers a 14-ft. vaulted ceiling and a luxurious private bath with a walk-in closet, a garden tub, a separate shower and a dual-sink vanity with a sit-down makeup area.
- An open-railed stairway leads up to another full bath that serves two additional bedrooms.

Plan B-89061

Bedrooms: 3	Baths: 2½
Living Area:	
Upper floor	436 sq. ft.
Main floor	1,490 sq. ft.
Total Living Area:	**1,926 sq. ft.**
Standard basement	1,490 sq. ft.
Garage	400 sq. ft.
Exterior Wall Framing:	2x4

Foundation Options:

Standard basement
(All plans can be built with your choice of foundation and framing. A generic conversion diagram is available. See order form.)

BLUEPRINT PRICE CODE: B

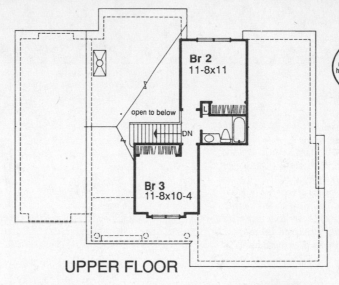

UPPER FLOOR

Br 2
11-8x11

open to below

DN

Br 3
11-8x10-4

NOTE:
The above photographed home may have been modified by the homeowner. Please refer to floor plan and/or drawn elevation shown for actual blueprint details.

MAIN FLOOR

55'-8"

Deck

Great Rm
14x18-6
vaulted

Glass Above

Kit
11x12

Brkfst
11x10
vaulted

Pantry

Desk

45'-0"

UP   DN

D W

Mas. Suite
13x16
vaulted

Dining
11-6x12-3

Garage
20x20

Photo by Felice Photographers

Classic Country-Style

- Almost completely surrounded by an expansive porch, this classic plan exudes warmth and grace.
- The foyer is liberal in size and leads guests to a formal dining room to the left or the large living room to the right.
- The open country kitchen includes a sunny, bay-windowed breakfast nook. A utility area, a full bath and garage access are nearby.
- Upstairs, the master suite is impressive, with its large sleeping area, walk-in closet and magnificent garden bath.
- Three secondary bedrooms share a full bath with a dual-sink vanity.
- Also note the stairs leading up to an attic, which is useful for storage space.

Plan J-86134

Bedrooms: 4	Baths: 3
Living Area:	
Upper floor	1,195 sq. ft.
Main floor	1,370 sq. ft.
Total Living Area:	**2,565 sq. ft.**
Standard basement	1,370 sq. ft.
Garage	576 sq. ft.
Exterior Wall Framing:	2x4

Foundation Options:

Standard basement
Crawlspace
Slab
(All plans can be built with your choice of foundation and framing. A generic conversion diagram is available. See order form.)

BLUEPRINT PRICE CODE: D

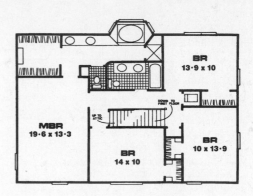

**NOTE:
The above photographed home may have been modified by the homeowner. Please refer to floor plan and/or drawn elevation shown for actual blueprint details.

UPPER FLOOR

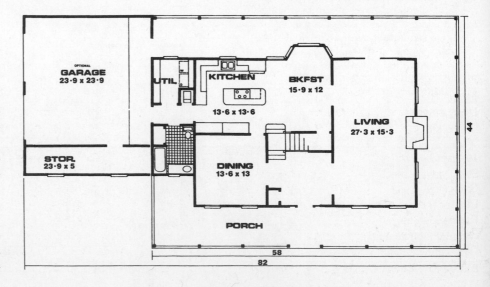

MAIN FLOOR

TO ORDER THIS BLUEPRINT, CALL TOLL-FREE 1-800-820-1283

Plan J-86134

PRICES AND DETAILS ON PAGES 12-15

Traditional Family

- A cute columned porch adds character to this traditional family home.
- A walk-in closet and a half-bath in the two-story foyer accommodate guests.
- To the right, the formal living and dining rooms make entertaining your guests a snap.
- The open kitchen includes a space-saving island and a windowed sink. Sliding glass doors in the bright dinette extend dining to an enormous patio that is perfect for a barbecue.
- A striking 11-ft. cathedral ceiling soars over the family room, where a cozy fireplace adds warmth.
- An open staircase leads up to the magnificent master bedroom, which is embellished with a 9½-ft. tray ceiling and a private whirlpool bath.
- Three secondary bedrooms share a conveniently located full bath.

Plan GL-2223

Bedrooms: 4	Baths: 2½
Living Area:	
Upper floor	1,007 sq. ft.
Main floor	1,216 sq. ft.
Total Living Area:	**2,223 sq. ft.**
Standard basement	1,207 sq. ft.
Garage	484 sq. ft.
Exterior Wall Framing:	2x6

Foundation Options:

Standard basement
(All plans can be built with your choice of foundation and framing. A generic conversion diagram is available. See order form.)

BLUEPRINT PRICE CODE: C

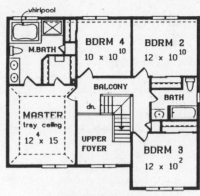

UPPER FLOOR

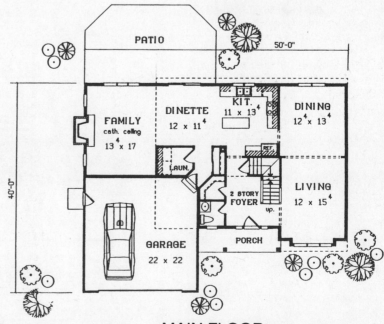

MAIN FLOOR

TO ORDER THIS BLUEPRINT,
CALL TOLL-FREE 1-800-820-1283

Plan GL-2223

PRICES AND DETAILS
ON PAGES 12-15

177

Country-Style Has Colonial Influence

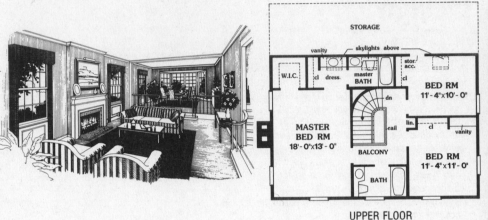

- This country-style-home is influenced by the Colonial saltbox design.
- A porch dominates the front and side of the house, while a terrace stretches across the rear.
- A large fireplace warms the spacious, sunken living room. A decorative railing separates the living room from the dining room, up two steps. Sliding glass doors set in a bayed window access the terrace.
- The roomy U-shaped kitchen and dinette flow together for a traditional family atmosphere.
- To the right of the foyer is a big family room with a built-in entertainment center.
- The upper-level bedrooms are accessed by a curved stairway in the foyer. The private master suite has a skylit bath and dressing area.

Plan HFL-1130-AM

Bedrooms: 3	Baths: 3
Space:	
Upper floor	797 sq. ft.
Main floor	1,238 sq. ft.
Total Living Area	**2,035 sq. ft.**
Basement	1,159 sq. ft.
Garage	439 sq. ft.
Exterior Wall Framing	**2x6**

Foundation options:
Standard Basement
Slab
(Foundation & framing conversion diagram available—see order form.)

Blueprint Price Code	C

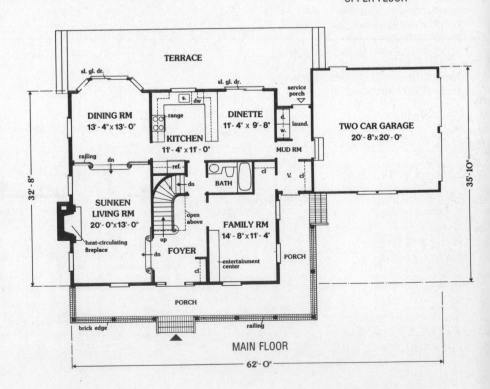

UPPER FLOOR

MAIN FLOOR

TO ORDER THIS BLUEPRINT, CALL TOLL-FREE 1-800-820-1283

Plan HFL-1130-AM

PRICES AND DETAILS ON PAGES 12-15

Easy-Going Design

- A relaxing front porch and airy, easy-going spaces inside make a wonderful combination in this charming country-style design.
- Family and visitors alike will gather in front of the fireplace in the large living room. The adjoining dining room features a bay window and opens to the efficiently designed kitchen. A back door leads to another covered porch.
- The main-floor master suite is brightened by a bay window overlooking the backyard. The private, compartmentalized bath includes a dual-sink vanity, a garden tub and a large walk-in closet.
- Another full bath is just across the hall from the second main-floor bedroom.
- Upstairs, two large bedrooms with double closets have private access to a nice-sized bathroom.

Plan J-91006

Bedrooms: 4	Baths: 3
Living Area:	
Upper floor	698 sq. ft.
Main floor	1,467 sq. ft.
Total Living Area:	**2,165 sq. ft.**
Standard basement	1,467 sq. ft.
Garage	459 sq. ft.
Exterior Wall Framing:	2x6

Foundation Options:

Standard basement

Crawlspace

Slab

(Typical foundation & framing conversion diagram available—see order form.)

BLUEPRINT PRICE CODE:	C

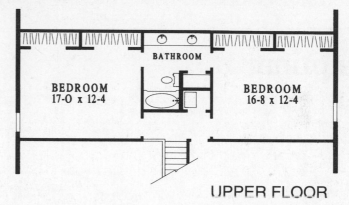

BATHROOM

BEDROOM 17-0 x 12-4

BEDROOM 16-8 x 12-4

UPPER FLOOR

46-6

53-6

KITCHEN 12-4 x 11-4

BEDROOM 10-4 x 12-2

MASTER BEDROOM 13-8 x 15-0

STORAGE

DINING 11-8 x 11-0

GARAGE 21-0 x 20-0

LIVING ROOM 19-5 x 17-2

PORCH 24-10 x 6-6

MAIN FLOOR

Warm Reception

- The inviting wraparound porch of this beautiful country-style home provides a warm reception for all who visit.
- Past the porch, the impressive reception hall boasts a 16½-ft.-high ceiling and a gorgeous curved staircase.
- The living room and the dining room combine to create an open feel. Sliding glass doors in the dining room open to a lovely rear terrace.
- The island kitchen includes a snack bar and a handy laundry closet. The adjoining dinette offers terrace access and a panoramic view of the outdoors.
- Enhanced by a 16½-ft.-high ceiling, the family room boasts a warm fireplace.
- The deluxe master suite features a 12-ft. cathedral ceiling, a walk-in closet and sliding glass doors to a private terrace. The master bath has a skylighted whirlpool tub.
- Upstairs, a railed balcony overlooks the main floor below. A second full bath is shared by three upper-floor bedrooms.

Plan K-801-R

Bedrooms: 4	Baths: 2½
Living Area:	
Upper floor	750 sq. ft.
Main floor	1,808 sq. ft.
Total Living Area:	**2,558 sq. ft.**
Standard basement	1,808 sq. ft.
Garage	483 sq. ft.
Exterior Wall Framing:	2x4 or 2x6

Foundation Options:

Standard basement

Slab

(All plans can be built with your choice of foundation and framing. A generic conversion diagram is available. See order form.)

BLUEPRINT PRICE CODE: D

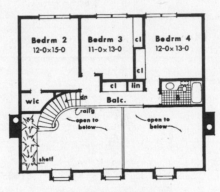

UPPER FLOOR

VIEW INTO
LIVING AND DINING ROOMS

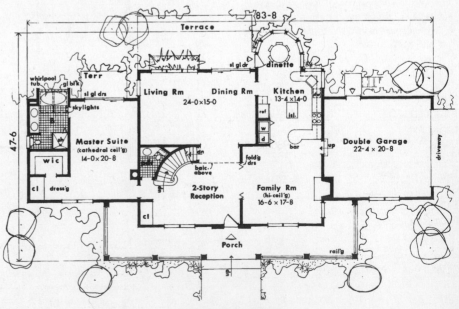

MAIN FLOOR

TO ORDER THIS BLUEPRINT, CALL TOLL-FREE 1-800-820-1283

Plan K-801-R

PRICES AND DETAILS ON PAGES 12-15

Warm Country Embrace

- A cozy fireplace warms the living room of this home, while a covered porch embraces the facade and extends to a sprawling backyard deck.
- Sidelights brighten the 17-ft.-high foyer, which is flanked on the right by a quiet study and on the left by the sunken living room.
- The spacious dining room is graced by a charming window seat and offers French-door deck access.
- An informal eating bar sets off the kitchen, with its handy work island. A powder room is nearby.
- Upstairs, a balcony hall leads to the master bedroom, which flaunts a cute window seat. A very large walk-in closet, a whirlpool tub and a separate shower highlight the master bath.
- Two roomy secondary bedrooms share a hall bath.
- Spacious laundry facilities are located on the upper floor for convenience.

Plan LMB-9852

Bedrooms: 3+	Baths: 2½
Living Area:	
Upper floor	980 sq. ft.
Main floor	1,104 sq. ft.
Total Living Area:	**2,084 sq. ft.**
Garage	500 sq. ft.
Exterior Wall Framing:	2x6

Foundation Options:
Crawlspace
(All plans can be built with your choice of foundation and framing. A generic conversion diagram is available. See order form.)

BLUEPRINT PRICE CODE:	C

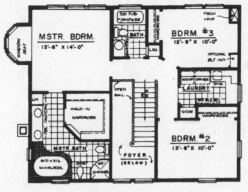

UPPER FLOOR

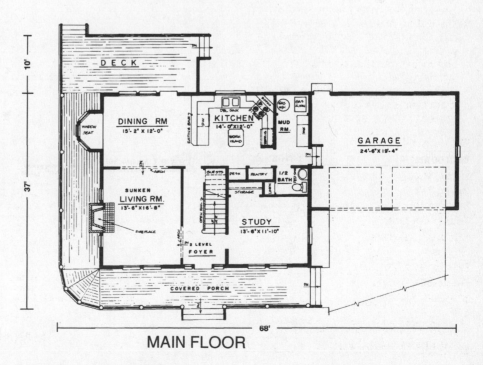

MAIN FLOOR

Spacious Great Room

- The efficient floor plan of this home centers around a stunning Great Room. The entire main floor is designed for those who enjoy casual living and entertaining, without the fuss of maintaining formal, rarely used living spaces.
- The Great Room is partially vaulted to the balcony overhead. The open-plan concept allows light, and traffic, to flow easily throughout the home.
- The two generous bedrooms on the lower level are separated from the master suite, which is located on the second level. The future bonus space can be finished as needed.
- The covered patio can be eliminated in favor of a two-story sunspace, accessible from the master bedroom and the lower-level dining room.
- This is a home for all seasons and has a modest size of 2,542 sq. ft., excluding the bonus space over the garage.

Plan LRD-41389	
Bedrooms: 2-4	Baths: 2-3
Space:	
Upper floor	910 sq. ft.
Main floor	1,632 sq. ft.
Bonus area	456 sq. ft.
Total Living Area:	**2,998 sq. ft.**
Standard basement	1,632 sq. ft.
Garage	567 sq. ft.
Exterior Wall Framing:	2x6

Foundation Options:
Standard basement
Crawlspace
(Typical foundation & framing conversion diagram available—see order form.)

BLUEPRINT PRICE CODE: D

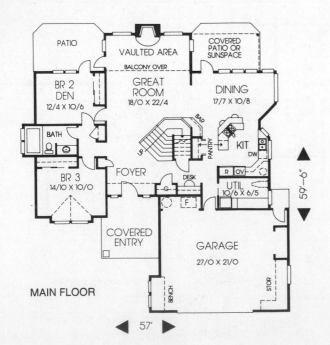

MAIN FLOOR

57'

UPPER FLOOR

TO ORDER THIS BLUEPRINT, CALL TOLL-FREE 1-800-820-1283

Plan LRD-41389

PRICES AND DETAILS ON PAGES 12-15

Open and Airy Design

- The open and airy design of this compact, affordable home makes the most of its space.
- Inside, the entry's 23½-ft. vaulted ceiling soars to the upper floor. Two decorative wood rails set off the entry from the living room. A corner fireplace topped by a wood mantel anchors the room, and French doors lead to the backyard.
- The good-sized dining room extends to the kitchen, where a handy island maximizes workspace, and a bright window adds light. Plenty of room is available for cooking and dining.
- Across the home, the secluded master bedroom is a great adult retreat. The private master bath boasts two separate vanities and a walk-in closet with convenient built-in shelves.
- At the top of the open staircase, a railed sitting area with a 16-ft. vaulted ceiling is ideal for a computer nook.
- Two spacious bedrooms are serviced by a centrally located hall bath.
- Plans for a detached two-car garage are also included in the blueprints.

Plan LS-94046-E

Bedrooms: 3	Baths: 2
Living Area:	
Upper floor	561 sq. ft.
Main floor	1,190 sq. ft.
Total Living Area:	**1,751 sq. ft.**
Standard basement	1,145 sq. ft.
Exterior Wall Framing:	2x6

Foundation Options:

Standard basement

(All plans can be built with your choice of foundation and framing. A generic conversion diagram is available. See order form.)

BLUEPRINT PRICE CODE: B

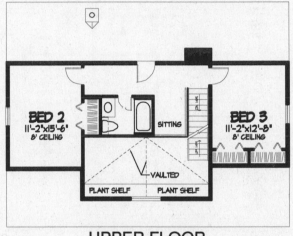

UPPER FLOOR

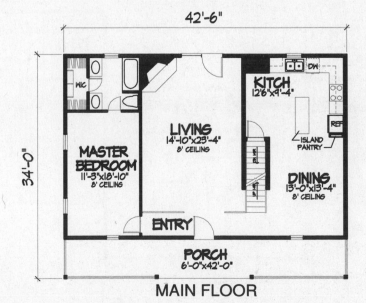

MAIN FLOOR

TO ORDER THIS BLUEPRINT,
CALL TOLL-FREE 1-800-820-1283

Plan LS-94046-E

PRICES AND DETAILS
ON PAGES 12-15

183

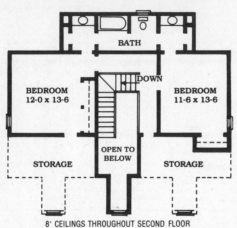

BATH

BEDROOM
12-0 x 13-6

DOWN

BEDROOM
11-6 x 13-6

OPEN TO
BELOW

STORAGE

STORAGE

8' CEILINGS THROUGHOUT SECOND FLOOR

◄74'►

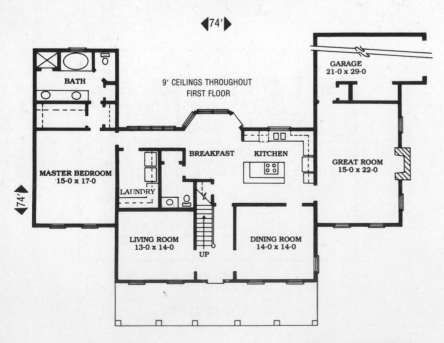

BATH

9' CEILINGS THROUGHOUT
FIRST FLOOR

GARAGE
21-0 x 29-0

MASTER BEDROOM
15-0 x 17-0

BREAKFAST

KITCHEN

GREAT ROOM
15-0 x 22-0

LAUNDRY

74'

LIVING ROOM
13-0 x 14-0

UP

DINING ROOM
14-0 x 14-0

Gulf-Style Plantation Home

This stately home is designed for those who love the look of the older houses found along the coastal regions of the Gulf of Mexico. A large breakfast area is planned for those who like spaciousness in this popular area, and a well-planned utility room is conveniently located near the kitchen and the master bedroom. Please note the tremendous amount of storage space both upstairs and down in this gracious house.

First floor:	2,026 sq. ft.
Second floor:	663 sq. ft.
Total living area:	2,689 sq. ft.

PLAN V-2689
WITHOUT BASEMENT
(CRAWLSPACE FOUNDATION)

Blueprint Price Code D
Plan V-2689

PRICES AND DETAILS
ON PAGES 12-15

Starter Home
Offers Options

- Country styling adds to the appeal of this two-story, ideal as a starter home.
- Beyond the wide front porch, the foyer flows to both the living room and the kitchen. Limited hall space maximizes the living area of the home.
- The large living room enjoys a view of the porch through a pair of shuttered windows. Sliding glass doors in the adjoining dining area offer a view of the backyard from either location.
- The open and efficient kitchen has easy access to the one-car garage and the main-floor laundry room. Closed off by a pocket door, the generous-sized laundry area has a convenient folding counter that can also serve as a work desk or planning center.
- Three bedrooms and two baths are located on the upper floor. An alternate one-bathroom version is included with the blueprints.
- An optional two-car garage adds four feet to the overall width of the home.

Plan GL-1430-P

Bedrooms: 3	Baths: 1½-2½
Living Area:	
Upper floor	720 sq. ft.
Main floor	710 sq. ft.
Total Living Area:	**1,430 sq. ft.**
Standard basement	710 sq. ft.
One-car garage	341 sq. ft.
Optional two-car garage	427 sq. ft.
Exterior Wall Framing:	2x4

Foundation Options:

Standard basement

(All plans can be built with your choice of foundation and framing. A generic conversion diagram is available. See order form.)

BLUEPRINT PRICE CODE:	A

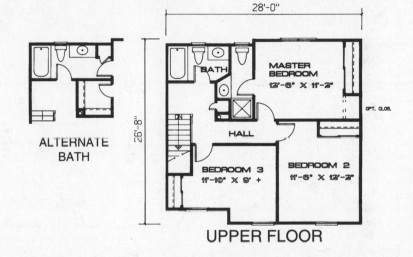

ALTERNATE BATH

UPPER FLOOR

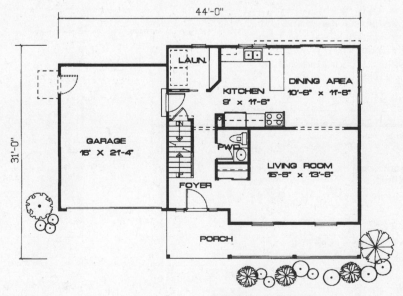

MAIN FLOOR

TO ORDER THIS BLUEPRINT,
CALL TOLL-FREE 1-800-820-1283

Plan GL-1430-P

PRICES AND DETAILS
ON PAGES 12-15

185

Saltbox with Style

- Beyond the saltbox exterior of this classic home is its stylish, updated floor plan, which is perfectly suited for today's active families.
- Past the inviting entry, the spacious living room boasts an impressive central fireplace. Sliding glass doors open to a relaxing screened porch with access to a backyard patio.
- Perfect for informal entertaining, the adjacent family room is warmed by a handsome woodstove.
- The efficient kitchen offers patio access and includes an open counter with a pass-through to the family room. The formal dining room, a half-bath and a laundry room with a service entrance are conveniently nearby.
- Upstairs, the master bedroom features a windowed walk-in closet and a private bath with an oversized shower.
- Three additional bedrooms share a second full bath.

Plan M-2214

Bedrooms: 4	Baths: 2½
Living Area:	
Upper floor	940 sq. ft.
Main floor	964 sq. ft.
Total Living Area:	**1,904 sq. ft.**
Standard basement	964 sq. ft.
Garage	440 sq. ft.
Exterior Wall Framing:	2x6

Foundation Options:

Standard basement

(All plans can be built with your choice of foundation and framing. A generic conversion diagram is available. See order form.)

BLUEPRINT PRICE CODE: B

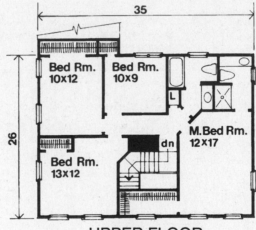

UPPER FLOOR

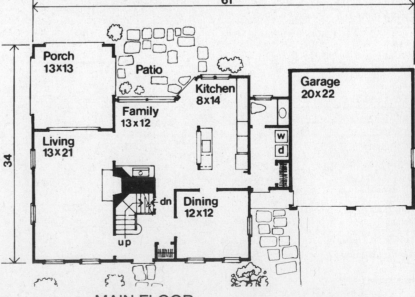

MAIN FLOOR

Plan M-2214

PRICES AND DETAILS ON PAGES 12-15

Narrow Lot Excitement

- A stylish entry invites guests into this exciting, narrow-lot, two-story home.
- The excitement continues inside with a two-story entry foyer and a view into the living room with fireplace and the dining room with sliders to the rear terrace.
- The U-shaped kitchen opens to a family eating/lounging area with side terrace.
- Upstairs, there are three large bedrooms and two full baths.
- The master bedroom offers two walk-in closets and a whirlpool tub in its private bath.

UPPER FLOOR

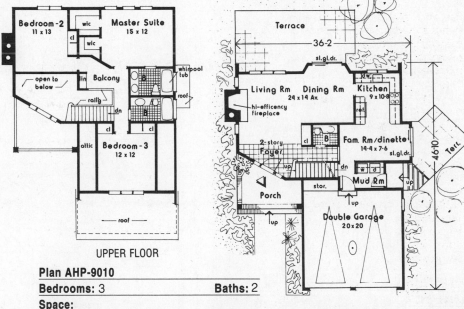

MAIN FLOOR

Plan AHP-9010

Bedrooms: 3	**Baths:** 2

Space:	
Upper Floor	826 sq. ft.
Main floor	794 sq. ft.
Total Living Area	**1,620 sq. ft.**
Basement	794 sq. ft.
Garage	444 sq. ft.
Exterior Wall Framing	**2x6**

Foundation options:
Standard Basement
Slab
(Foundation & framing conversion diagram available—see order form.)

Blueprint Price Code	**B**

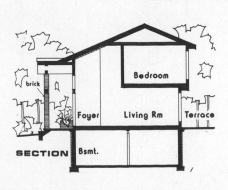

SECTION

Rustic Relaxation

- A covered front porch, a pair of dormers and a combination of wood and brick create a rustic exterior for this traditional home. An expansive screen porch doubles as a breezeway connecting the home with the garage.
- The front porch opens directly into the large Great Room, with its handsome fireplace. With a nearby snack bar and French-door access to the screen porch, a dining area would fit nicely between the Great Room and the kitchen.
- Also adjoining the kitchen is an oversized utility room with space for a washer, a dryer and an extra freezer.
- The deluxe master suite offers a private bath with a separate tub and shower and a dual-sink vanity with knee space for a makeup table. Generous closet space for two is also provided.
- The second main-floor bedroom uses the full bath across the hall. Two more bedrooms, each with a window seat and storage space access, share a full bath on the upper floor.

Plan C-7746

Bedrooms: 4	Baths: 3
Living Area:	
Upper floor	773 sq. ft.
Main floor	1,694 sq. ft.
Total Living Area:	**2,467 sq. ft.**
Daylight basement	1,694 sq. ft.
Screen porch	353 sq. ft.
Garage	552 sq. ft.
Exterior Wall Framing:	2x4

Foundation Options:

Daylight basement
Crawlspace
(All plans can be built with your choice of foundation and framing. A generic conversion diagram is available. See order form.)

BLUEPRINT PRICE CODE: C

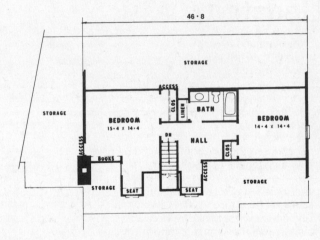

UPPER FLOOR

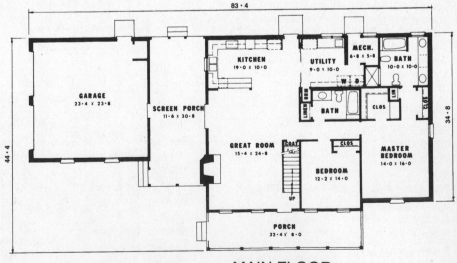

MAIN FLOOR

Updated Classic

- Light-filled and airy, this classic country-style home is filled with modern amenities.
- Brightened by high transom windows, the inviting two-story-high foyer flows into the spacious living room and the formal dining room.
- The efficient kitchen features a breakfast bar and a window over the sink. The adjoining dinette offers sliding glass doors to a backyard terrace. The nearby mudroom/laundry room has garage and backyard access.
- The friendly family room enjoys a view of the backyard through a row of three windows. The handsome fireplace is flanked by glass.
- Upstairs, the spectacular master bedroom boasts a 10-ft. cathedral ceiling and a roomy walk-in closet. The skylighted master bath showcases a whirlpool tub, a separate shower and a dual-sink vanity.
- Another skylighted bath services the three remaining bedrooms.

Plan AHP-9402

Bedrooms: 4	Baths: 2½
Living Area:	
Upper floor	1,041 sq. ft.
Main floor	1,129 sq. ft.
Total Living Area:	**2,170 sq. ft.**
Standard basement	1,129 sq. ft.
Garage and storage	630 sq. ft.
Exterior Wall Framing:	2x4 or 2x6
Foundation Options:	
Standard basement	
Crawlspace	
Slab	

(All plans can be built with your choice of foundation and framing. A generic conversion diagram is available. See order form.)

BLUEPRINT PRICE CODE: C

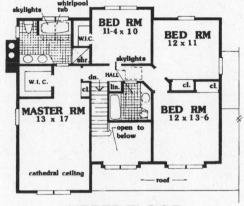

UPPER FLOOR

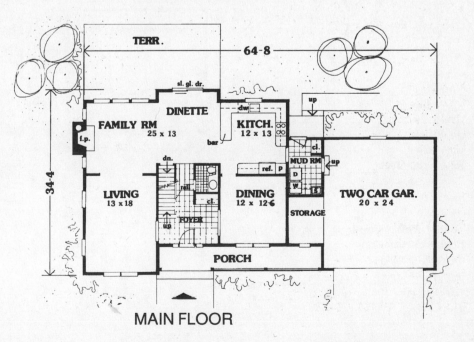

MAIN FLOOR

TO ORDER THIS BLUEPRINT,
CALL TOLL-FREE 1-800-820-1283

Plan AHP-9402

PRICES AND DETAILS
ON PAGES 12-15

189

Victorian Touches

- A huge covered porch and fishscale shingles bring Victorian elements to the facade of this country-style home.
- The spacious foyer leads to the formal living and dining rooms on either side.
- The informal living areas flow together at the back of the home for easy entertaining.
- The island kitchen features a pantry and a bright corner sink. The oversized, bayed dinette offers sliding glass doors to the backyard.
- The sunken family room boasts a rear window wall and a large fireplace.
- Upstairs, the master suite offers a private bath with corner whirlpool tub, a separate shower and a dual-sink vanity. The two remaining bedrooms share a hall bath.
- A large bonus room over the garage could be used as a hobby area, home office or playroom.
- Central to the upper floor is an inviting sitting area with lovely oval window.

Plan PI-91-567

Bedrooms: 3+	Baths: 2½
Living Area:	
Upper floor	1,194 sq. ft.
Main floor	1,258 sq. ft.
Bonus room	369 sq. ft.
Total Living Area:	**2,821 sq. ft.**
Standard basement	1,244 sq. ft.
Garage	672 sq. ft.
Exterior Wall Framing:	2x6

Foundation Options:

Standard basement

(Typical foundation & framing conversion diagram available—see order form.)

BLUEPRINT PRICE CODE: D

UPPER FLOOR

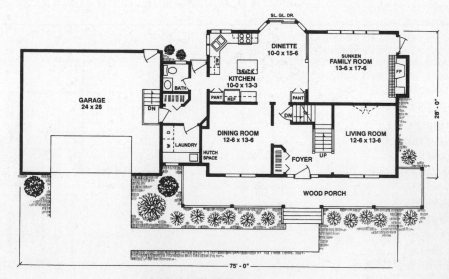

MAIN FLOOR

Plan PI-91-567

PRICES AND DETAILS
ON PAGES 12-15

Elegant Simplicity

- From the covered front porch to the main-floor master suite, this simple yet elegant home is filled with surprises.
- The vaulted dining room is graced by arched openings leading from the vaulted foyer and the family room.
- A sunny breakfast nook overlooks the vaulted family room and floods the kitchen with light.
- The family room offers a rear window wall, an inviting fireplace and built-in shelving topped by attention-getting plant shelves.
- The main-floor master suite includes an elegant tray ceiling and a vaulted bath with an oval whirlpool tub and an adjacent shower.
- A beautiful open staircase leads to the upper floor with a balcony overlook. Also included are two large bedrooms, each with a walk-in closet, plus an optional bonus space.

Plan FB-5019-WAVE

Bedrooms: 3	Baths: 2½
Living Area:	
Upper floor	502 sq. ft.
Main floor	1,414 sq. ft.
Bonus room	208 sq. ft.
Total Living Area:	**2,124 sq. ft.**
Daylight basement	1,414 sq. ft.
Garage	420 sq. ft.
Storage	28 sq. ft.
Exterior Wall Framing:	2x4

Foundation Options:
Daylight basement
(Typical foundation & framing conversion diagram available—see order form.)

BLUEPRINT PRICE CODE: **C**

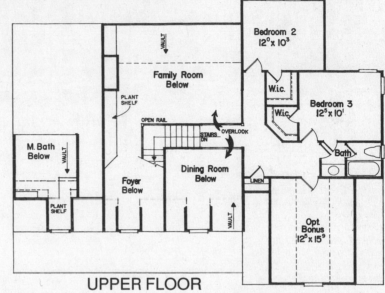

UPPER FLOOR

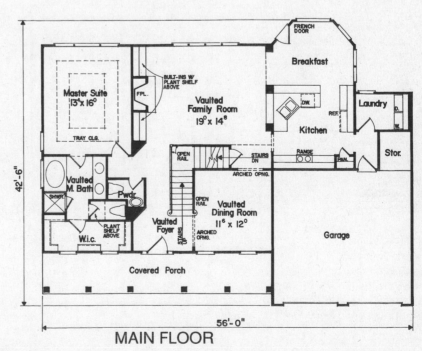

MAIN FLOOR

TO ORDER THIS BLUEPRINT,
CALL TOLL-FREE 1-800-820-1283

Plan FB-5019-WAVE

PRICES AND DETAILS
ON PAGES 12-15

191

Surprises at Every Angle

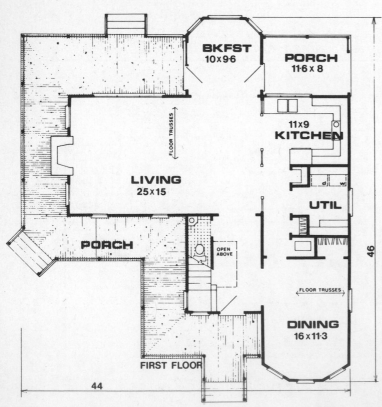

BKFST 10 x 9-6

PORCH 11-6 x 8

11 x 9 **KITCHEN**

LIVING 25 x 15

PORCH

OPEN ABOVE

FLOOR TRUSSES

UTIL

46

DINING 16 x 11-3

FLOOR TRUSSES

FIRST FLOOR

44

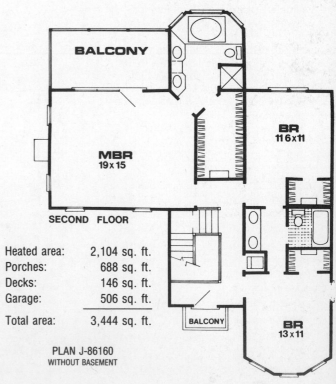

BALCONY

MBR 19 x 15

BR 11-6 x 11

SECOND FLOOR

BALCONY

BR 13 x 11

Heated area: 2,104 sq. ft.
Porches: 688 sq. ft.
Decks: 146 sq. ft.
Garage: 506 sq. ft.
─────────────────────
Total area: 3,444 sq. ft.

PLAN J-86160
WITHOUT BASEMENT

Blueprint Price Code C

Plan J-86160

TO ORDER THIS BLUEPRINT,
CALL TOLL-FREE 1-800-820-1283

PRICES AND DETAILS
ON PAGES 12-15

Traditional Treat

- A covered front porch and ornamental columns and brackets make this two-story a traditional treat.

- The airy 17-ft. vaulted foyer is open to the upper floor and may be viewed from a dramatic bridge above.

- Arched, columned openings set off the living room and the adjoining formal dining room. The living room also shows off a beautiful fireplace.

- The kitchen and the adjacent informal spaces may be closed off from the dining room and the main hallway with pocket doors. The kitchen offers a functional cooktop island/snack bar. A corner window brightens the breakfast nook.

- The fabulous family room features a warm woodstove and a French door to the backyard patio.

- Double doors keep the den or guest room quiet and private.

- The upper floor includes four more bedrooms and two full baths. The master bath boasts a relaxing spa tub.

Plan CDG-2026

Bedrooms: 4+	Baths: 2½
Living Area:	
Upper floor	1,089 sq. ft.
Main floor	1,295 sq. ft.
Total Living Area:	**2,384 sq. ft.**
Daylight basement	1,233 sq. ft.
Garage	452 sq. ft.
Exterior Wall Framing:	2x6

Foundation Options:

Daylight basement

Crawlspace

(All plans can be built with your choice of foundation and framing. A generic conversion diagram is available. See order form.)

BLUEPRINT PRICE CODE: C

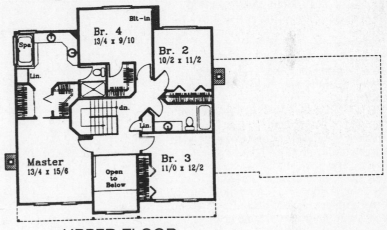

UPPER FLOOR

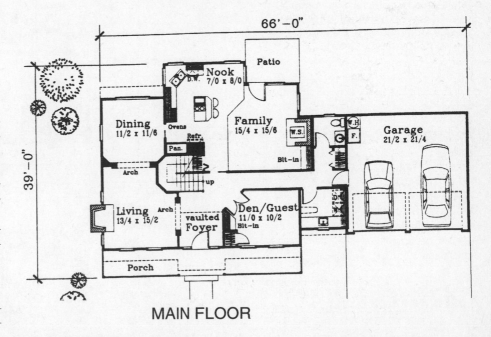

MAIN FLOOR

TO ORDER THIS BLUEPRINT,
CALL TOLL-FREE 1-800-820-1283

Plan CDG-2026

PRICES AND DETAILS
ON PAGES 12-15

193

Open Country

- With its covered porch and shutters, this home exudes country styling outside and offers an open, expansive interior.
- The two-story entry flows between the formal spaces, and an open-railed stairway overlooks the family room.
- The raised ceiling extends into the central family room, where windows flank a soothing fireplace.
- The open kitchen is a chef's dream, with its central work island, storage room and pantry. Its angled counter allows service to the family room and the breakfast nook. The nook includes a corner window seat and backyard access.
- Nearby, a door opens from the garage, and a utility area has room for a freezer.
- The main-floor master suite boasts a huge, divided walk-in closet, dual vanities and a garden tub.
- The upper floor includes two more bedrooms and a second full bath. A bonus room allows space for another bedroom or a home studio.

Plan RD-2168

Bedrooms: 3+	Baths: 2½
Living Area:	
Upper floor	521 sq. ft.
Main floor	1,647 sq. ft.
Bonus room	240 sq. ft.
Total Living Area:	**2,408 sq. ft.**
Standard basement	1,639 sq. ft.
Garage and storage	576 sq. ft.
Exterior Wall Framing:	2x4

Foundation Options:
Standard basement
Crawlspace
Slab

(All plans can be built with your choice of foundation and framing. A generic conversion diagram is available. See order form.)

BLUEPRINT PRICE CODE: C

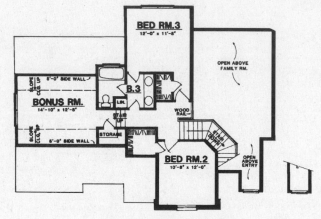

UPPER FLOOR

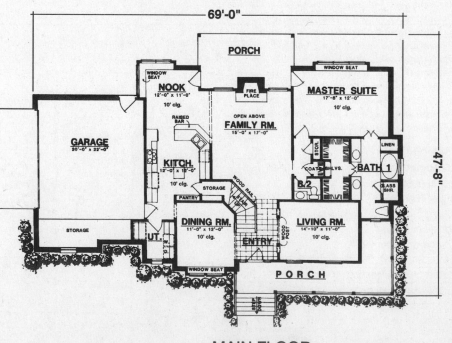

MAIN FLOOR

TO ORDER THIS BLUEPRINT,
CALL TOLL-FREE 1-800-820-1283

Plan RD-2168

PRICES AND DETAILS
ON PAGES 12-15

Colonial-Style Farmhouse

- This gracious farmhouse is enhanced by authentic Colonial styling.
- The inviting covered porch welcomes guests into the central foyer, where a beautiful curved stairway ascends to the upper floor.
- On the left, the living room is large enough to host any occasion. On the right, the formal dining room is easily served by the galley-style kitchen.
- The adjoining dinette is the perfect spot for casual meals, with a view to the outdoors. A half-bath is nearby.
- The informal family room features an exposed-beam ceiling, wood paneling and a brick fireplace wall. Sliding glass doors open to a large patio.
- A decorative railing and a planter adorn the upper-floor balcony, which overlooks the foyer below.
- The quiet master bedroom boasts a private bath and a walk-in closet. A second full bath with two sinks serves the remaining three bedrooms.

Plan HFL-1010-CR

Bedrooms: 4	Baths: 2½
Living Area:	
Upper floor	932 sq. ft.
Main floor	1,099 sq. ft.
Total Living Area:	**2,031 sq. ft.**
Standard basement	998 sq. ft.
Garage and storage	476 sq. ft.
Exterior Wall Framing:	2x4

Foundation Options:
Standard basement
Slab
(All plans can be built with your choice of foundation and framing. A generic conversion diagram is available. See order form.)

BLUEPRINT PRICE CODE: C

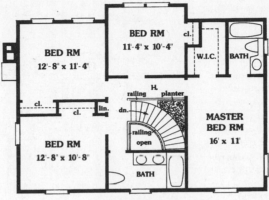

UPPER FLOOR

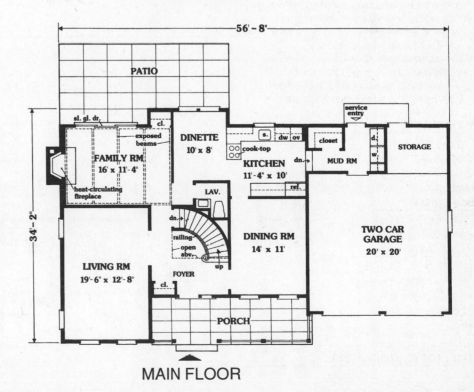

MAIN FLOOR

Good Looks, Great Design

- An enchanting exterior coupled with a super-efficient floor plan make this a great design.
- With only a little more than 1,500 sq. ft., the home offers three bedrooms and 1½ baths, plus the option of having either a laundry room or a second full bath on the upper floor.
- The first floor is laid out to maximize space. The appealing Great Room flows into the bayed dinette and U-shaped kitchen to create one large, comfortable living area.
- A formal dining room, an accommodating foyer, a mud room and a powder room round out the first floor.
- The upper level is available with two different floor plans (both are provided in the blueprints). In addition to three large bedrooms, one option offers an upstairs laundry room and a full bath. The second option includes two full baths, one of which is private to the master bedroom.

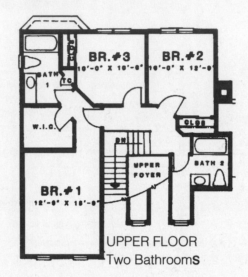

UPPER FLOOR
Two Bathroom**s**

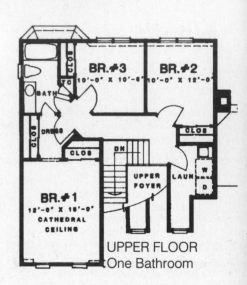

UPPER FLOOR
One Bathroom

Plan A-2259-DS

Bedrooms: 3	Baths: 1½-2½
Space:	
Upper floor	726/742 sq. ft.
Main floor	792 sq. ft.
Total Living Area	**1,518/1,534 sq. ft.**
Basement	792 sq. ft.
Garage	484 sq. ft.
Exterior Wall Framing	**2x6**
Foundation options:	
Standard Basement	
(Foundation & framing conversion diagram available—see order form.)	
Blueprint Price Code	**B**

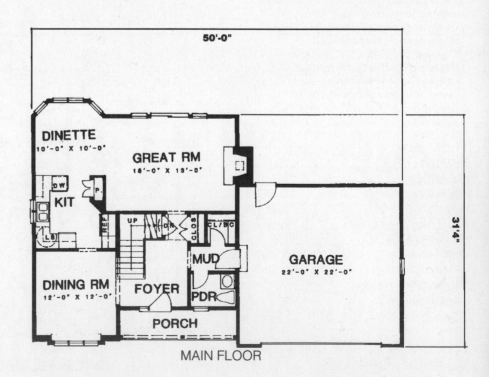

MAIN FLOOR

Plan A-2259-DS

PRICES AND DETAILS ON PAGES 12-15

Neatly Arranged

- Four bedrooms and good-sized living areas are found in this well-planned compact home.
- Off the foyer and open to the upper floor, the skylighted living room boasts a 16-ft.-high cathedral ceiling. The living room flows into the dining room, for plenty of entertainment space.
- The expansive family room features a large masonry fireplace and easy outdoor access through sliding glass doors. Over a half-wall, a wide bay window enhances the inviting country kitchen. A pantry, a washer/dryer and extra storage space are provided in the adjoining utility room.
- Also on the main floor, the secluded master suite offers a skylighted bath and a separate dressing area.
- Three additional bedrooms and a second full bath share the upper floor. More storage space and a balcony overlooking the living room are also featured.

Plan AX-8817-A

Bedrooms: 4	Baths: 2½
Living Area:	
Upper floor	600 sq. ft.
Main floor	1,110 sq. ft.
Total Living Area:	**1,710 sq. ft.**
Standard basement	1,110 sq. ft.
One-car garage	240 sq. ft.
Optional two-car garage	413 sq. ft.
Exterior Wall Framing:	2x4

Foundation Options:

Standard basement
Slab

(All plans can be built with your choice of foundation and framing. A generic conversion diagram is available. See order form.)

BLUEPRINT PRICE CODE:	B

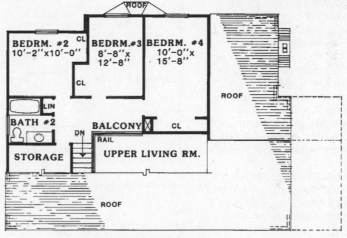

UPPER FLOOR

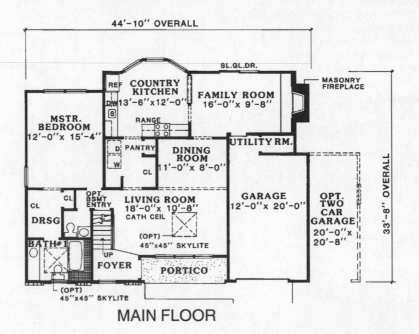

MAIN FLOOR

TO ORDER THIS BLUEPRINT,
CALL TOLL-FREE 1-800-820-1283

Plan AX-8817-A

PRICES AND DETAILS
ON PAGES 12-15

197

Farmhouse with Style

- Modern rooflines and arched window treatments dress up this farmhouse-styled home.
- A skylit, cathedral-ceilinged foyer opens to the upper level. It is flanked by a formal dining room and a sunken living room with cathedral ceiling.
- Merging with the living room is a sunken family room with a huge fireplace and sliders that access an attached rear deck.
- A massive island kitchen adjoins a breakfast area with a rear deck view and a pantry. A nearby half-bath and a laundry room buffer the garage entrance.
- The upper level houses the large master bedroom with a cathedral ceiling and large dressing area. The private bath features a circular tub, separate shower and skylit vanity area.
- Three additional bedrooms and a second full bath complete this level.

Plan AX-9032

Bedrooms: 4	Baths: 2 ½
Space:	
Upper floor	1,181 sq. ft.
Main floor	1,240 sq. ft.
Total Living Area	**2,421 sq. ft.**
Basement	1,240 sq. ft.
Garage	493 sq. ft.
Exterior Wall Framing	2x4

Foundation options:

Standard Basement

Slab

(Foundation & framing conversion diagram available—see order form.)

Blueprint Price Code	C

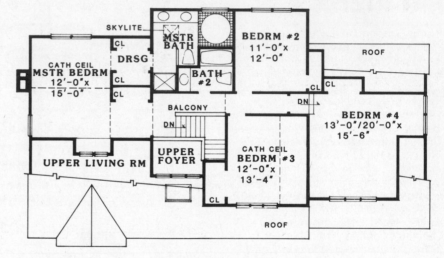

UPPER FLOOR

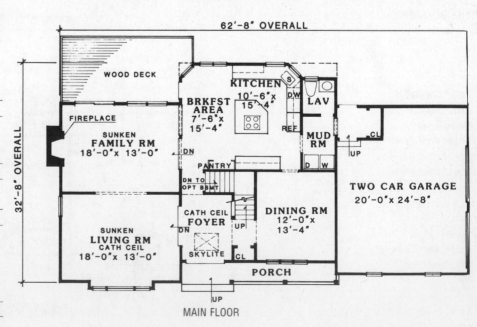

MAIN FLOOR

Plan AX-9032

PRICES AND DETAILS ON PAGES 12-15

Warm, Friendly and Inviting

- This two-story plan offers a nostalgic front porch, multiple gables, divided windows and lap siding, lending a warm, friendly and inviting feeling to the home.
- The volume entry gives an immediate sense of spaciousness, as it flows between the formal areas, which are set off by columns rather than solid walls.
- The entire rear of the main floor is devoted to informal family living with a cozy fireplace, an island cooktop and a sunny breakfast room with deck access.
- The four upstairs bedrooms include a lavish master suite complete with a stunning, spacious private bath.
- The three additional bedrooms share another full bath and a laundry room.

Plan UDG-90013

Bedrooms: 4	Baths: 2½
Living Area:	
Upper floor	1,248 sq. ft.
Main floor	1,059 sq. ft.
Total Living Area:	**2,307 sq. ft.**
Standard basement	1,059 sq. ft.
Garage	460 sq. ft.
Exterior Wall Framing:	2x6

Foundation Options:

Standard basement
(All plans can be built with your choice of foundation and framing. A generic conversion diagram is available. See order form.)

BLUEPRINT PRICE CODE:	C

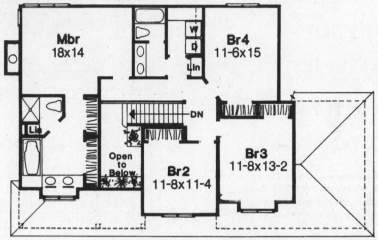

UPPER FLOOR

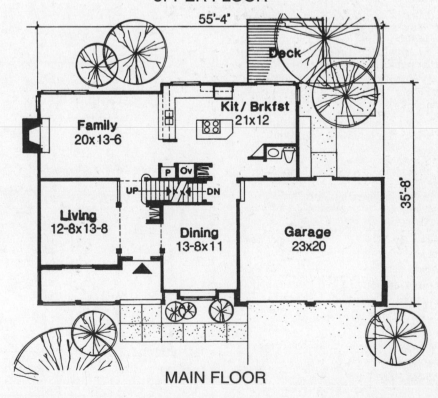

MAIN FLOOR

Country-Style Comfort

The large front porch and charming window treatments give added appeal to this country-style design. Inside, the vaulted foyer leads to the luxurious master bedroom, the dining room, or the Great Room at the rear of the home.

The Great Room features vaulted ceilings, with exposed beams and a balcony above lending a rustic feel. A raised-hearth fireplace, built-in wet bar and access to a backyard deck add extra livability and comfort. The adjoining breakfast room is brightened by a bay window, and a breakfast bar supplements the formal eating area.

The master suite includes a walk-in closet, oversized vanity, and a garden tub. Vaulted ceilings highlight the bathing area, which also features a large linen closet and a shower.

An open stairway leads to the second floor, with views of the Great Room below. Each of the upstairs bedrooms has a walk-in closet, plus there's a large storage room for overflow. A full bath completes the second floor.

First floor:	1,494 sq. ft.
Second floor:	853 sq. ft.
Total living area:	2,347 sq. ft.
(Not counting basement or garage)	
Basement:	897 sq. ft.
Garage:	484 sq. ft.
Porch:	250 sq. ft.
Deck:	200 sq. ft.

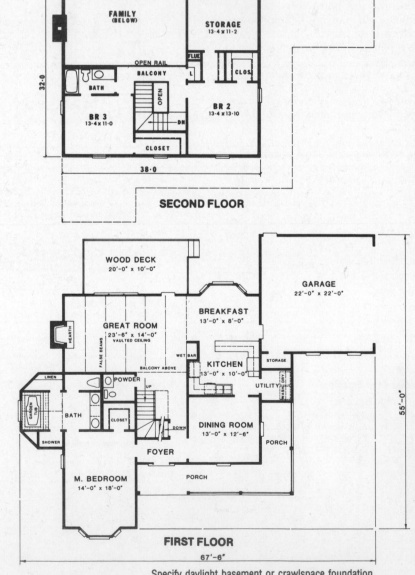

SECOND FLOOR

FIRST FLOOR

Specify daylight basement or crawlspace foundation.

Blueprint Price Code C

Plan C-8655

A Natural Setting

- The large front porch of this traditionally styled home offers a warm accent to its durable stone exterior.

- The open and informal interior has a country feel.
- The spacious living and dining rooms allow for good traffic flow and large get-togethers. A fireplace, sloped ceilings open to the balcony above, and rear views to the large deck make this a perfect conversation area.
- A modern island kitchen and a sunny morning room are separated by a pantry and a counter bar.
- Privacy and relaxation are found in the master suite at one end of the home; the private sitting area has a cozy fireplace and a lovely corner window. The master bath offers a huge tub, a separate shower and twin vanities.
- A third bedroom and optional bonus space are found on the upper level.

UPPER FLOOR

BONUS SPACE · GALLERY

BEDROOM 3
14⁴ X 14²

BATH 3 · LINEN

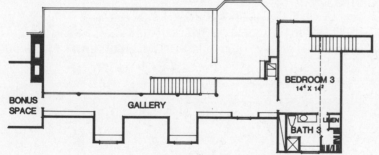

MAIN FLOOR

99⁰

52⁶

DECK

BEDROOM 2
17⁰ X 12⁰

BATH 2

MORNING
12⁰ X 14⁰

UTIL.

SITTING
11⁰ X 14⁰

LIVING
27⁴ X 19⁰

DINING
12⁰ X 15⁴

PANTRY

MASTER SUITE
15⁴ X 15⁰

FOYER

LOGGIA

ISLAND KITCHEN
14⁴ X 17⁰

GARAGE
21⁴ X 23⁰

M. BATH

PORCH

PWDR.

Plan DD-3467	
Bedrooms: 3	**Baths:** 3½
Living Area:	
Upper floor	822 sq. ft.
Main floor	2,645 sq. ft.
Bonus space	215 sq. ft.
Total Living Area:	**3,682 sq. ft.**
Basement	2,645 sq. ft.
Garage	491 sq. ft.
Exterior Wall Framing:	2x4

Foundation Options:
Standard basement
Crawlspace
Slab
(Typical foundation & framing conversion diagram available—see order form.)

BLUEPRINT PRICE CODE: **F**

Tradition Rekindled

- Stylish half-round windows and a quaint front porch rekindle family tradition in this warm country home.
- The porch opens to a spacious living and dining room combination that unfolds to the rest of the main floor. The open railing to the left provides a view of the stairway to the upper floor.
- Beyond the living room, an angled hallway flows past a convenient powder room and the luxurious master suite to the informal spaces.

- The comfortable family room features a 17-ft. vaulted ceiling and sliding glass doors that open to a covered patio.
- The kitchen's handy pass-through allows easy transporting of food and beverages into the family room. If desired, the opening could be closed off with bi-fold doors. A pantry and a sunny breakfast nook are also featured.
- The quiet master suite boasts a walk-in closet and a private bath with a spa tub.
- Off the upper-floor balcony are two nice-sized bedrooms, a full bath and a dramatic view into the family room.
- The optional bonus room above the garage could be finished and tailored to your needs.

Plan S-11993

Bedrooms: 3+	**Baths:** 2½

Living Area:	
Upper floor	489 sq. ft.
Main floor	1,128 sq. ft.
Total Living Area:	**1,617 sq. ft.**
Optional bonus room	256 sq. ft.
Standard basement	1,128 sq. ft.
Garage and shop	488 sq. ft.
Exterior Wall Framing:	2x6

Foundation Options:

Standard basement

Crawlspace

Slab

(All plans can be built with your choice of foundation and framing. A generic conversion diagram is available. See order form.)

BLUEPRINT PRICE CODE:	B

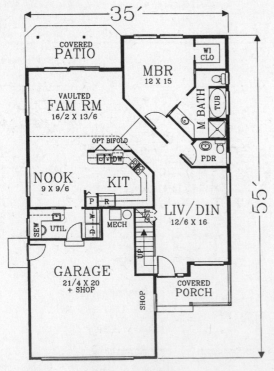

MAIN FLOOR

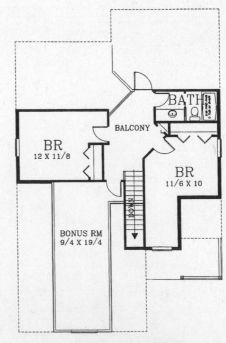

UPPER FLOOR

Plan S-11993

TO ORDER THIS BLUEPRINT, CALL TOLL-FREE 1-800-820-1283

PRICES AND DETAILS ON PAGES 12-15

Fantastic Farmhouse

- Endless amenities are found in this exciting two-story.
- The vaulted entry opens to a den or study, a formal living room with raised ceiling and the island kitchen and breakfast area to the rear.
- The adjoining rear deck and vaulted sun room provide outdoor excitement.
- The large family room offers a fireplace, corner windows and refreshing wet bar.
- Laundry facilities are conveniently located on the upper level with the three bedrooms; the master has vaulted ceiling, plant shelf and dual walk-in closets.

Plan UDG-91005

Bedrooms: 3-4	Baths: 2 ½
Space:	
Upper floor	1,015 sq. ft.
Main floor	1,336 sq. ft.
Total Living Area	**2,351 sq. ft.**
Basement	1,336 sq. ft.
Garage	504 sq. ft.
Exterior Wall Framing	2x4

Foundation options:

Standard Basement

(Foundation & framing conversion diagram available—see order form.)

Blueprint Price Code	C

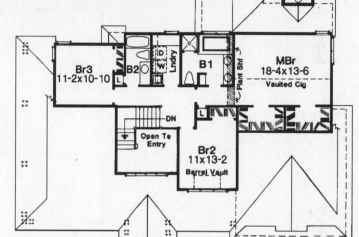

UPPER FLOOR

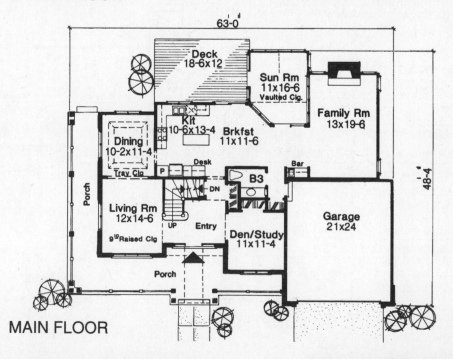

MAIN FLOOR

Warm Rural Feel

- Round-top windows, a wrap-around covered porch and brick chimney give a warm rural feel to this innovative plan.
- The entry opens to the spacious living room with fireplace and soaring ceiling, leading the eye up the stairs to the second floor family room with dormer and balcony.
- The kitchen overlooks the dining room, with French doors to the side porch.
- Two secondary bedrooms are located on the main level, while the lavish master suite with dormered sitting area and private bath is on the second level.

Plan NW-297

Bedrooms: 3	Baths: 2

Space:

Upper floor:	663 sq. ft.
Main floor:	1,470 sq. ft.
Total living area:	**2,133 sq. ft.**
Exterior Wall Framing:	**2x6**

Foundation options:
Crawlspace.
(Foundation & framing conversion diagram available — see order form.)

Blueprint Price Code: C

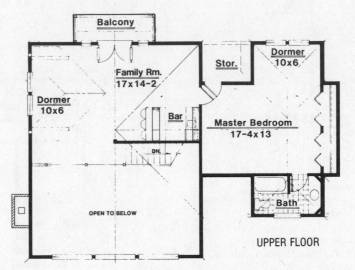

UPPER FLOOR

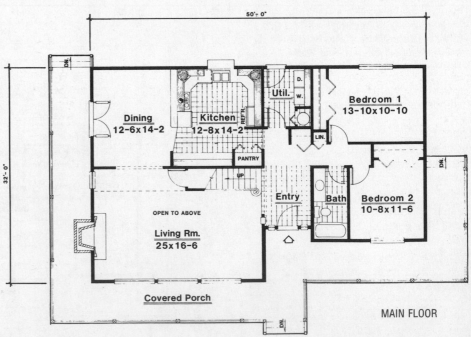

MAIN FLOOR

TO ORDER THIS BLUEPRINT, CALL TOLL-FREE 1-800-820-1283

Plan NW-297

PRICES AND DETAILS ON PAGES 12-15

Surprising Features!

- The exciting exterior of this charming home reflects traditional country style, while its enticing interior is filled with surprising luxurious features.
- The bright foyer boasts a 17-ft. vaulted ceiling highlighted by a high plant shelf set into a classy dormer.
- The adjacent formal dining room enjoys an elegant 10 ft., 10-in. tray ceiling.
- The efficient galley-style kitchen includes a pantry and a sunny breakfast area. A powder room and a laundry closet are nearby.
- Graced by a 17-ft. vaulted ceiling, the Great Room offers a fireplace and a French door to the backyard.
- The deluxe master suite features a 9½-ft. tray ceiling. The master bath has a 13-ft. vaulted ceiling and offers a spa tub, a separate shower and a dual-sink vanity.
- Upstairs, a second full bath is shared by two additional bedrooms. The bonus room may be finished as an extra bedroom, a den or a playroom.

Plan FB-5231-NAPL

Bedrooms: 3+	Baths: 2½
Living Area:	
Upper floor	435 sq. ft.
Main floor	1,065 sq. ft.
Bonus room	175 sq. ft.
Total Living Area:	**1,675 sq. ft.**
Daylight basement	1,065 sq. ft.
Garage and storage	458 sq. ft.
Exterior Wall Framing:	2x4

Foundation Options:

Daylight basement

(All plans can be built with your choice of foundation and framing. A generic conversion diagram is available. See order form.)

BLUEPRINT PRICE CODE: B

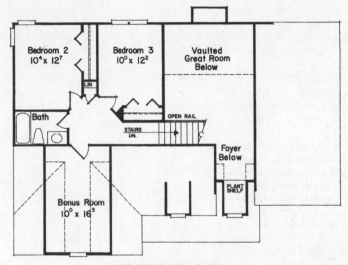

UPPER FLOOR

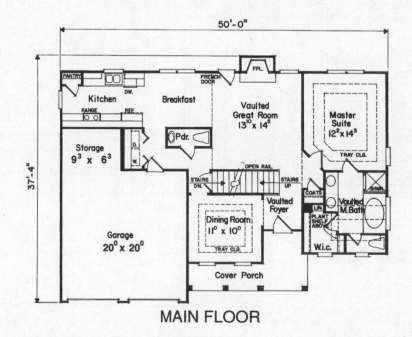

MAIN FLOOR

TO ORDER THIS BLUEPRINT,
CALL TOLL-FREE 1-800-820-1283

Plan FB-5231-NAPL

PRICES AND DETAILS
ON PAGES 12-15

205

Traditional Charmer with Lots of Space

- This plan is loaded with charming traditional design elements, including a cozy gazebo attached to the veranda sweeping across the front of the house.
- Inside, a spacious foyer leads guests to a formal living room on the left or a dining room on the right.
- A large study can be utilized for strictly private pursuits or can be used for extra entertaining space when needed for large groups.
- The family room, kitchen and dinette combine to create an expansive area for casual family living.
- The second floor master suite is luxurious, and includes a splendid bath and large closet.
- Three secondary bedrooms, another full bath, a balcony, loft and storage area complete the second floor.

Plan GL-3027

Bedrooms: 4	Baths: 2½

Space:

Upper floor:	1,400 sq. ft.
Main floor:	1,627 sq. ft.
Total living area:	**3,027 sq. ft.**
Basement:	1,627 sq. ft.
Garage:	529 sq. ft.

Exterior Wall Framing:	2x4

Foundation options:
Standard basement only.
(Foundation & framing conversion diagram available — see order form.)

Blueprint Price Code:	E

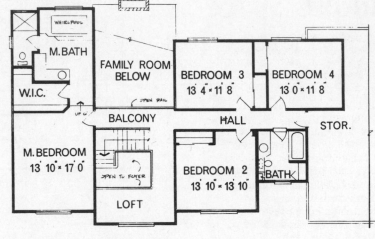

UPPER FLOOR

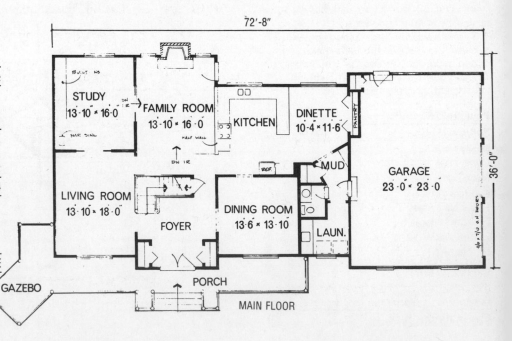

MAIN FLOOR

Plan GL-3027

PRICES AND DETAILS
ON PAGES 12-15

Luxurious Space

- This design manages to look both cozy and impressive at the same time, with its covered porch, gables and large divided-pane windows.
- The interior is loaded with features, starting with the interesting angled foyer area which provides easy access to all parts of the home.
- The large and interesting kitchen/breakfast/family room area provides abundant space for family activities and household tasks, especially with the adjacent laundry/mudroom area.
- The formal living room boasts a vaulted ceiling, fireplace and bright windows at two corners.
- Upstairs, a gorgeous master suite includes a private master bath with a skylight, and a large closet.
- Two other bedrooms share another full bath. The second floor also features a den or fourth bedroom as well as a loft area which can be used as a sitting room, library, playroom or studio.

Plan B-87115-L

Bedrooms: 3-4	Baths: 2½
Space:	
Upper floor	1,186 sq. ft.
Main floor	1,369 sq. ft.
Total Living Area	**2,555 sq. ft.**
Basement	1,369 sq. ft.
Garage	572 sq. ft.
Exterior Wall Framing	2x4

Foundation options:

Standard Basement
(Foundation & framing conversion diagram available — see order form.)

Blueprint Price Code	D

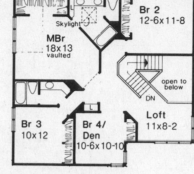

UPPER FLOOR

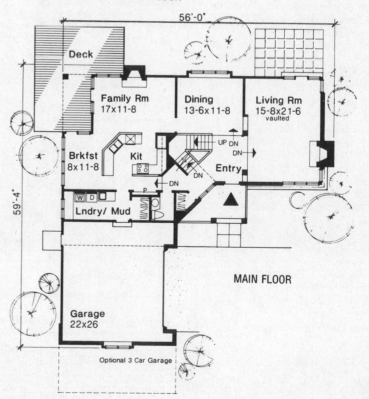

MAIN FLOOR

TO ORDER THIS BLUEPRINT,
CALL TOLL-FREE 1-800-820-1283

Plan B-87115-L

PRICES AND DETAILS
ON PAGES 12-15

207

Family Living with a Flair

- Dormer windows and an inviting front porch give this four-bedroom home its warm, country appeal. That warmth is carried inside, where the spacious rooms are well integrated to create an elegant yet cordial atmosphere.
- The vaulted entry soars to a height of 17 feet, which is further emphasized by the beautiful open stairway. The upstairs balcony overlooks the foyer, and a plant shelf is tucked into the alcove of the dormer window above.
- The well-planned entry hall leads to the formal living spaces on the left side of the home. The living room features a focal-point fireplace and an archway to the dining room. To the right of the entry hall French doors open to a secluded den that includes built-in bookshelves. A bath is close by.
- The informal living area is sure to be a family favorite. The large country kitchen and nook are angled out toward the backyard and open to the family room for casual everyday living. An island counter separates the kitchen and nook from the family room, which is highlighted by a wood stove.
- Upstairs, the centrally located laundry room is a real treat. The master suite is a private haven, with its sumptuous spa bath. The two front-facing bedrooms feature cozy window seats. A full bath and another bedroom round out the second floor.

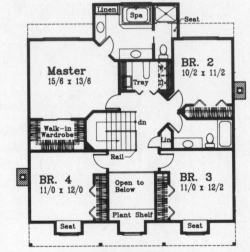

UPPER FLOOR

Plan CDG-2029	
Bedrooms: 4-5	**Baths:** 3
Space:	
Upper floor	1,144 sq. ft.
Main floor	1,222 sq. ft.
Total Living Area	**2,366 sq. ft.**
Garage	494 sq. ft.
Exterior Wall Framing	2x4
Foundation options:	
Crawlspace	
(Foundation & framing conversion diagram available—see order form.)	
Blueprint Price Code	C

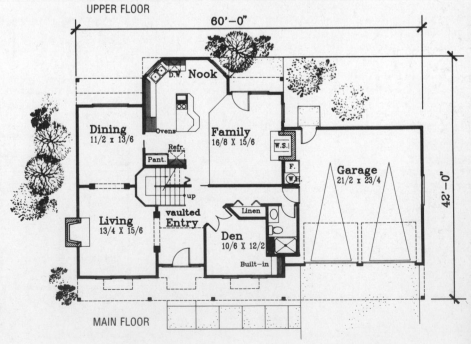

MAIN FLOOR

Plan CDG-2029

New Traditional

- A lovely front porch and an open floor plan give this new traditional its modern appeal.
- The foyer opens to a fabulous living room with a 16-ft. vaulted ceiling, a fireplace and an open staircase. Railings introduce the bayed breakfast area. The efficient galley-style kitchen leads to a covered back porch.
- The sizable master suite is enhanced by a 10-ft. raised ceiling and a cozy bay window. The compartmentalized bath includes a dual-sink vanity and a walk-in closet. Another bedroom is nearby, along with a convenient laundry closet.
- Upstairs, a third bedroom has private access to a full bath. A large future area provides expansion space.

Plan J-8636

Bedrooms: 3	Baths: 3
Living Area:	
Upper floor	270 sq. ft.
Main floor	1,253 sq. ft.
Bonus room	270 sq. ft.
Total Living Area:	**1,793 sq. ft.**
Standard basement	1,287 sq. ft.
Garage	390 sq. ft.
Exterior Wall Framing:	2x4

Foundation Options:

Standard basement

Crawlspace

Slab

(All plans can be built with your choice of foundation and framing. A generic conversion diagram is available. See order form.)

BLUEPRINT PRICE CODE: B

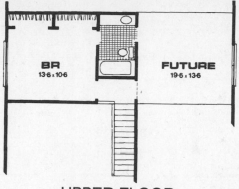

UPPER FLOOR

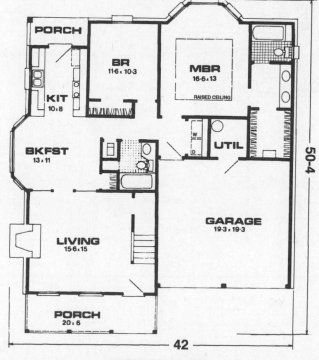

MAIN FLOOR

Quaint Country Design

- The renewed "country" look is evident in this simply designed two-story with wrap-around front porch.
- Functional living areas flank the entryway and stairs.
- A beautiful and spacious Great Room, with masonry fireplace and wrap-around windows, is to the left, and a nice-sized den which could serve as a library, office, guest room or fourth bedroom is to the right.
- The kitchen is a lovely space with two separate areas, an efficient work area and a distinct bay windowed dining area with center door leading to the rear yard.
- The second floor includes a master bedroom with full private bath and two large closets, plus two secondary bedrooms.

Plan AX-89311

Bedrooms: 3	Baths: 2½

Space:	
Upper floor:	736 sq. ft.
Main floor:	1,021 sq. ft.

Total living area:	**1,757 sq. ft.**
Basement:	approx. 1,021 sq. ft.
Garage:	440 sq. ft.

Exterior Wall Framing:	2x4

Foundation options:
Standard basement.
Slab.
(Foundation & framing conversion diagram available — see order form.)

Blueprint Price Code:	B

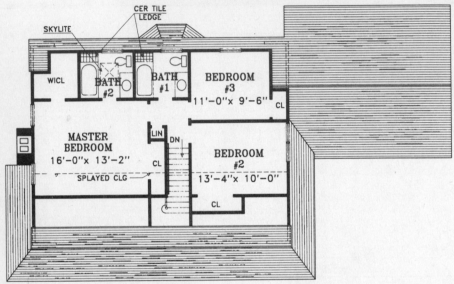

UPPER FLOOR

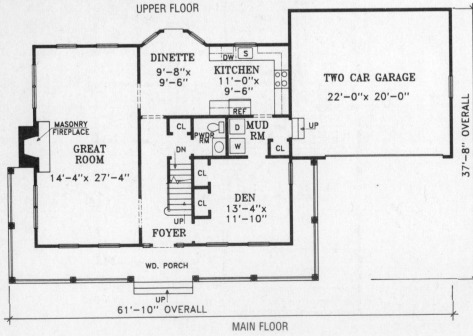

MAIN FLOOR

TO ORDER THIS BLUEPRINT, CALL TOLL-FREE 1-800-820-1283   Plan AX-89311   *PRICES AND DETAILS ON PAGES 12-15*

Cozy and Compact

- While cozy and compact, this design proves that small can be beautiful and comfortable as well.
- A covered entry porch leads into the spacious living and dining rooms, which flow together for plenty of entertaining space. The living room's two-story-high ceiling shows off the balcony above.
- The open, walk-through kitchen extends an angled serving counter to the living and dining rooms.
- A laundry closet and an outside storage area are nearby.
- The master suite is a quiet retreat, complete with a bayed sitting area. Other features include a walk-in closet and private access to the hall bath.
- Upstairs, a roomy balcony/bedroom has its own bath and offers views into the living room below.

Plan E-1007

Bedrooms: 1+	Baths: 2
Living Area:	
Upper floor	208 sq. ft.
Main floor	811 sq. ft.
Total Living Area:	**1,019 sq. ft.**
Standard basement	811 sq. ft.
Storage	15 sq. ft.
Exterior Wall Framing:	2x4

Foundation Options:
Standard basement
Crawlspace
Slab
(All plans can be built with your choice of foundation and framing. A generic conversion diagram is available. See order form.)

BLUEPRINT PRICE CODE: A

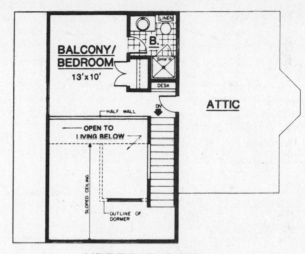

UPPER FLOOR

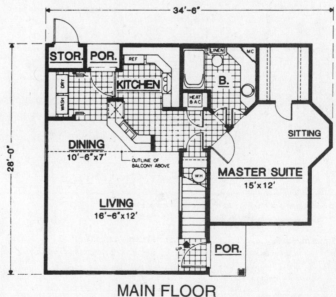

MAIN FLOOR

TO ORDER THIS BLUEPRINT,
CALL TOLL-FREE 1-800-820-1283

Plan E-1007

PRICES AND DETAILS
ON PAGES 12-15

211

Victorian Farmhouse

- Fish-scale shingles and horizontal siding team up with the detailed front porch to create a look of yesterday. Brickwork enriches the sides and rear of the home.
- The main level features 10-ft.-high ceilings throughout the central living space. The front-oriented formal areas merge with the family room via three sets of French doors.

- The island kitchen and skylighted eating area have 16-ft. sloped ceilings.
- A breezeway off the deck connects the house to a roomy workshop. A two-car garage is located under the workshop and a large utility room is just inside the rear entrance.
- The main-floor master suite offers an opulent skylighted bath with a garden vanity, a spa tub, a separate shower and an 18-ft.-high sloped ceiling.
- The upper floor offers three more bedrooms, two full baths and a balcony that looks to the backyard.

Plan E-3103

Bedrooms: 4	Baths: 3½
Living Area:	
Upper floor	1,113 sq. ft.
Main floor	2,040 sq. ft.
Total Living Area:	**3,153 sq. ft.**
Daylight basement	2,040 sq. ft.
Tuck-under garage and storage	580 sq. ft.
Workshop and storage	580 sq. ft.
Exterior Wall Framing:	2x6

Foundation Options:

Daylight basement
Crawlspace
Slab
(All plans can be built with your choice of foundation and framing. A generic conversion diagram is available. See order form.)

BLUEPRINT PRICE CODE:	E

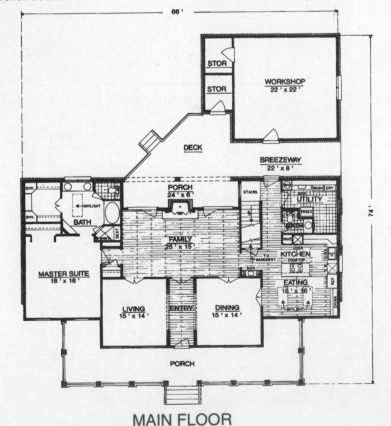

MAIN FLOOR

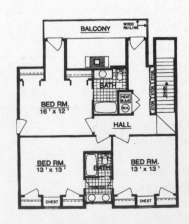

UPPER FLOOR

Plan E-3103
PRICES AND DETAILS
ON PAGES 12-15

Attractive and Cozy Cottage

- This cozy country cottage is attractive, economical and easy to build.
- A striking front door with oval glass and sidelights opens directly into the huge living room, which is warmed by a nice fireplace. French doors provide access to the expansive covered front porch.
- The dining room is brightened by a boxed-out area with lots of glass.
- The efficient kitchen includes a snack bar, a windowed sink and a lazy Susan.
- The quiet main-floor master bedroom offers porch access through French doors. The master bath boasts a garden tub, a separate shower, two vanities and a walk-in closet.
- A powder room and a convenient laundry room round out the main floor.
- Upstairs, two bedrooms share another full bath. Hall closets provide additional storage space.
- A storage area for outdoor equipment is offered in the secluded carport.

Plan J-86131

Bedrooms: 3	Baths: 2½
Living Area:	
Upper floor	500 sq. ft.
Main floor	1,369 sq. ft.
Total Living Area:	**1,869 sq. ft.**
Standard basement	1,369 sq. ft.
Carport and storage	540 sq. ft.
Exterior Wall Framing:	2x4

Foundation Options:

Standard basement

Crawlspace

Slab

(All plans can be built with your choice of foundation and framing. A generic conversion diagram is available. See order form.)

BLUEPRINT PRICE CODE:　　　　B

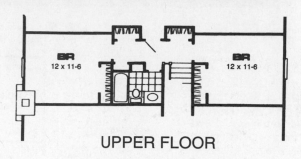

UPPER FLOOR

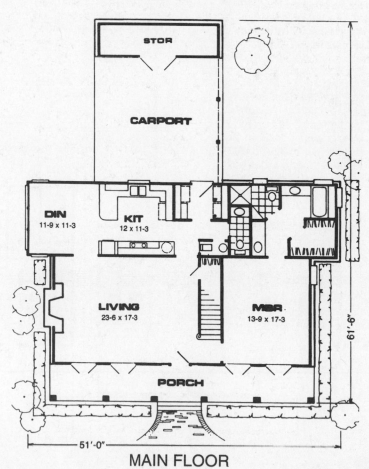

MAIN FLOOR

Warm, Rustic Appeal

- This quaint home has a warm, rustic appeal with a stone fireplace, paned windows and a covered front porch.
- Just off the two-story-high foyer, the living room hosts a raised-hearth fireplace and flows into the kitchen.
- The open L-shaped kitchen offers a pantry closet and a bright sink as it merges with the bayed dining room.
- The secluded master bedroom boasts a walk-in closet and a private bath with a dual-sink vanity. A laundry closet and access to a backyard deck are nearby.
- Upstairs, a hall balcony overlooks the foyer. A full bath serves two secondary bedrooms, each with a walk-in closet and access to extra storage space.
- Just off the dining room, a stairway descends to the daylight basement that contains the tuck-under garage.

Plan C-8339

Bedrooms: 3	Baths: 2
Living Area:	
Upper floor	660 sq. ft.
Main floor	1,100 sq. ft.
Total Living Area:	**1,760 sq. ft.**
Daylight basement/garage	1,100 sq. ft.
Exterior Wall Framing:	2x4

Foundation Options:

Daylight basement

(All plans can be built with your choice of foundation and framing. A generic conversion diagram is available. See order form.)

BLUEPRINT PRICE CODE: B

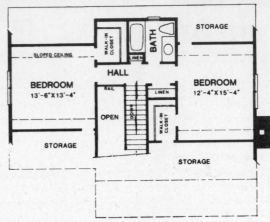

UPPER FLOOR

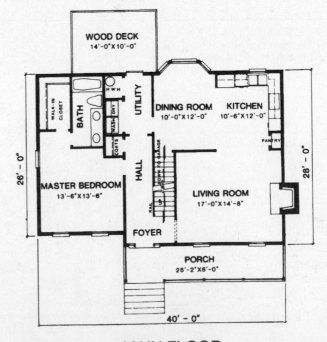

MAIN FLOOR

TO ORDER THIS BLUEPRINT, CALL TOLL-FREE 1-800-820-1283   Plan C-8339   *PRICES AND DETAILS ON PAGES 12-15*

Today's Tradition

- This two-story country home combines traditional standards with the exciting new designs of today.
- Visitors are welcomed by the wrap-around porch and the symmetrical bay windows of the living and dining rooms.
- The front half of the main floor lends itself to entertaining as the angled entry creates a flow between the formal areas.
- French doors lead from the living room to the spacious family room, which boasts a beamed ceiling, a warm fireplace and porch access.
- The super kitchen features an island cooktop with a snack bar. A nice-sized laundry room is nearby.
- The spacious upper level hosts a master suite with two walk-in closets and a large bath with a dual-sink vanity, a tub and a separate shower. Three more bedrooms share another full bath.

Plan AGH-2143

Bedrooms: 4	Baths: 2½
Living Area:	
Upper floor	1,047 sq. ft.
Main floor	1,096 sq. ft.
Total Living Area:	**2,143 sq. ft.**
Daylight basement	1,096 sq. ft.
Garage	852 sq. ft.
Exterior Wall Framing:	2x6

Foundation Options:

Daylight basement

(All plans can be built with your choice of foundation and framing. A generic conversion diagram is available. See order form.)

BLUEPRINT PRICE CODE:	C

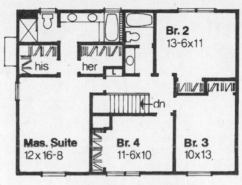

UPPER FLOOR

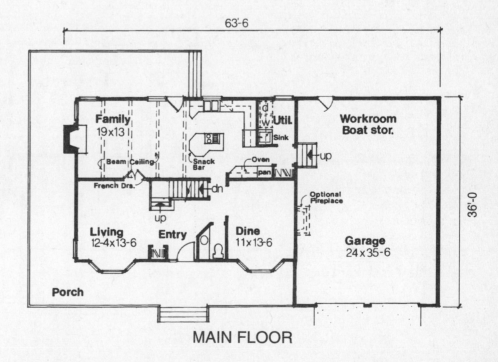

MAIN FLOOR

TO ORDER THIS BLUEPRINT,
CALL TOLL-FREE 1-800-820-1283

Plan AGH-2143

PRICES AND DETAILS
ON PAGES 12-15

215

Combining Past and Present

- This home combines the best from the past and the present. The shed roof is reminiscent of a New England saltbox, while the gabled dormers and half-circle windows recall the Victorian era.
- Inside, the cozy kitchen features an island cooktop and a breakfast counter. A built-in pantry and a china closet are centrally located between the dining room and the kitchen.

- The sunny nook is popular for everyday meals. The formal dining room offers a view to the living room over a railing.
- The sunken living room boasts a soaring 25-ft.-high vaulted ceiling, a nice fireplace and built-in shelves for an entertainment center. Sliding glass doors open to a backyard deck.
- The larger of the two main-floor bedrooms provides additional deck access. The full bath is conveniently located nearby.
- The upper floor is devoted to the master bedroom, which features a hydro-spa, a separate shower and a walk-in closet.

Plan H-1453-1A

Bedrooms: 3	Baths: 2
Living Area:	
Upper floor	386 sq. ft.
Main floor	1,385 sq. ft.
Total Living Area:	**1,771 sq. ft.**
Garage	438 sq. ft.
Exterior Wall Framing:	2x6

Foundation Options:

Crawlspace
(All plans can be built with your choice of foundation and framing. A generic conversion diagram is available. See order form.)

BLUEPRINT PRICE CODE: B

MAIN FLOOR

UPPER FLOOR

TO ORDER THIS BLUEPRINT, CALL TOLL-FREE 1-800-820-1283

Plan H-1453-1A

PRICES AND DETAILS ON PAGES 12-15

Simply Beautiful

Photo by Mark Englund/HomeStyles

- The beautiful symmetry of this home is marked by the double-door entry with overhead dormer windows and the full-width porch with columns and railings. The clean-cut lines of the design belie the home's 2,360 sq. ft. of luxurious living space.
- Guests are greeted by a two-story-high foyer that is flooded with light from the elegant, half-round dormer window above. Abundant closet space and a half-bath are just ahead.
- The home's spaciousness is enhanced by 9-ft. ceilings throughout the first floor. The large living room features a centrally located fireplace that can also be enjoyed from the adjoining dining room.
- Storage space is again well accounted for in the kitchen. An island cooktop counter is convenient to the full-glass nook. A French door in the nook opens to a covered porch for outdoor entertaining.
- An oversized utility room has plenty of space for a freezer, plus a clothes-folding table with extra storage below.
- The first-floor master suite is an appreciated feature, with an enticing master bath that includes a whirlpool tub, shower, dual vanities and a walk-in closet.
- The two spacious bedrooms upstairs share a compartmentalized bath.

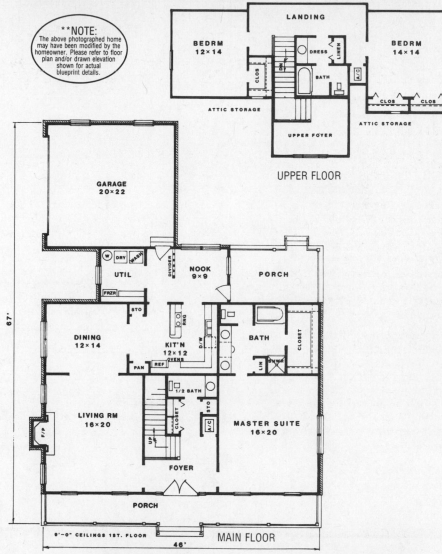

NOTE:
The above photographed home may have been modified by the homeowner. Please refer to floor plan and/or drawn elevation shown for actual blueprint details.

UPPER FLOOR

MAIN FLOOR

Plan VL-2360	
Bedrooms: 3	**Baths:** 2 ½
Space:	
Upper floor	683 sq. ft.
Main floor	1,677 sq. ft.
Total Living Area	**2,360 sq. ft.**
Garage	458 sq. ft.
Exterior Wall Framing	2x4
Foundation options:	
Crawlspace	
Slab	
(Foundation & framing conversion diagram available—see order form.)	
Blueprint Price Code	C

Up-to-Date Country Styling

- Nearly surrounded by a covered wood porch, this traditional 1,860-sq.-ft. farm-styled home is modernized for today's active, up-to-date family.
- Inside, the efficient floor plan promotes easy mobility with vast openness and a minimum of cross-traffic.
- The spacious living and dining area is warmed by a fireplace with a stone hearth; sliding glass doors off the dining room open to the porch.
- The U-shaped country kitchen is centrally located and overlooks a bright breakfast nook and a big family room with a woodstove and its own sliding glass doors to a patio.
- On the upper floor is a large master bedroom with corner windows, a dressing area and a private bath. Two secondary bedrooms share a second bath with a handy dual-sink vanity.

Plans P-7677-2A & -2D

Bedrooms: 3	Baths: 2½
Living Area:	
Upper floor	825 sq. ft.
Main floor	1,035 sq. ft.
Total Living Area:	**1,860 sq. ft.**
Daylight basement	1,014 sq. ft.
Garage	466 sq. ft.
Exterior Wall Framing:	2x6
Foundation Options:	**Plan #**
Daylight basement	P-7677-2D
Crawlspace	P-7677-2A

(All plans can be built with your choice of foundation and framing. A generic conversion diagram is available. See order form.)

BLUEPRINT PRICE CODE:	**B**

UPPER FLOOR

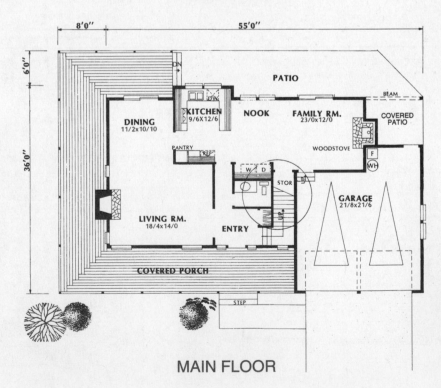

MAIN FLOOR

TO ORDER THIS BLUEPRINT, CALL TOLL-FREE 1-800-820-1283

Plans P-7677-2A & -2D

PRICES AND DETAILS ON PAGES 12-15

Classic Flair

- Prominent gables and a railed front porch lend a classic flair to this gorgeous country home.
- To either side of the sidelighted, two-story foyer, arched openings introduce the formal living and dining rooms.
- Straight ahead, the family room is warmed by a handsome fireplace and crowned by an impressive 18-ft. ceiling.
- A corner study with private bath access may be used as a bedroom.

- From the family room, a wide archway leads to the breakfast nook and the large island kitchen. A French door opens to the backyard.
- Upstairs, the master suite is topped by a 10-ft., 8-in. tray ceiling. The master bath enjoys a 13½-ft. vaulted ceiling above a delightful garden tub and a separate shower.
- Along the balcony hall, arched openings give great views to the family room. Three more bedrooms offer private bath entrances.

NOTE: The above photographed home may have been modified by the homeowner. Please refer to floor plan and/or drawn elevation shown for actual blueprint details.

Plan FB-5016-MARY

Bedrooms: 4+	Baths: 4
Living Area:	
Upper floor	1,408 sq. ft.
Main floor	1,426 sq. ft.
Total Living Area:	**2,834 sq. ft.**
Daylight basement	1,426 sq. ft.
Garage and storage	442 sq. ft.
Exterior Wall Framing:	2x4

Foundation Options:
Daylight basement
Crawlspace
(All plans can be built with your choice of foundation and framing. A generic conversion diagram is available. See order form.)

BLUEPRINT PRICE CODE:	D

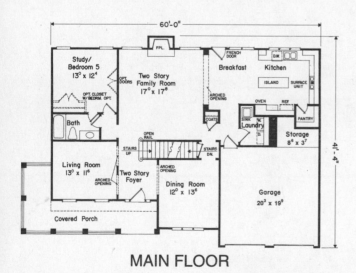

MAIN FLOOR

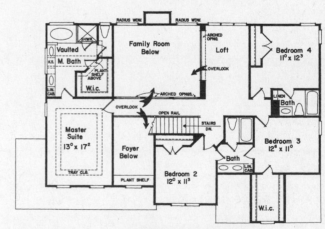

UPPER FLOOR

Photo by Mark Englund/HomeStyles

Modern Elegance

- Half-round transom windows and a barrel-vaulted porch with paired columns lend elegance to the facade of this post-modern design.
- Inside, the two-story-high foyer leads past a den and a diagonal, open-railed stairway to the sunken living room.
- A 17-ft. vaulted ceiling and a striking fireplace enhance the living room, while square columns introduce the adjoining formal dining room.
- The adjacent kitchen is thoroughly modern, including an island cooktop and a large pantry. A sunny bay window defines the breakfast area, where a sliding glass door opens to the angled backyard deck.
- Columns preface the sunken family room, which also sports a 17-ft.-high vaulted ceiling and access to the deck.
- Upstairs, the master suite features a 10-ft. vaulted ceiling, a private bath and a large walk-in closet.

NOTE: The above photographed home may have been modified by the homeowner. Please refer to floor plan and/or drawn elevation shown for actual blueprint details.

Plan B-89005

Bedrooms: 4+	Baths: 2½
Living Area:	
Upper floor	1,083 sq. ft.
Main floor	1,380 sq. ft.
Total Living Area:	**2,463 sq. ft.**
Standard basement	1,380 sq. ft.
Garage	483 sq. ft.
Exterior Wall Framing:	2x4

Foundation Options:

Standard basement

(All plans can be built with your choice of foundation and framing. A generic conversion diagram is available. See order form.)

BLUEPRINT PRICE CODE:	C

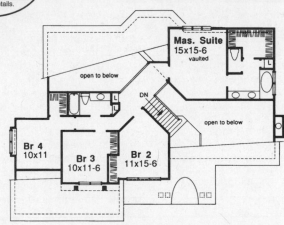

UPPER FLOOR

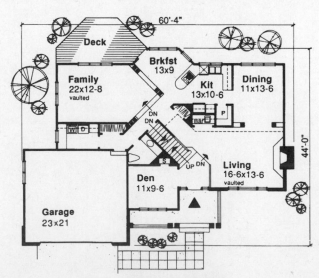

MAIN FLOOR

UPPER FLOOR

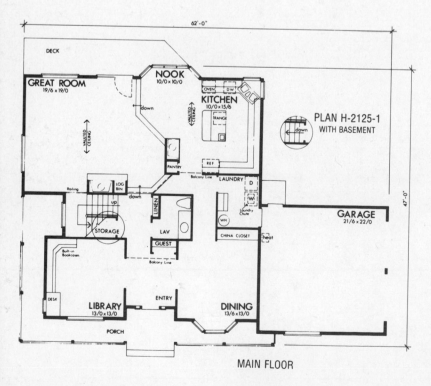

PLAN H-2125-1
WITH BASEMENT

MAIN FLOOR

Delightful Blend of Old and New

- A contemporary floor plan is hidden in a traditional farmhouse exterior.
- Vaulted entrance is open to the upper level; adjacent open stairwell is lit by a semi-circular window.
- French doors open into a library with built-in bookcase and deck.
- Sunken Great Room features a fireplace, vaulted ceiling open to the upstairs balcony, and French doors leading to a backyard deck.
- Roomy kitchen has center cooking island, eating bar, and attached nook with corner fireplace.
- Upper level has reading area and exciting master suite with hydro-spa.

Plans H-2125-1 & -1A

Bedrooms: 3	Baths: 2½
Space:	
Upper floor:	1,105 sq. ft.
Main floor:	1,554 sq. ft.
Total living area:	2,659 sq. ft.
Basement:	approx. 1,554 sq. ft.
Garage:	475 sq. ft.
Exterior Wall Framing:	2x6

Foundation options:
Standard basement (Plan H-2125-1).
Crawlspace (Plan H-2125-1A).
(Foundation & framing conversion diagram available — see order form.)

Blueprint Price Code:	D

Angled Four-Bedroom

- A covered front porch, half-round windows and an angled garage with an attractive window arrangement give this two-story an inviting look.
- Inside, the spacious foyer boasts a 17-ft. ceiling and a view of the formal living room, which includes a warm fireplace and plenty of windows.
- Between the formal dining room and the island kitchen and breakfast area is the generous-sized sunken family room. The family room boasts a 17½-ft. ceiling and a second fireplace flanked by patio doors to a rear patio.
- Upstairs, the lush master suite features an 11-ft. ceiling and a private bath with a garden tub, a separate shower and a dual-sink vanity.
- Three additional bedrooms are serviced by a hall bath. The two front bedrooms include striking 11-ft. ceilings.

Plan AX-90309

Bedrooms: 4	Baths: 2½
Living Area:	
Upper floor	1,148 sq. ft.
Main floor	1,190 sq. ft.
Total Living Area:	**2,338 sq. ft.**
Standard basement	1,082 sq. ft.
Garage	545 sq. ft.
Exterior Wall Framing:	2x4

Foundation Options:

Standard basement

Slab

(All plans can be built with your choice of foundation and framing. A generic conversion diagram is available. See order form.)

BLUEPRINT PRICE CODE: C

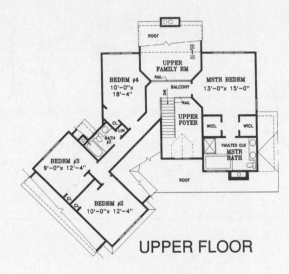

UPPER FLOOR

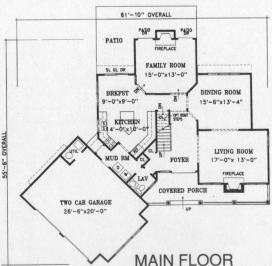

MAIN FLOOR

TO ORDER THIS BLUEPRINT, CALL TOLL-FREE 1-800-820-1283

Plan AX-90309

PRICES AND DETAILS ON PAGES 12-15

Classic Homestead

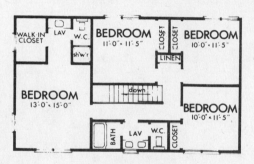

SECOND FLOOR

WALK-IN CLOSET

LAV

W.C.

sh'w'r

BEDROOM 11'-0" x 11'-5"

CLOSET CLOSET

LINEN

BEDROOM 10'-0" x 11'-5"

BEDROOM 13'-0" x 15'-0"

down

BEDROOM 10'-0" x 11'-5"

BATH

LAV

W.C.

CLOSET

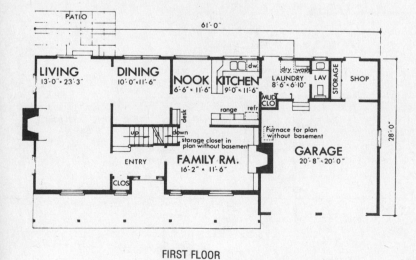

FIRST FLOOR

PATIO

61'-0"

LIVING 13'-0" x 23'-3"

DINING 10'-0" x 11'-6"

NOOK 6'-6" x 11'-6"

KITCHEN 9'-0" x 11'-6"

dw

LAUNDRY 8'-6" x 6'-10"

dry wash

LAV

STORAGE

SHOP

desk

range

refr

MUD CLO

Furnace for plan without basement

up

down

storage closet in plan without basement

ENTRY

FAMILY RM. 16'-2" x 11'-6"

GARAGE 20'-8" x 20'-0"

CLOS

28'-0"

Plans H-3678-3 & H-3678-3A

Bedrooms: 4	**Baths:** 2½

Finished space:
Upper floor:	960 sq. ft.
Main floor:	1,036 sq. ft.

Total living area:	**1,996 sq. ft.**
Basement:	900 sq. ft.
Garage:	413 sq. ft.

Features:
Spacious living room and large family room.
Convenient nook/kitchen/laundry arrangement.
Inviting porch and roomy entry area.

Exterior Wall Framing:	2x4

Foundation options: (Specify)
Standard Basement:	Plan H-3678-3
Crawlspace:	Plan H-3678-3A

(Foundation & framing conversion diagram available — see order form.)

Blueprint Price Code:
Without finished basement design:	B
With finished basement design:	D

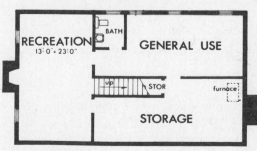

RECREATION 13'-0" x 23'-0"

BATH

GENERAL USE

up

STOR

furnace

STORAGE

BASEMENT

TO ORDER THIS BLUEPRINT,
CALL TOLL-FREE 1-800-820-1283

Plans H-3678-3 & -3A

PRICES AND DETAILS
ON PAGES 12-15

223

Exterior Excitement Abounds

- Exterior excitement is created by repeated front-projecting gables, a covered front porch, and half-round transom windows.
- Upon entering the home, guests are greeted with a dramatic view into the living/dining room, with a cathedral ceiling, fireplace and transom window.
- Continuing back from the entry brings you to the informal living area made up of the kitchen with interesting angled counter, the family room and the sunny breakfast room, each with cathedral ceilings.
- An optional loft or third bedroom overlooks the family area.
- There are two bedrooms on the main floor, including a spacious master bedroom with cathedral ceiling and lavish master bath.

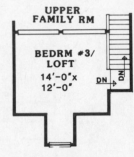

UPPER FAMILY RM

BEDRM #3/ LOFT
14'-0"x 12'-0"

DN

PART PLAN OF (OPT) LOFT/ BEDRM #3

Plan AX-89321-A

Bedrooms: 2-3	Baths: 2

Space:

Upper floor: (opt.)	184 sq. ft.
Main floor:	1,514 sq. ft.
Total living area:	**1,698 sq. ft.**
Basement:	1,514 sq. ft.
Garage:	491 sq. ft.
Exterior Wall Framing:	**2x4**

Foundation options:
Daylight basement.
Slab.
(Foundation & framing conversion diagram available — see order form.)

Blueprint Price Code:	**B**

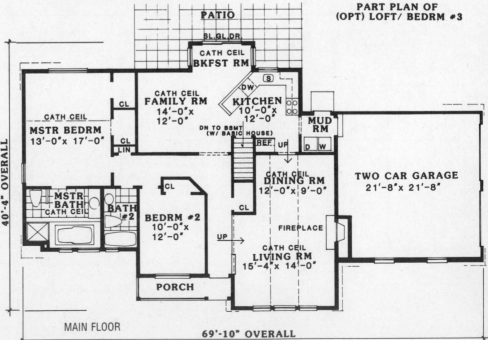

PATIO
SL.GL.DR.
CATH CEIL BKFST RM
CATH CEIL FAMILY RM 14'-0"x 12'-0"
KITCHEN 10'-0"x 12'-0"
DW
S
CATH CEIL MSTR BEDRM 13'-0"x 17'-0"
CL
CL
LIN
DN TO BSMT (W/ BASIC HOUSE)
REF
UP
MUD RM
D W
MSTR BATH CATH CEIL
BATH #2
CL
BEDRM #2 10'-0"x 12'-0"
CATH CEIL DINING RM 12'-0"x 9'-0"
TWO CAR GARAGE 21'-8"x 21'-8"
CL
UP
FIREPLACE
CATH CEIL LIVING RM 15'-4"x 14'-0"
PORCH
40'-4" OVERALL
MAIN FLOOR
69'-10" OVERALL

TO ORDER THIS BLUEPRINT, CALL TOLL-FREE 1-800-820-1283

Plan AX-89321-A

PRICES AND DETAILS ON PAGES 12-15